How Pilots Live

How Pilots Live

An Examination of the Lifestyle of Commercial Pilots

SIMON ASHLEY BENNETT

PETER LANG

Oxford · Bern · Berlin · Bruxelles · Frankfurt am Main · New York · Wien

Bibliographic information published by Die Deutsche Nationalbibliothek
Die Deutsche Nationalbibliothek lists this publication in the Deutsche Nationalbibliografie;
detailed bibliographic data is available on the Internet at http://dnb.d-nb.de.

A catalogue record for this book is available from the British Library.

Library of Congress Control Number: 2014931826

ISBN 978-3-0343-1722-1

Peter Lang AG, International Academic Publishers, Bern 2014
Hochfeldstrasse 32, CH-3012 Bern, Switzerland
info@peterlang.com, www.peterlang.com, www.peterlang.net

This publication has been peer reviewed.

Printed in Germany

*This book is dedicated to the late
Captain Ralph Kohn FRAeS – a wise and generous man.*

Contents

Introduction

As a piece of applied science the aeroplane has a place alongside the wheel,
gunpowder, the printing press and the steam engine as one of the great
levers of change in world history.

— RENDALL, 1988: 7

We can pull and haul and push and lift and drive,
We can print and plough and weave and heat and light,
We can run and race and swim and fly and dive,
We can see and hear and count and read and write ...
But remember, please, the Law by which we live,
We are not built to comprehend a lie.
We can neither love nor pity nor forgive –
If you make a slip in handling us, you die!

— KIPLING, The Secret of the Machines

Commercial aviation is economically and culturally significant. It creates
wealth and opportunity and allows the traveller to experience different
cultures (Sarker, Hossan and Zaman, 2012). By bringing people together it
reduces the chances of global cleavage. Commercial aviation is an *artifact*.
As such it reflects the dominant ideologies and fashions of the day. Britain's
state-run airline Imperial Airways and its successor the British Overseas
Airways Corporation served the needs of Empire. Aircraft were designed to
serve the so-called Empire Routes.[1] The post-War loss of Empire removed
BOAC's *raison d'etre*. Becoming British Airways in 1974 it was sold off in
1987 in a 'yard sale' of state-owned companies. The ownership pattern,

---

1   With reference to theories of the social construction of technology (SCOT)
     (MacKenzie and Wajcman, 1985; Latour, 1991; Bjiker, 1994; Pinch, 1996), the design

structure and *modus operandi* of the industry cannot be divorced from its social, economic and political milieu. The *praxis*[2] of commercial aviation both reflects and reproduces that milieu. In his 1984 book *Empires of the Sky*, Sampson charted BOAC's metamorphosis:

> Over ... six decades Britain's 'chosen instrument' [has] undergone every kind of metamorphosis: it [has] been a pioneers' airline, an imperialists' airline, a pilots' and engineers' airline, and now it [is] a marketer's airline (Sampson, 1984: 219).

As the industry's ownership pattern, structure and *modus operandi* have evolved, so has its culture and behaviour. The following quotations illustrate the industry's cultural trajectory:

> The airman ... delights in the ever-changing patchwork of light and shadow on the earth's surface, the toylike aspect of everything beneath, the wonderful variety of patterns which roads, rivers, valleys, forests and hedgerows provide in unbroken succession (Supf cited in Duke and Lanchbery, 1964: 243).

> A Boeing 707 captain, looking back at the huge aircraft he [sic] has just brought down through fog to a silk-soft landing, has every right to be proud of the disciplined skills which enabled him to do it ... If a magic sort of X-ray photograph that showed the psychological factors inside him could ... be taken ... they would reveal an intelligent human being, conscious of his enormous responsibilities ..., highly skilled, courageous, conscientious—and very vulnerable (Beaty, 1969: 16–25).

> Are we going to apologise when something goes wrong? No, we're f***ing not. Please understand. It does not matter how many times you write to us complaining that we wouldn't put you up in a hotel because there was fog in Stansted. You didn't pay us for it (O'Leary cited in Johnson, 2004).

Commercial aviation, transformed by privatisation and market liberalisation, is a hard-edged business. It is as cut-throat and unsentimental as High Street

---

of the Empire Flying Boats reflected a political imperative, namely the need to connect Britain with her scattered and vulnerable Empire. To paraphrase Latour (1991), technology makes politics tangible. NASA's ground-breaking Saturn V rocket expressed President Kennedy's desire to regain the lead in the space race (Bennett, 1998).

2   How a discrete set of skills (like surgery, banking, driving or aviating) is realised or rendered is termed the praxis of that skill-set.

retail. While pilots' professionalism and romantic attachment endures, airline Chief Executive Officers maintain an unsentimental focus on the bottom line. The mantra of every airline CEO is shareholder value. Maximise it and you are a success. Fail to meet shareholder expectations and you might as well pack your bags. In this febrile atmosphere cost-cutting is *de-rigueur*. The author remembers working for an airline where cost-cutting measures included not supplying pilots with a small company diary (which when bought in bulk would have cost just a few pence) and not supplying pilots with a sustaining meal, even though most rosters involved flying between 23:00 and 07:00 (when food was unobtainable at *en route* bases) (Bennett, 2010a). While the first cost-saving measure had no safety implications, the second did: human beings need sustenance to function properly (British Air Line Pilots Association Medical Study Group, 1988; Rhodes and Gil, 2002).

Considering the intensity of airline competition and hostility of the natural environment, aviation is a remarkably safe form of transportation (Brookes, 2002; Rickard, 2010). Pilots underwrite aviation's good safety record. Witness how Captain Chesley Sullenberger saved the lives of 150 passengers by landing his stricken US Airways Airbus on New York's Hudson River. Despite the aircraft's automatic features (a bone of contention for some pilots) it was the liveware component that saved the day. A case of *deus ex machina*? Because pilots are pivotal in delivering safe and efficient air service it is important that we monitor how evolutionary changes (for example, in employment practices and terms and conditions) affect their habits, morale, commitment, physical capacities and mental state. We ignore the nexus between what happens off the flight deck and what happens on it at our peril.

It is accepted in aviation circles that the pilot lifestyle is under-researched. There are few sociological studies of the lifestyles of the women and men who fly commercial aircraft, which is surprising given the size of the industry and the wealth and opportunity it creates. Understanding the pilot lifestyle is not only important from an academic or intellectual point of view. Understanding the pilot lifestyle is also important from a safety standpoint. It is important because regulations made without reference to the 'lived reality' of the pilot lifestyle create 'resident pathogens' or 'latent errors' – the necessary preconditions for incident and accident (Reason, 1990, 2013).

In 2010–2011 the author researched the pilot lifestyle using sleep/activity logs and an on-line questionnaire. The fifty-four question on-line questionnaire generated 433 responses. Many of the questions allowed free-text answers. The sleep/activity logs (SLOGs) generated a significant amount of data. One-hundred and thirty-three pilots kept a sleep-diary for three weeks. SLOGs contained up to 9,000 words of description. Pilots described their working life *and* home life. Finally, half a dozen pilots were interviewed. The longest interview took two hours. Responses were taped and transcribed.

Although participants were subject to the relatively strict Flight Time Limitation/Flight Duty Period (FTL/FDP) regulations that applied at the time (like the United Kingdom's CAP371 FTL/FDP standard), the data revealed that pilots routinely experienced acute and chronic fatigue. If that was the situation under relatively strict FTL/FDP regulations like CAP371, what might happen under more relaxed regulations like those proposed by the European Aviation Safety Agency?

A Change for the Better?

In July 2008 the European Aviation Safety Agency (EASA) introduced EU OPS 1 Subpart Q. Intended to be the EU-wide FTL regulation, it was rejected by countries with more stringent FTLs. In a political compromise these countries were allowed to retain their FTLs:

> As this new scheme ... was considered by the UK and a number of other EU states to set standards well below those required by their current legislation, EASA issued a derogation permitting the UK to continue using CAP371 and for other states to continue using their current schemes if more restrictive that Subpart Q (Rickard, 2010).

By the early Spring of 2011 EASA had received some 30,000 comments from across Europe on its proposed new FTL/FDP scheme. The Agency took months to digest the feedback, publishing its *Comment-Response Document 2010–14* on 18 January 2012. Discussions reached a crescendo. In a sharply polarised debate the European Cockpit Association (ECA) argued against the proposals (in, for example, its *2012 Barometer on Pilot Fatigue*) while the Association of European Airlines (AEA), the International Air Carrier Association (IACA) and European Regional Airlines Association (ERA) argued for the proposals.[3] ERA (2013a) claimed:

> [A]irlines will never compromise on safety. The final proposed FTL rules are not a relaxation of today's rules as the unions suggest. On the contrary, they harmonise the different FTL requirements that exist across Europe and even include some new and more restrictive requirements and limitations. EASA's final proposals are the result of an extensive review involving all stakeholders including national safety regulators, airlines and trade unions, and are based on robust safety data, including the review of almost 50 different scientific studies.

The ECA (2013a) said:

> ECA insists that the EU's current FTL rules are replaced by safe, science-based fatigue prevention rules. EASA's 3 proposals – the NPA, CRD and Final Opinion – are not a credible basis for such rules. The Opinion, issued on 1 Oct. 2012, disregards decades of scientific evidence, including several studies commissioned by EASA itself, and is contrary to the precautionary principle. If not changed, the Opinion will reduce safety standards in many parts of Europe ... Therefore, the EASA Opinion must be substantially revised, be put on a solid medical and scientific basis, and aligned with the safety levels of existing state-of-the art FTL rules, best operational safety practices, and the precautionary principle.

The trench warfare around EASA's proposals continued throughout the Summer of 2013. Then, on September 30, the European Parliament's Transport Committee rejected the proposals by a margin of 21–13. Despite this defeat, those in favour of EASA's proposals were determined to have them accepted by the European Parliament. Hostilities resumed. The British Airline Pilots Association's General Secretary said:

---

3   The conservative 2008 EASA/Moebus report was the focus of a 2009 critique written by Alertness Solutions's Dr Mark Rosekind and Kevin Gregory. The report was titled *The Moebus Aviation Report on 'Scientific and Medical Evaluation of Flight Time Limitations': Invalid, Insufficient and Risky*. The Eire-based low-cost carrier Ryanair reproduced this report on its web-site.

The Commission must now go back to the drawing board and work with pilots and scientists to develop rules on flying time and tiredness that are based on evidence and expert experience (McAuslan cited in BBC News, 2013).

Some feared the new rules could require pilots to:

... land an aircraft after being awake for 22 hours; fly on the longest-haul flights with only two crew rather than the three at present; and work up to seven early starts in a row rather than the current three allowed (BBC News, 2013).

Long periods of wakefulness add to operational risk:

[Fatigue results] from sleep loss, extended wakefulness, phase of the circadian rhythm or workload. As fatigue increases, declines occur in many aspects of human performance, especially alertness. Alertness is fundamental to many cognitive tasks (The Canadian Nuclear Safety Commission, 2013: 2).

Hersman (2009: 39) observes:

The NTSB's 1994 study of flight crew-related major aviation accidents found that captains who had been awake for more than about 12 hours made significantly more errors than those who had been awake fewer than 12 hours.

Caruso and Hitchcock (2010: 193) note:

Fatigue-related impairments can lead to reduced performance on the job ... [T]he odds for a nurse making an error at work increased by three times when work shifts lasted 12.5 hours or longer, compared with 8.5-hour shifts.

The Institute of Medicine of the National Academies (2009: 12) notes:

Prolonged wakefulness in excess of 16 hours at work, reduced or disturbed periods of sleep, more consecutive days or nights of work, shift variability and the volume of work all increase fatigue and thus can contribute to errors.

Rhodes and Gil (2002: 15) observe:

By the 18th hour [of wakefulness] the pilot will have great difficulty remembering things he has done or said a few moments ago (short-term memory) and his reaction time will have almost doubled in duration. By the 24th hour his ability to think creatively and make decisions will be dangerously low.

The Civil Aviation Authority (2007: 16) explains:

> A blood alcohol concentration (BAC) level of 0.085% ... is just over the permitted level for drivers of road vehicles in the UK. This is approximately the level reached ... After 24 hours of continuous wakefulness.

Put another way, after 24 hours awake the subject will perform as if mildly intoxicated. If that subject is trying to land an aircraft at an unfamiliar airport at night in a strong crosswind in the company of an inexperienced First Officer, the consequences could be serious. Despite the warnings, on 9 October 2013 the EU Parliament voted to accept EASA's proposed new Europe-wide FTL scheme.[4] The Agency (European Aviation Safety Agency, 2013) emphasised what it considered the safety benefits of the new scheme:

> This [new scheme] will bring a series of clear safety improvements in crew protection against fatigue. In particular, night flight duty will be reduced to 11h in the new regulation, instead of 11h45 today, more flights will be considered night flights and subject to shorter duty periods. Total flight time in 12 consecutive months will be limited to 1,000 hours instead of 1,300 hours. The weekly rest will be increased by 12 hours twice a month. The combination of standby at the airport with flight duty will be capped at 16 hours. It is currently 20 hours or 26 hours, or even without limit at all in some Member States.

Important though it is, the book is about much more than the debate over FTL/FDP regulations. It paints a picture of the pilot lifestyle so as to reveal – perhaps for the first time in detail – the *lived reality* of flight-deck labour.

Commuting – A Resident Pathogen?

Regulators and airlines take little interest in the pilot lifestyle, even though that lifestyle has an important bearing on pilots' physiological and psychological well-being. The book's premise is that what happens off the

---

4   The vote went 387 to 218 in favour, with 66 abstentions.

flight-deck influences what happens on it. The book argues that flight-crew performance cannot be dissociated from factors like terms and conditions, commute-to-work times, the duration and quality of sleep and the quality of support available from airline managements, the medical profession, colleagues, friends and partners.

One of the more worrying findings was the distances pilots commute each day before operating their four (or more) sectors. Industry volatility has created a 'pilot diaspora', a spatially dislocated workforce of commercial pilots who, because of airline bankruptcies, mergers and reorganisations, have no choice but to commute. Novice pilots commute because they can't afford to live in expensive airport catchments – many British pilots are saddled with debts in excess of £120,000. The same situation pertains in the United States where fees are high and starting salaries low:

> According to ALPA, an average First Officer at a US regional with one year of service earns only around $20,567 ... Even new pilots who graduate from four-year universities with highly-regarded training curricula can't expect well-paying jobs (Ray, 2010).

Those who fly for regional carriers (the 'nurseries' for early-career pilots) are poorly rewarded:

> As of 2012, the salary range for regional airline pilots was $16,500 to $60,000, according to AvScholars, an organization that guides would-be aviators in education and career. The wide salary range reflects the disparity in pay between inexperienced and veteran pilots (Johnson, 2013).

The Air Line Pilots Association International (2013: 4) notes:

> Beginning salaries for first officers range from $26,000 ... at major airlines, and from $12,000 ... at non-major airlines, depending on the size of the airplane flown.

Some of the industry's unskilled workers earn more than pilots:

> New-hire, full-time airline baggage handlers at large US airlines earn gross average salaries of around $21,000 annually ... Smaller regional airline baggage handler gross annual salaries are less, at about $17,600 annually (Guerra, 2013).

To make ends meet newly-qualified pilots live as cheaply as possible with family, friends or partners. Experienced pilots commute because they have children in school, partners in local jobs and mortgages to pay (following the 2007 crash, some are in negative equity). Commuting adds to the physiological and psychological stress of high-tempo operations in congested airspace. Despite this fact, politicians, regulators and airline managements take little interest in pilots' lifestyles – even though aspects of the pilot lifestyle impinge on safety. Aviation officials Balkanise. They attend to those things that happen inside the airport perimeter and ignore what happens outside. The private sphere is dismissed as irrelevant. For example, while the CAA's CAP371 acknowledges the fatigue-inducing potential of long-distance commuting, the Authority does no more than remind pilots who live more than 90 minutes' commute from base that they should *consider* taking temporary accommodation:

> Travelling time, other than that time spent on positioning, shall not be counted as duty. Travelling time, from home to departure aerodrome, if long distances are involved, is a factor influencing any subsequent onset of fatigue. If the journey time from home to normal departure airfield is usually in excess of 1½ hours, crew members should consider making arrangements for temporary accommodation nearer to base (Civil Aviation Authority, 2004: B7).

The question of pilots' ability to pay for temporary accommodation is nowhere addressed. Commuting is treated as a discrete activity. It is divorced from context. The reasons for long commutes (geographical dislocation, indebtedness, overheating airport catchments, etc.) are not explored.[5] The nexus between the private realm and safety is barely considered. The Federal Aviation Administration (2010: 55874) describes the CAA's advice in this way:

> CAP–371 provides that if journey time from home to normal home base is more than 1.5 hours, crew members should consider making arrangements for temporary accommodation nearer to base. This provision is not mandatory.

5   In October 2013 the average price of a house in London was over £544,000. The average price of a house in London's commuter belt was £300,000 (Binns, 2013). Newly-qualified pilots may have training academy debts of over £120,000. They may also be paying off a university loan. Indebtedness limits choice. In 2013 the starting salary for a UK-based pilot was circa £21,000 (National Careers Service, 2013).

Another finding with a potential safety impact was pilots' inability to get adequate sleep before night-duties. Night-flying is especially onerous because pilots work through the circadian low. During this period (for most people it spans 03:00–06:00) a sleep-deprived pilot may find it difficult to stay awake.[6] Sleep debt and the circadian nadir are uneasy bedfellows:

> Sleep is a basic need and no matter how hard we try, when we are sleep-deprived we may find it impossible to stay awake (Rhodes and Gil, 2002: 46).

Because of the risks inherent in the circadian low it is important that pilots scheduled for night duties are able to sleep before report. The research showed that many pilots find it difficult to get adequate sleep before report. They go to bed but find they cannot sleep. Consequently they may operate for many hours on little sleep. Long periods of wakefulness impinge on performance. Reactions slow and problem-solving abilities degrade.

Models – Panacea or Problem?

By definition, models or ideal-types are out of step with reality. Models average or summate. Consequently they fail to capture the full range of human experience. It follows that rules or regulations informed by a model or ideal-type create latent errors or resident pathogens – the preconditions for incident or accident. At one night-freight airline, those responsible for rostering made a number of assumptions about pilot behaviour, including a) that pilots could reliably obtain top-up sleep prior to report, b) that they could maintain an adequate level of performance through the circadian low (between roughly 03:00 and 06:00) and c) that they could work

6   A 2013 BALPA-commissioned survey of 500 commercial pilots revealed a worrying trend: "56% of pilots admit to having fallen asleep on the flight deck and … of those who admitted this nearly 1 in 3 (29%) said they woke to find the other pilot asleep" (British Airline Pilots Association, 2013).

through the night without adequate sustenance. In reality pilots could neither reliably obtain top-up sleep, maintain performance through the circadian low, nor maintain performance without a meal (Bennett, 2010a). Because the model that informed rostering was out of kilter with reality, operational risk increased. Rosters based on the model created latent errors or resident pathogens – the preconditions for incident or accident. Had rosters reflected actual capacities, operational risk could have been reduced. Instead they reflected the assumed abilities of an ideal-type pilot – effectively a superman.

Because policy-informing models rarely accommodate the full range of human experience, ability or need, they are problematic in any context. Some years ago the United Kingdom's National Health Service (NHS) developed a care model to help elderly or terminally-ill patients die with dignity. Propagated throughout the NHS, the Liverpool Care Pathway (LCP) proved popular with doctors and nurses. Its prescriptions were easy to follow. Ambiguities and time-consuming assessments were eliminated. Human variety was swallowed up "within a singular, overarching characterisation" (Bennett, 2013b). Casework and individual circumstance were irrelevancies. Over time doctors' and nurses' zealous application of the LCP depersonalised – and in some cases, dehumanised – patient care:

> Introduced to improve patients' end-of-life experience the LCP [could] involve heavy sedation (such that patients [could] no longer communicate with nursing staff and loved-ones) and the withdrawal of food and water. Popular with medical staff, the LCP became feared and reviled by those forced to watch family members die a frightening and undignified death. Instead of easing pain and suffering in too many cases the pathway amplified it. Some of those who gave dying relatives water were admonished by nurses... Too often the Pathway had more to do with euthanasia than care (Bennett, 2013b).

Because they replace discretion with formulaic responses, models (like the LCP) are authoritarian in nature. Imposition empowers those who administer the model, and disempowers those subject to it. The relationship between actor and subject is one of coercion.

As with the NHS, so too with aviation: models (of human performance) subsume variety within a singular characterisation. This loss of detail adds to the overall level of risk in aviation.[7] For example, planning duties on the assumption that pilots can get top-up sleep before report, when research suggests many cannot, creates a situation where pilots may go for 24 hours or more without sleep (Bennett, 2011). Performance models assume pilots can 'sleep-to-order'. Many cannot. Because the assumption is wrong it creates a resident pathogen in the form of an overly-tiring roster. The solution? Document the pilot lifestyle. Then use the data to develop a more accurate model of pilots' physical capacities. Ideally, match pilots to rosters:

> Preferential rostering provides a way both of shifting the locus of control more towards flight crew and of accommodating the physiological limitations of individual pilots (Bennett, 2011: 185).

Chittick (1998: 17) observes:

> [Preferential rostering] enables crew members to match their schedules with their circadian rhythms, helping to preclude fatigue. Thus a person whose peak performance usually is reached late in the day can shape the schedule to eliminate or minimise early duties while accepting more late duties, a schedule that a 'morning' person would find fatiguing and undesirable ... Preferential scheduling is an inexpensive tool for airlines, and it may also help reduce the problem of aircrew fatigue.

Australia's Civil Aviation Safety Authority (2012: 81) notes:

> Many people prefer to be on permanent night duty. For some, this preference ... suits their 'night owl' chronotype.

Jones (2009: 10) explains:

> For the long-haul pilot contending with sleep pattern and circadian rhythm disruption, a good ... awareness of their own personal physiological traits are important to predict the best times to take rest periods when sleep can be achieved and, if the facility is available, *bid for the roster patterns that most appropriately conform to the diurnal variations of their metabolism*. For the airline some alleviation from fatigue risk is achieved through sympathetic and preferential rostering where pilots can influence their allocation of trips [my emphasis].

---

7   Risk is the probability of exposing someone or something to danger, harm or loss.

Unsurprisingly, EASA's proposed new EU FTL/FDP regulations do not reference the pilot lifestyle. The fatigue impacts of ever-longer commutes-to-work (caused by the dislocation of the pilot workforce) are ignored. Because EASA has based its regulations on an idealised model of the pilot, they introduce the necessary conditions for incident and accident. Seen through the lens of Professor Jim Reason's (1990, 2013) theory of latent error, EASA's regulations amount to 'an accident waiting to happen'.

The research described in this book proves that pilots suffer acute and chronic fatigue *even under Britain's strict CAP371 regulations*. It is reasonable to conclude that the problem of pilot fatigue will worsen if the rules are relaxed. Safety-margins will be squeezed – perhaps to the point where there are more incidents and accidents. Should this happen, lives may be lost and the industry's reputation will be tarnished. This would be an enormous shame given how hard those at the sharp end (pilots, cabin crew, controllers, dispatchers, engineers, etc.) work to keep aviation safe. It would be a betrayal of a dedicated workforce. It would be a betrayal of the travelling public.

The United States's Federal Aviation Administration (FAA) is moving in the opposite direction to EASA. Following the 2009 Colgan Air disaster that drew attention to issues like training, pilot fatigue and flight-crew dislocation, the FAA, under pressure from the National Transportation Safety Board, politicians, pilots and travelling public, tightened its FTL/FDP regulations. Tombstone regulation it may be. But at least the FAA acted on the lessons learned from Colgan.

The Colgan Air disaster foregrounded risky practices. It revealed in a very public way the US regional pilot lifestyle that saw flight-crew flying thousands of miles, grabbing some sleep in a grubby, poorly-serviced crew room, then flying a four-sector duty. It was only after working a full day that the pilot, exhausted and dirty, got to sleep in a bed. The regional pilot lifestyle involved heavily indebted cadet pilots saving money by sleeping on loungers or under desks. Seen through the lens of Diane Vaughan's (1997) normalisation of deviance theory, habituation, the passing of time, and the industry's knack of 'getting away with it' from a safety standpoint, conspired to normalise pilots' risky behaviour. It took the loss of fifty lives and the glare of media attention to persuade Congress and the FAA to correct the deviation.

Conclusion

Aviation has a good safety record. But it is not perfect. Further improvement requires that new regulations reference the sorts of lifestyle factors described in this book. The book's premise is simple: what happens outside of the flight-deck influences what happens on it. Regulations that objectify pilots – that assume they exist in a social and economic vacuum – add to operational risk. A pilot is more than a factor of production. S/he is a social being.

The models used by many regulatory agencies assume things most pilots can't deliver, like always turning up for work fully rested, or always turning up for work stress-free. If a cadet First Officer spends two hours driving to work (a not-unusual scenario) it is unlikely s/he will be either fully rested or stress-free. The commutes will squeeze the time s/he has available for sleep. They will stress the driver. Repeat the process for four or five days (four hours driving each day) and the pilot may end up carrying a significant amount of sleep-debt. Regulations that assume pilots (or train drivers, ships' captains, doctors, etc.) exist in a vacuum cannot deliver the intended level of safety. Regulations that deny the social component undermine safety.

Structure of the Book

Chapter Two

The second chapter, 'The *Realpolitik* of Commercial Aviation', views aviation through multiple lenses: sociology, economics, politics, geography, globalisation, and philosophy. It recognises commercial air service as a socio-technical enterprise, and locates it in a wider context. It shows that the tenor and behaviour of the industry both reflects and reproduces society's dominant value system. It suggests that rules and regulations also reflect and reproduce society's values. It links industry mind-set to Zeitgeist.

Chapter Three

The third chapter, 'Diarising Our Lives', reproduces a representative sample of the sleep/activity logs kept by pilots. The SLOGs record both the pilots' working lives and home lives, thereby creating a longitudinal, holistic (three-dimensional) record. The premise that what happens off the flight-deck influences what happens on it, and *vice-versa*, informs this methodology. The data challenges the idea that there is no need to reference the social and economic context of commercial aviation when designing rules and regulations.

Chapter Four

The fourth chapter, 'Quantitative and Qualitative', presents the most important findings from the on-line questionnaire survey. Many of the questions invited narrative responses, enabling pilots to describe their experiences. The questionnaires, together with the SLOGs, create a powerful and detailed ethnographic account of the pilot lifestyle. Ethnographic accounts allow us to 'get under the skin' of an activity:

> There are no formulae or systems of classification. Ethnography is inductive. Understanding emerges from observation, analysis of subjects' testimony and, as Gilbert (1993) puts it, 'some effort to "think" oneself into the perspective of the members, the introspective, empathetic process Weber called "verstehen"' (Bennett, 2010a: 4).

Chapter Five

Chapter five, 'The Lived Reality of Commercial Flying', draws the data presented in chapters three and four together to create a panoptic on the pilot lifestyle. It talks about every facet of the pilot lifestyle, including: The emergence of a 'pilot diaspora'; longer commutes-to-work; the impact of pilot impoverishment on geographical mobility and standards of accommodation; pilots' inability to sleep/rest to order and the consequences for pilots' flight-deck performance (especially at night when the circadian low is a factor); the interplay between work stress and home-life, and stress experienced at home and work; the perceived lack of support for stressed pilots; disillusionment and the impact on morale; whether pilots are their own worst enemies – because of their visceral attachment to the profession, many pilots will do almost anything to secure/retain a job; whether the airlines exploit pilots' desire to fly for their own selfish ends?

Chapter Six

Chapter six, 'What Have We Learned?', suggests that referencing the lived reality of a socio-technical activity improves the quality, relevance and effectiveness of the regulations that govern it.[8] Because rules and regulations generally do not reference the lived reality of the pilot lifestyle, they harbour organisational pathogens – embedded weaknesses that surface inexplicably and without warning to create a risk of incident or accident (Reason, 1990, 2013). Not grounding rules and regulations in reality creates an affordance for mishap. Sociological study can help agencies like the Federal Aviation Administration and European Aviation Safety Agency improve the relevance and effectiveness of rules and regulations. If the industry is serious about further improving safety it can no longer afford to ignore what happens outside the airport perimeter.

8   All regulated activities, from oil and gas production to air service, can benefit from this approach.

CHAPTER TWO

The *Realpolitik* of Commercial Aviation

Introduction

This chapter locates the enterprise that is commercial aviation in a wider social, economic and political context. Every business activity, from banking to aviation, is acted upon by social, economic and political forces. Economic activities like commercial aviation reify (express) society's beliefs and values. Industries and their practices are *socially produced*. To understand an industry's behaviour one must understand the beliefs and values of the society from which it springs. Zeitgeist influences perceptions and practice. One just has to think of the 2007–2013 world banking crisis to understand the degree to which society's values influence business practice: it is widely accepted that rising social expectations influenced banks to lend to parties who were unlikely to be able to repay their loans (the 'sub-prime' crisis).[1] When those parties failed to meet their financial obligations the world economy crashed (Cable, 2009). A society where profit is valued over all other considerations will encourage employers to work their resources – plant and employees – as hard as possible and to challenge anything (for example, health and safety legislation or working-time directives) that favours labour.

Perceptions and behaviours reference broader social, economic and political conditions. No-one can cut themselves off entirely from the spirit of the age (Zeitgeist). A society where, for example, it is permissible for

---

1   In his speech to the 2010 Liberal Democrat conference Dr Vince Cable, the Conservative–Liberal Democrat coalition government's Business Secretary, referred to bankers as "spivs and gamblers" (Cable cited in Oborne 2010).

employers to sub-contract will see a gradual 'hollowing-out' of industrial establishments. Individual and corporate behaviour can only be understood if located in a wider social, economic and political context. This chapter does that for pilots and their industry.

The Impact of Politicised Consumerism

In 1978 US President Jimmy Carter, ever the populist, signed the Airline Deregulation Act (ADA). In doing so he started a cycle of competition, cost-cutting and employee dislocation that created the circumstances of the 12 February 2009 Colgan Air disaster that killed fifty people. Both of Flight 3407's pilots commuted long distances to their base at Newark (EWR). The Captain travelled from Tampa, Florida; the First Officer from Seattle, Washington State:

> The Captain spent the night of February 11/12 in Colgan's crew room. The First Officer spent the night dead-heading to EWR via Memphis on FedEx flights. The Captain logged into Colgan's computer system at 03:10 and 07:26. He can't have slept well. The First Officer arrived at EWR at 06:30 on February 12, some 33 hours after waking in Seattle. Although she slept on her FedEx flights and in the crew room, these sleeps amounted to no more than nine hours in total (Bennett, 2010b: 2).

Commuting long distances and sleeping in less-than-ideal conditions can induce fatigue.[2] The National Transportation Safety Board (NTSB) concluded:

> Because the effects of fatigue can exacerbate performance failures, its role in the pilots' performance during the flight cannot be ruled out. The NTSB concludes

---

2   Bunks provide the best environment for efficient, restorative sleep. Other sleeping arrangements, like reclining seats, are less likely to deliver restorative sleep (European Transport Safety Council, 2013).

that the pilots' performance was likely impaired because of fatigue ... (National Transportation Safety Board, 2010: 108).

Actions have consequences. By lowering the bar to market entry, removing controls on ticket prices and giving airline managements significantly more freedom, Carter's ADA created an affordance for practices that contributed to disaster (like reducing salaries to a level where pilots are unable to afford to buy or rent in expensive airport catchments and operating with a spatially dislocated workforce). Bennett (2010b: 2) notes:

> Thirty-six percent of Colgan Air's Newark-based pilots lived more than 400 miles from Newark International. A culture of long-distance commuting existed amongst Colgan's pilots. According to the Federal Aviation Authority's (FAA's) accident report the senior pilot responsible for Colgan's Newark operation 'did not know the number of commuting pilots at EWR'.

As far as the aviation industry is concerned there is no link between terms and conditions, lifestyle and safety. The industry believes safety levels to be a function of the quality of the hardware, liveware, rules and regulations that comprise the aviation system.

Often it takes a disaster to reveal risky practices. This was the case with the North Sea oil industry where the 1988 Piper Alpha disaster (that killed 167 oil platform workers) highlighted numerous latent risks, both technical and organisational. Reflecting on his Piper Alpha inquiry some twenty-five years later, Lord Cullen summarised the latent errors that contributed to the fire and explosions that destroyed the platform:

> I examined the significance of whatever had a tenable connection with the chain of events which led up to the catastrophe, and I also took account of other factors which played no part in bringing about the result ... [A]s I dug down ... *I discovered it was not just a matter of technical or human failure.* As is often the case, such failures are indicators of underlying weaknesses ... Management shortcomings emerged in a variety of forms. For example there was no clear procedure for shift handover. The permit to work system was inadequate ... Training, monitoring and auditing had been poor, the lessons from a previous relevant accident had not been followed through. Evacuation procedures had not been practised adequately. There had not been an adequate assessment of the major hazards and methods for controlling them ... I was conscious that no amount of regulations can make up for deficiencies

in the quality of management of safety. That quality depends critically on effective
safe leadership at all levels ... It is essential to create a corporate atmosphere or culture where safety is understood to be and accepted as the number one priority ...
[The report on the 2003 loss of STS Columbia observed] '*If reliability is preached
as organisation bumper-stickers but leaders constantly emphasise keeping on schedule
and saving money, workers will soon realise what is important and change accordingly*'
[my emphasis] (Cullen cited in Jeffrey, 2013).

In Cullen's opinion the disaster had both immediate and proximate causes.
The latter included a safety regime that was superficial and tokenistic and
managers who emphasised production targets over other considerations.
It is unsurprising that Piper's almost *laissez-faire* organisational culture was
visited by disaster. At Colgan Air managers saw nothing wrong with pilots
being frequently shunted between bases to meet business objectives. They
saw nothing wrong with pilots commuting across the continental United
States to report for duty.[3] They could not, or would not make the connection between low salaries and pilots not residing in airport catchments.[4]
They were reluctant to acknowledge that cross-country commutes-to-work
could cause or exacerbate fatigue. In short, Colgan's management refused
to accept that terms and conditions, lifestyle and flight-deck performance
were in any way linked. Unlike Colgan Air, the National Transportation
Safety Board (in the person of Board Member Deborah Hersman) recognised that safety could be affected by contextual factors like commuting
and management's broader economic objectives:

> Flight crew commuting is particularly challenging. A regional flight crew's home
> base changes often, and to offset the disruption of frequent relocations, pilots may

3   Colgan Air's *Flight Crewmember Policy Handbook* stated: "[C]ommuting by Flight
     Crewmembers is understood and accepted by the Company" (cited in National
     Transportation Safety Board, 2010: 47).
4   Interviewed by the NTSB, one of Colgan Air's pilots claimed there was a link between
     compensation and commuting: "[A]nother EWR-based pilot stated that the reason
     for the large number of commuting pilots was the high cost of living in the EWR area
     and the low wages that company pilots received" (National Transportation Safety
     Board, 2010: 47).

commute from a home location. The Colgan Air pilots were commuting pilots. Both pilots were based in EWR but the captain lived in Florida and the first officer in Seattle. During the previous 14 months, the first officer lived in Phoenix (when hired by the company), then expected to be based in Houston before being sent to Norfolk, Virginia, and then at the time of the accident, was based in Newark, New Jersey but lived in Seattle, Washington. Flight crew salaries are also problematic. It is financially challenging for pilots, whether earning $60,000 or $16,000, to regularly relocate their families or hold down multiple residences. When the FAA convened the fatigue ARC [Aviation Rulemaking Committee] in the summer of 2009, they took commuting off the table, and neither Colgan, nor ALPA [Airline Pilots Association] addressed the issue of commuting in their accident submission documents, even though 70% of the pilots based in Newark commute and 20% commute from over 1,000 miles away. I recognize that an objective analysis of commuting will be a difficult, and perhaps, uncomfortable discussion. But we should not be afraid to confront this issue in the context of understanding fatigue and its effect on pilot performance ... Unfortunately, in the aviation industry, fatigue-related decisions – such as minimum crew hires, flight crew schedules and commuting – are decisions that too often reflect the economics of the industry, rather than the ... science of fatigue and human performance (Hersman cited in National Transportation Safety Board, 2010: Notation 8090A: 6–7).

Despite Hersman's comment that the Federal Aviation Administration 'took the commuting issue off the table' in the Fatigue Aviation Rulemaking Committee, the FAA does talk about commuting. For example:

Commuting is common in the airline industry, in part because ... of economic reasons associated with low pay and regular furloughs by some carriers that may require a pilot to live someplace with a relatively low cost of living (Federal Aviation Administration, 2010: 89–90).

The 2009 Colgan Air disaster did for the US aviation industry what the 1988 Piper Alpha disaster did for the North Sea oil industry: it revealed latent errors and suggested a link between economic context and safety. Specifically, the Colgan Air disaster suggested links between the organisation of the air transport industry, terms and conditions, pilot lifestyle and safety. It suggested that what happened off the flight-deck influenced what happened on it.

Aviation as a Capitalistic Enterprise?

In this analysis the meaning and character of capitalistic enterprise is informed by the work of thinkers like Marx (1992) and Braverman (1974). Following the demise of communism in the 1980s and 1990s capitalism became the pre-eminent economic model (Fulcher, 2004). Capitalism's hegemony has been cemented by the fetishisation and deification of consumption (you are what you wear, drink, eat, drive; where you school, holiday, live, shop, exercise, etc.), privatisation of public space (the rise of the shopping mall; sale of parkland and school playing fields, etc.), sale of state-owned assets (like the United Kingdom's British Gas, British Telecom, British European Airways and British Overseas Airways Corporation), rise of powerful transnational corporations (TNCs) and globalisation – a process that sees the increasingly free movement of data, capital (money), labour (skilled and unskilled), food, raw materials, finished goods, ideas, ideologies and cultural products across international borders (Waters, 1995; Cerny, 2010). Thanks to globalisation the world order is today characterised by 'complex interdependencies' (Keohane and Nye, 1977). In the over-developed states it is also characterised by the replacement of the ideologies of massification and conformity with those of individuation, self-interest, self-expression, conspicuous consumption and label-derived identity (Leadbeater, 1989; Fulcher, 2004).

Capitalism, today the dominant economic form, has several engines or drivers, including the division of labour, deskilling and the maximisation of what Marx (1992) called surplus value.[5] Gambles, Lewis and Rapoport (2006: 48) talk about the *intensification* of work in a rapidly globalising world. Extracting as much value as possible from the labour process maximises returns to owners and shareholders. Maximising returns to owners and shareholders is the *primary* objective of capitalistic enterprise. Following an incident or accident a Chief Executive Officer will frequently claim

---

5   Marx's *Capital: A critique of political economy, Volume 3* was originally published in 1894, eleven years after the philosopher's death.

safety to be 'my/our number one priority'. Actually this is not the case. The number one priority for the officers of any capitalistic enterprise is profit – because profit helps ensure market survival:

> [C]apitalist employment is essentially exploitative ... The need for capital accumulation demands employers' constant attention to subjugating labour in order to extract enough profit from it to enable the employer to survive within the capitalist market economy (Watson, 2003: 44).

Ames and Hlavacek (1990) see cost-reduction as the key to corporate success. As Lawton (2002: 3) explains:

> [They] argue that managing costs is at the heart of every successful company and that four related cost truisms apply ... These are, first, over the long-term, it is essential to be a lower cost supplier; second, to maintain a competitive position, the inflation-adjusted costs of producing and supplying ... *must continuously decrease*; the true cost and profit ... must always be transparent; and fourth, a company should focus on cash-flow as much as on profit generation [my emphasis].

Although the search for profit colours corporate thinking, it is usually concealed by a polished rhetoric of safety and concern for the consumer. For example, following claims made in two television programmes (one Dutch (Katholieke Radio Omroep, 2012) the other British (Channel 4 Dispatches, 2013)) that Ryanair's corporate culture inhibits the confidential reporting of safety concerns, a 2010 incident in which a Ryanair aircraft declared a fuel emergency, the subsequent investigation report from Spain's Comisión de Investigación de Accidentes e Incidentes de Aviación Civil that stated "The company's fuel savings policy, though it complies with the minimum legal requirements, tends to minimise the amount of fuel with which its airplanes operate and leaves none for contingencies below the legal minimums ... This contributed to the amount of fuel used being improperly planned and to the amount of fuel onboard dropping below the required final fuel reserve" (Comisión de Investigación de Accidentes e Incidentes de Aviación Civil, 2013: 29) and a later 26 July 2012 incident in which three diverted Ryanair aircraft declared fuel emergencies (Massey, 2012), on 14 August 2013 the airline's Director of Flight and Ground Operations David O'Brien (2013) stated: "... safety is and will remain our No. 1 priority".

Following the Spanish incidents Ryanair's Chief Executive Officer stated: "The only pressure put on Ryanair's pilots on every flight on every day is to operate safely. Safety at Ryanair takes priority over cost" (O'Leary cited in *The Sydney Morning Herald*, 2012). Ryanair's 2013 Annual Report stated: "Safety is the primary priority of Ryanair and its management" (Ryanair Holdings plc., 2013: 60). Such statements should be considered against the International Civil Aviation Organisation's (2002: 1.1–1.2) claim that running an airline involves *striking a balance between production and safety goals* (see below).

Petzinger (1995) suggests that cost-cutting, the 'natural inclination' of airline CEOs, may have a negative impact on safety. Nevertheless, aviation safety continues to improve: "[T]oday, despite … an enormous increase in traffic, there are fewer fatal accidents" (Ramsden cited in Rickard, 2010: 3). Brookes (2002: 7) says: "Notwithstanding the massive growth in air travel over the last 50 years … flying is safer now than it has ever been … [I]t is nearly twenty times safer to get airborne in a commercial airliner than to drive to the airport in the first place". In the United States in the late 1930s there was one fatality for every 50,000 passengers carried. By 1950 this figure had been reduced to one fatality per 100,000 passengers carried. In 2011 the fatality rate was one per 8.2 million passengers carried. In 2012 it was one per 9.9 million passengers (Hayes, 2013: 42–43):

> Although there were still 10 fatal accidents on revenue passenger flights and 362 passenger fatalities in 2012 … it will be noted that the passenger fatality rate last year was 100 times better than in 1950, and perhaps 1000 times better than in the 1930s (Hayes, 2013: 43).

The paradox of aggressive cost-cutting, exploitation of hardware and live-ware and steadily improving safety is difficult to explain. How can safety improve when resources like pilots are worked harder? The answer may lie in the willingness of pilots (and cabin-crew, controllers, dispatchers, engineers, loaders, etc.) to use all their physical and psychological reserves to see the job through. There may come a point, however, when operational demands are so great, and pilots' reservoir of physical and psychological resources so depleted, that the accident rate begins to rise. Human beings have only so much they can give. Like you and me, pilots have limitations. This raises the possibility that decades of safety progress will begin to unravel. In August 2013 the crew operating a Virgin Atlantic Orlando–Manchester service reported to the Civil Aviation Authority that they had obtained five hours sleep in the previous thirty-six. Virgin Atlantic responded that their roster was legal. "[The pilots were] tired but able to fly" a spokesperson told the press. The CAA said: "The airline is now taking steps to adjust its rostering arrangements for flight crew" (Civil Aviation Authority cited in Edmonds, 2013).

The division of labour involves the breaking-down of complex tasks into discrete activities (often monotonous and unchallenging) that are allocated to suitably trained employees. While productivity improves, workers' satisfaction and commitment declines (Beynon, 1973). Deskilling involves employees surrendering skills, expertise and knowledge to machinery (like programmable machine-tools, pocket calculators or flight-management computers (FMCs)) (Braverman, 1974). Like the division of labour, deskilling alienates employees. Maximising the value of labour involves the extraction of as much output as possible (screws, chair legs, spreadsheets, sandwiches, telephone cold-calls, sectors flown, etc.) for the least input in terms of salary or wage and other necessities/benefits (like protective clothing, uniforms, workplace showers, canteen facilities, hotel accommodation, subsidised transport, training, health-care schemes, etc.).

Other things being equal, the longer and harder an employee can be made to work, the greater the value derived from their labour. Other things being equal, the lower an employee's wage or salary, the greater the value derived from their labour. Other things being equal, the more meagre an employee's fringe benefits, the greater the value derived from their labour. The more desirable an employee's outputs (tangible or intangible), the greater the value derived from their labour. The more malleable an employee, the greater the potential for employee exploitation. The more ineffectual the trade union movement, the greater the potential for exploitation. The weaker a labour force's legal protections, the greater the potential for exploitation. The greater the desire to enter a profession, the greater the potential for exploitation (because employers know they can capitalise on employees' professionalism and sense of vocation). The more pressure an employee can absorb, the greater the potential for exploitation.

Employers are best placed when absorbing pressure and doing more with less are behavioural attributes of a particular work-culture (like offshore oil and gas production – the roustabout culture – or commercial flying).[6] Labour value and economic efficiency (productivity) are linked. Owners' and managers' desire to maximise the value of labour encourages automation, de-skilling, the division of labour, lengthening of shifts, salary freezes, salary reductions, lobbying of politicians, civil servants and regulators to weaken employee protections and the passing on of as many costs as possible to employees (like the funding of job-specific training, purchase of uniforms, cost of meals and beverages while at work, cost of hotel accommodation necessitated by late-working, cost of mandatory medical checks, etc.). Profit-seeking behaviour underpins the capitalist mode of production. It is the *primary* concern of all capitalists:

> [T]he specific and defining feature that belongs only to the capitalist system is 'the privileged position accorded the search for economic efficiency' ... [T]he privileged significance given to the pursuit of economic ends over other values [like social justice or equity] ... may not be shared equally by all members of society ... Reducing manning levels, or the deskilling of work, is clearly in the interests of efficiency, but it is not necessarily 'efficiency' from the point of view of those experiencing job or skill loss (Watson, 2003: 55).

Aviation conspicuously displays two capitalistic behaviours: deskilling and employers' concern to maximise the value generated by employees. In 2004 the British Airline Pilots Association (BALPA) published an article titled 'From airline pilot to airline machine-minder' in its house journal *The Log*. The author, a commercial pilot, claimed that his airline had set in motion a comprehensive programme of flight-deck de-skilling:

6   Dekker (2013: 9) argues that the attributes of those who work in safety-critical industries, like "[a] willingness to show self-confidence ... a mastery and control of complex and changing situations, a decisiveness", enable the smooth accommodation of "... production pressures, design problems, equipment malfunctions [and] cost cuts ... External pressure ... gets internalised". Pilots' 'can-do' work ethic almost invites abuse.

[T]he airline for [which] I work has increasingly discouraged manual flying and the use of manual thrust control on the Airbus fleet. This has led to a de-skilled pilot force with a consequent rise in manual flying errors. The airline's response ... was to ban the use of manual thrust in normal operations ... Since Airbus sidestick inputs are mediated by flight control computers this means there is no longer any direct pilot control of the aircraft. This ban is likely to lead to further de-skilling and further increases in errors (Scott, 2004: 5).

According to Scott the locus of aircraft control has shifted from the Captain (and her/his First Officer) to, as he puts it, 'automatics and managements':

[T]here has been a *historical shift from fully human control towards fully automatic control of aircraft.* Currently we have a hybrid system in which control and decision-making are shared in an ambiguous and poorly understood way between pilots and computers. With *airline managements firmly committed to constraining pilots* rather than supporting them we have reached the point of no return. The stick and throttle are history. The airline pilot era has ended; *the airline machine-minder era has begun'* [my emphasis] (Scott, 2004: 6).

While some dissent from Scott's analysis[7] there is no doubt that flight-deck automation and implementation of tighter controls on pilot behaviour under normal flying conditions proceed apace. Discretion is being constrained:

In today's aviation industry the automation paradigm dominates. As with all paradigms [this] paradigm supports and reproduces a particular mind-set or world-view that is reified in, for example, the way pilots are trained and the way aircraft are flown (Bennett, 2012b).

---

7   Consider, for example, this observation from a pilot who started his flying career on Douglas DC-2s and ended it on Boeing 747s: "Because of the computers and programming, 'wise' people like to say that the pilot has become a systems manager. This expression grates on my sensibilities, because whether you're pushing buttons or moving old-fashioned controls, you'd better have a lot of flying knowledge, background and judgment – which makes you a pilot, not a systems manager. The computer for all its miscellany is just another tool for the trade" (Buck, 1994: 183).

What is happening in aviation supports Braverman's vision of an increasingly de-skilled and more programmed workforce. Theobald (1994: 111) summarises Braverman's vision:

> [I]n an era dominated by large corporations ... managers ... must constantly seek to redesign and modify the labour process in order to achieve maximum profit. To reach this goal management needs to assert as much control over the labour force as possible.

The drive to reduce airline costs (including wage costs) evidences employers' concern to maximise the value generated by employees (Petzinger, 1995; Koehler, Esquivias and Varadarajan, 2009; Massachusetts Institute of Technology, 2011). It is notoriously difficult to make money in aviation, largely because of significant and unpredictable fluctuations in the price of oil, and fluctuations in demand (Petzinger, 1995; *The Economist*, 1998). A fall in seat demand following the September 11 2001 terrorist attacks in New York and Washington D.C. catapulted the industry into a spiral of decline, bankruptcy and restructuring. Some airlines took a decade to recover. Others disappeared. Volatility is the *bête-noir* of the airline CEO. In September 2011 a *New York Times* journalist observed:

> A lot of frequent flier miles have been piling up in the 10 years since the terrorist attacks brought the domestic airline industry to its knees in autumn 2001. Airlines in the United States lost $55 billion and shed 160,000 jobs during that decade. But the industry has worked through the economic tumult (Sharkey, 2011).

Intense airline competition means keener pricing (Morrison and Winston, 1995). The real cost of air travel to the consumer has dropped to the point where travelling by air is commonplace. Lowering the bar to market entry has democratised air travel. In 2009 William Swelbar (cited in Freeman, 2009), a researcher at the International Centre for Air Transportation at the Massachusetts Institute of Technology, observed:

> When adjusted for inflation over the last 30 years, fares are down some 50-plus percent. And that just does not make for a sustainable business model. It doesn't make a model that allows them [the airlines] to compensate their people well, like they have in the past.

Johnston (2013) comments:

Adjusted for inflation, airfare has risen less than 2 percent since 2008, according to the Department of Transportation. Since 1995, ticket prices have dropped nearly 15 percent, adjusted for inflation.

Bennett (2012a: 155) observes:

> Like vacuum cleaner, refrigerator or automobile prices, airline ticket prices have dramatically fallen in real terms.

To counter uncertainty over costs they can't control (like fuel, hardware, third-party maintenance and airport landing charges), airline CEOs bear down on costs they *can* control. This puts salaries (compensation) and general terms-and-conditions (like who pays for training, uniforms, food and emergency accommodation) in their sights. In the United States, airlines' determination to control costs means that many pilots are paid less than manual workers. Those who fly for regional airlines are often the lowest paid. At the time of her death in the 2009 Buffalo air crash, Colgan First Officer Rebecca Shaw earned around $23,900 per annum. To save money, Shaw lived with her parents in Seattle.[8] She occasionally waited tables to boost her income. As can be seen from the following table, a First Officer's salary compares unfavourably with several manual occupations, including brickmason, carpenter, carpet installer, bus driver and labourer.

Occupation	May 2008 Mean annual wage $US	May 2012 Mean annual wage $US
Dishwasher	17,700	18,930
Short-order cook	20,200	21,240
Baggage porter/bellhop	23,200	23,090
Filing clerk	25,300	28,030
Construction labourer	32,200	34,490
Bus driver	35,700	38,470
Carpet installer	41,300	40,930
Carpenter	42,900	44,520

8   This necessitated a lengthy commute by freighter to her East coast base.

Occupation	May 2008 Mean annual wage $US	May 2012 Mean annual wage $US
Brickmason	47,700	50,370
Source: United States Bureau of Labour Statistics (2013). *Occupational Employment Statistics: Occupational Employment and Wages, May 2012.*		

It is worth remembering that while a pilot may be responsible for several hundred lives at any one time, this psychological burden is not borne by labourers, carpet installers, carpenters or brickmasons.

The following table provides estimated pilot salary levels for 2013:

Position	Note	Annual salary $
First Officer	Entry level, regional airline	20,000
Senior First Officer	Several years experience, regional airline	30,000–40,000
First Officer	Entry level, major carrier	30,000–50,000
Senior First Officer	Several years experience, major carrier	100,000
Captain	Turboprop operations, regional airline	35,000
Captain	Turbojet operations, regional airline	50,000
Captain	Junior Captain, major carrier	120,000–140,000
Captain	Junior Captain, successful major	>200,000
Source: Anonymous (2013). *The Truth About The Profession.* <http://thetruthabouttheprofession.weebly.com>		

The originator of the data observes:

> Unfortunately, the six figure numbers ... are the salaries that are thrown around by the media, and the slick-talking flight school/university salesmen trying to get you to enroll in their flight program. Those salaries are assumed by the flying public to be the 'average' or 'normal' salaries for the typical airline pilot ... nothing could be further from the truth (Anonymous, 2013).

Before deregulation, many aviators enjoyed a glamorous, privileged lifestyle. They were also respected. After deregulation the economic and social landscape changed. Pilots were worked harder while privileges were eliminated (Bennett, 2003, 2006).

While regional flying is not especially well rewarded, even those lucky enough to work for America's majors have felt the chill wind of salary and benefits cuts: between 2001 and 2005 America's legacy carriers cut average wage rates by 7% (Massachusetts Institute of Technology, 2011). In 2009 Chesley Sullenberger, the US Airways Captain who successfully ditched his Airbus in New York's Hudson River, addressed the House of Representatives:

> It is my personal experience that my decision to remain in the profession I love has come at a great financial cost to me and my family. My pay has been cut 40%, my pension, like most airline pensions, has been terminated ... (Sullenberger, 2009).

Thanks to the ever-increasing global demand for oil and onward march of liberalisation those who run the airlines inevitably obsess about costs (Petzinger, 1995). The world's airlines are locked in a battle for survival. Surveying the industry in the early 1990s Zellner and Rothman (1992) noted the "endless price wars". Robert Crandall, Chief Executive Officer (CEO) of American Airlines, claimed the industry was "... intensely, vigorously, bitterly, savagely competitive" (Crandall cited in *Businessweek*, 1992).

Donald Burr, CEO of pioneering US low-cost carrier People Express, considered airlines "a low-end commodity ... capital intensive, labour-intensive, fuel-intensive" (Burr cited in Sampson, 1984: 136). Michael O'Leary, CEO of Ryanair, claims airlines "are very hard to run" (O'Leary cited in Ashcroft, 2004). Virgin Atlantic's founder Richard Branson famously said: "If you want to be a Millionaire, start with a billion dollars and launch a new airline". So hard is it to make a reasonable return that some have called for the industry to be *re-regulated*:

> Unfettered competition just doesn't work very well in certain industries, as amply demonstrated by our airline experience ... In my view, it is time to acknowledge that airlines ... are more like utilities than ordinary businesses ... [We could] establish minimum fares sufficient to cover full costs and produce a reasonable return. While

I would fully support such an approach, the idea is deeply offensive to those who
cling to the belief that the markets can solve everything (Crandall, 2008).

Given the onward march of market liberalisation and laissez-faire economics (Cable, 2009) it is unlikely that Crandall's re-regulation idea will
gain traction.

The Myth and Reality of Aviation Operations

As mentioned above, it is usual for airline Chief Executive Officers to
claim safety to be their top priority. This is understandable in an industry
where passenger confidence is a key concern. Because flying creates a 'dread
risk' in the minds of many (Bennett, 2012a) airline professionals deem it
necessary to talk-up safety.

The unsurprising reality is that airline operations balance two impera-
tives: safety and economic efficiency. At the end of the day an airline that
consistently loses money will eventually fail or be acquired. Witness the
fate of Skytrain, People Express, Eastern, Pan Am, Trans World Airlines,
Swissair and Sabena (to name but a few). As far as struggling American
airlines are concerned Chapter 11 bankruptcy protection may only delay
the inevitable. In *Line Operations Safety Audit (LOSA)* the International
Civil Aviation Organisation (2002: 1.1–1.2) captures the essence of the
safety-efficiency tradeoff that shapes airline employees' decision making:

> [D]ecision making in aviation operations is considered to be 100 per cent safety-
> oriented ... this is hardly realistic. *Human decision making in operational contexts
> is a compromise between production and safety goals* ... The optimum decisions to
> achieve the actual production demands ... may not always be fully compatible with
> the optimum decisions to achieve theoretical safety demands. All production systems
> ... generate a migration of behaviours: due to the need for economy ... people are
> forced to operate at the limits of the system's safety space. Human decision making
> in operational contexts ... is ... a compromise ... [T]he trademark of experts is not
> years of experience ... but ... how effectively they have mastered the necessary skills to
> manage the compromise between production and safety ... [I]n order to understand
> human performance ... the industry needs to systematically capture the mechanisms

underlying successful compromises when operating at the limits of the system [my emphasis].

Commercial aviation is an interactively complex socio-technical system (that is, it is composed of myriad social and technical elements whose interactions are complex, sometimes unpredictable and sometimes difficult to comprehend). System failure is always a possibility. According to Perrow (1984; 1999), in interactively complex and tightly coupled systems, accidents are 'normal'. According to the literature, system breakdown may result from:

- inherent structural vulnerability (Perrow, 1984, 1999; Reason, 1990, 2013)
- a sequential process of failure: the 'six stage model' (Turner, 1976, 1978)
- gradual degradation occasioned by reactive patching (Weir, 1996)
- the emergence of deviant cultural norms (Vaughan, 1997; Snook, 2000; Dekker, 2012; Reason, 2013)
- the Efficiency-Thoroughness Trade-Off (ETTO) which involves the subordination of safety to economic objectives (Hollnagel, 2004)
- safety migration: a gradual and difficult-to-detect migration towards the boundary of safe operation (Rasmussen, 1997; Reason, 1997).[9]

Given that the International Civil Aviation Organisation accepts safety migration to be a possibility (see above), claims by CEOs that safety is invariably the one and only priority should be treated with caution. Competitive and other pressures require compromises to be made – compromises that

---

9   In *The Right Stuff*, Tom Wolfe (1991: 23–24) describes how stretching the envelope was the norm in test flying: "[In test flying it] seemed to be that a man should have the ability to go up in a hurtling piece of machinery and put his hide on the line and then have the moxie, the reflexes, the experience, the coolness, to pull it back in the last yawning moment ...". Safety migration is less deliberate and obvious – but no less risky – in commercial flying.

are *essential* to viability.[10] Such compromises, however, may create a situation where the aviation system no longer operates as originally envisaged. That is, it no longer operates as per the approvals. Commercial pressures are *transformative*.

For Rosness (2009), the efficiency-thoroughness trade-off theorised by Rasmussen "may lead to ... an increasing gap between design assumptions and work as it is in reality". Such a gap may render approvals obsolete. Any mis-match between a system design or approval document and the current necessary method of working (MOW) creates a resident pathogen – an embedded and difficult-to-detect flaw that under certain conditions may lead to incident or accident (Reason, 1990; 2013). Put another way, managers' necessary pursuit of economic efficiency could sow the seeds of disaster (Bennett and Shaw, 2003). As the ICAO statement confirms, decision-making involves striking a balance between safety and production goals. Usually the right balance is struck and all goes well. Sometimes, however, it is not.

10   Knowing what balance to strike between production and safety goals is problematic: "The dilemma of production/safety conflicts is this: if organisations never sacrifice production pressure to follow-up warning signs, they are acting much too riskily. On the other hand, if uncertain 'warning' signs always lead to sacrifices ... can the organisation operate within ... stakeholder demands?" (Woods *et al.*, 2010: 88). The issue of safety assurance becomes more acute when businesses respond to competition and reduced margins by working human and physical capital harder. To ensure survival, resources are switched to production just at the point where *more* time and money should be spent on safety: "[S]afety investments are most important when least affordable" (Woods *et al.*, 2010: 88).

The Challenger Lesson

In January 1986 the Challenger space shuttle (STS-51-L) exploded shortly after launch killing all on board and severely denting NASA's reputation. Although aware that the shuttle's solid rocket booster (SRB) O-ring seals performed less well when cold, NASA decided to launch. Given that previous cold-weather launches had gone according to plan, NASA expected the same for STS-51-L. Because the agency had 'got away with it' for years, it had no reason to expect anything different with the January 1986 mission. Successful cold-weather launches had 'normalised' the O-ring seals' under-performance:

> One of the specific factors in [the Challenger disaster] was what came to be called 'the normalisation of deviance' ... NASA and the Morton Thiokol Company, the contractor who made the O-rings, had noted problems in earlier flights. They knew there was a design flaw; they also knew that the malfunction increased under cold conditions. Nevertheless, in flight after flight, nothing really bad had happened. Over time, management increased the amount of damage considered 'acceptable' (Gunn and Gullickson, 2004: 1).

The subsequent inquiry into the disaster concluded that, in the matter of the decision to launch STS-51-L, safety goals had been subsumed by production goals. During a pre-launch conference-call between NASA and Morton-Thiokol, Thiokol went off-line for a time. While off-line, Thiokol decision-makers were told to 'wear their management hats'. One interpretation of this exhortation was that, in coming to a decision on whether or not to recommend a launch, Morton-Thiokol managers should evaluate not only the engineering data (which was somewhat contradictory), but also the company's desire to be considered a reliable contractor keen to secure further work, and the wider social, economic and political dimensions of the shuttle programme. As the stage for the Teacher in Space Project, the Challenger mission was a high-profile event. Because it had generated significant public and media interest the programme was politically useful to NASA – an ambitious agency determined to increase its funding. The Teacher in Space Project also created political capital for the Reagan administration.[11]

During the fateful off-line discussion Morton-Thiokol's Jerry Mason urged his fellow managers (each of whom had been an engineer) to make a 'management' decision. Mason dealt firmly with one manager, Robert Lund, who seemed reluctant to recommend a launch:

> Thiokol Senior Vice President Jerry Mason took charge of the discussion. It soon became clear that he was not persuaded by the argument against launching. In response [engineers] Roger Boisjoly and Arnie Thompson strongly defended the recommendation not to launch, pointing out that the temperatures predicted for the next day at Cape Canaveral were 20°F below the temperatures at which anyone had had previous launch experience with the O-rings. Then Mason said if the engineers could not come forward with any new data to decide the issue, 'We have to make a management decision', indicating that the four senior Thiokol managers present would make the decision ... The four Thiokol managers spoke some more and then held a vote (Boisjoly [and] Thompson ... did not get to vote). Three voted in favour of launching; the fourth, Robert Lund paused. (Lund had been the recipient of Boisjoly's July, 1985, memo warning of 'the seriousness of the current O-ring erosion problem'). Mason then asked if Lund would 'take off his engineering hat and put on his management hat' ... Lund voted for launching (Rossow, 2012: 16).

It could be argued that NASA's desire to maintain STS programme momentum allied with Morton-Thiokol's desire to support that momentum and

---

11   Sometimes politics and science make unhappy bedfellows. On 12 April, 1961 the USSR stole a march on the USA by putting the first man into space. Having also put the first man-made satellite into orbit – Sputnik 1 – some feared the USA was losing the Cold War. In a speech to Congress on May 25, 1961, President John F. Kennedy committed the United States to "... landing a man on the moon and returning him safely to the earth" before the end of the 1960s. This ambitious, politically-motivated target put NASA under pressure. Although given a blank cheque by Congress, the need to run the programme at top speed created resident pathogens. On January 27, 1967, several of these were made apparent when a fire destroyed the Apollo 1 Command/Service Module (CSM) during a launch-pad test. Three astronauts were killed. Doubts had been raised about the CSM about a year before the tragedy. Resident pathogens included a hatch that took minutes to open, flammable materials and a high-pressure pure oxygen atmosphere. A redesign was initiated.

secure further work 'generated a migration of behaviours' that led the STS programme to operate 'at the limits of the system's safety space' (to paraphrase ICAO). With reference to Hollnagel's (2004) efficiency-thoroughness dictum, thoroughness was sacrificed to efficiency.

The same pressures that bore down on decision-makers at NASA and Morton-Thiokol prior to Challenger bear down on airline CEOs. They, too, must maintain momentum and seek efficiencies. As discussed, volatile fuel prices oblige airlines to pare down what costs they can. Reasons for fuel-price volatility include political events like coups and wars and longer-term trends like the accelerating economic development of Brazil, Russia, India and China (the 'BRIC' countries). As energy demand skyrockets, oil prices rise. Executives find themselves caught in a whirlwind:

> If we look at the cost side of the business, the biggest item is fuel. We expect it to be 31 percent of costs this year [2013] and 30 percent in 2014 ... [There is a] spike in oil prices from concerns over Syria ... Jet fuel is expected to average at $126.4/barrel in 2013. That should fall slightly to $122.9 in 2014. A decline is good news. But the price is still high. For reference, the average price for jet kerosene in 2004 was $49.70/barrel (Tyler cited in Bellamy, 2013).

As suggested by ICAO (2002), aviation is an industry susceptible to safety migration: Competition is intense. Costs are high. Consumer demand is unpredictable. Margins are slim. Resources are worked as hard as possible.[12] Senior managers hunger for commercial success (in part because of a bonus culture). Shareholders and markets expect good returns. Light-touch regulation is fashionable. As shown by industrial disasters like Flixborough, Bhopal, Piper Alpha and Buncefield,[13] such conditions induce companies to operate at the limits of the safety space:

12 The successful low-cost model requires that aircraft fly the maximum number of sectors in any 24-hour period. To help achieve this, crews must turn their aircraft around as quickly as possible (Broadbent, 2013). Flight and Duty-Time limitations may be viewed as productivity targets rather than as a means of managing pilot fatigue.

13 In its 2011 report into the Buncefield, Hertfordshire, England oil storage depot fire, the Health and Safety Executive noted the role played by production pressures: "Pressures on staff had been increasing before the incident ... Throughput had increased at the

A deeper analysis of accident causation indicates that the observed coincidence of multiple errors cannot be explained by a stochastic [chance] coincidence of independent events. Accidents are more likely caused by a systematic migration toward accident by an organization operating in an aggressive, competitive environment. *Commercial success depends on exploitation of the benefit from operating at the fringes of the usual, accepted practice.* Closing in on, and exploring the boundaries of established practice ... necessarily imply the risk of crossing the limits of safe practices. Court reports from several accidents such as Bhopal, Flixborough, Zeebrügge, and Chernobyl demonstrate this effect. This effect seems now to be increasingly critical, since we are facing some changes of the conditions of industrial risk management: Companies live in an increasingly aggressive and competitive environment; A very fast pace of change of technology is found at the operative level of society, faster than the pace of change found in management structures and regulatory rules [my emphasis] (Rasmussen, 1999: 1–2).

In September 2013 the European Parliament Transport Committee rejected the EU Commission's proposed new Flight and Duty Time limitations. Although roundly criticised by pilot associations and special interest groups for undermining safety,[14] the proposals had been welcomed by Europe's airlines and representative bodies like the European Regions Airline Association (ERA).[15] Another example of a financially hard-pressed industry attempting to survive by migrating itself to the fringes of the safety space? As mentioned in Chapter 1, despite the Committee's rejection the

---

site. This put more pressure on site management and staff and further degraded their ability to monitor the receipt and storage of fuel ... *Cumulatively, these pressures created a culture where keeping the process operating was the primary focus and process safety did not get the attention, resources or priority that it required*" [my emphasis] (Control of Major Accident Hazards Competent Authority, 2011: 4).

14   For example, both the United Kingdom's Air Safety Group (Rickard, 2010) and the European Transport Safety Council (2013) criticised the new proposals on safety grounds.

15   In supporting the new proposals the ERA claimed safety to be its 'paramount' concern. "Safety is, of course, paramount to ERA and its member airlines" said the ERA's Director General (McNamara cited in International Airport Review, 2013). In the United Kingdom both the Government and Civil Aviation Authority supported the new scheme.

Parliament accepted EASA's proposals on 9 October 2013. ERA's Director General welcomed the news:

> It is excellent news that MEPs have based their decision to endorse the FTL proposal on the grounds of a robust three-year consultation process by EASA (McNamara cited in European Regions Airline Association, 2013b).

Aviation as a Post-Fordist or Late-Modern Enterprise

In this analysis the meaning and character of post-Fordist or late-modern forms of social and economic organisation is informed by the work of thinkers like Professors Stuart Hall and Anthony Giddens. Post-Fordist or late-modern economies exhibit the following characteristics:

- the decline of large-scale manufacture
- the hegemony of the service sector
- labour market duality (a sharp divide between core and peripheral employees)
- a widening income and opportunity gap between the top two thirds and bottom third of society
- niche-outlets selling niche-products
- identity as a malleable private construct (you are what you drive, wear, eat, drink, etc.) and life as a process of re-invention (single, then married, then divorced, then married again, etc.)
- greater geographical mobility

The post-Fordist or late-modern features most visible in commercial aviation are contracting out and labour-market duality. In late-modern economies there is a "... hiving off or contracting-out of functions and services hitherto provided 'in house'" (Hall, 1989: 118). This trait is evident in aviation:

[T]he ongoing reorganisation of the aviation sector has led to the disintegration of the traditional operating model for airlines and its gradual replacement with outsourcing, global sub-contracting chains and increased use of hired employees (Koivu, 2013: 61).

As networks become larger and more complex, co-ordination and quality-assurance become more of an issue:

> How can the sprawling network of actors, including those abroad whose actions affect the domestic situation, be effectively supervised? (Koivu, 2013: 61).

In aviation contracting-out encompasses activities as varied as recruitment, publicity and maintenance. It is not uncommon for British-based aircraft to be flown to the Far East for heavy maintenance.[16] Cost is a major driver of industrial practice:

> The continual financial pressures in the air transport market ... has forced further change on the existing MRO [maintenance, repair, overhaul] providers, with a reduction in prices and a transfer of work to lower cost providers and countries. In geographical terms, there is a developing trend to move into China, the Far East and South America in pursuit of lower labour costs. In the survey ... most MRO providers said that the concerns over service quality in these emerging areas were gradually receding (MSP Solutions, 2007: 3).

In post-Fordist or late-modern societies the labour market polarises between securely-employed core workers (like middle and senior managers) and insecurely-employed support and peripheral workers (like junior office staff on temporary or part-time contracts, caterers, cleaners, etc.). Murray (1989: 49) comments: "The most pressing danger from post-Fordism ... is the way it is widening the split between core and periphery in the labour market". In post-Fordist or late-modern societies labour-market bifurcation exacerbates income inequality. As employers bear down on wage costs the

---

16   The author recalls talking to a shop assistant at East Midlands Airport (EMA), England. He said he used to work for British Midland's EMA-based engineering department as an aircraft engineer until the airline decided to outsource its maintenance.

income gap between the securely and insecurely employed, the experienced and inexperienced, women and men grows:

> Today more than one in three [British] people aged 16–30 ... are low-paid, compared with one in five in the 1970s ... In 2007, the median hourly wage for a new employee stood at almost £8.50; it has now fallen to just below £8. Women continue to be hit harder than men (Helm, 2013).

In the United Kingdom soaring living costs, the expansion of part-time and insecure employment and employers' determination to trim costs have driven down real wages:

> British workers have suffered one of the biggest falls in real wages among European countries over the past three years ... New [2013] figures collated by the House of Commons Library show a 5.5 per cent drop in wages after inflation since 2010 (Cusick, 2013).

In recent years so-called 'zero-hours'[17] contracts have become popular with employers determined to control costs. In the UK there is disagreement over what proportion of the workforce is employed on a zero-hours basis. Estimates range from less than one percent of the workforce to between three and four percent (Chartered Institute of Personnel and Development, 2013b). Zero-hours contracts are Janus-faced. On the plus side they suit people whose lifestyles prevent them committing to a full-time contract. On the minus side they can be oppressive and disruptive. The Labour Research Department (2013) offers this summary:

> There are occasions when a 'no strings attached' arrangement might suit the worker, such as sometimes occurs with bank nursing or supply teaching. But it is increasingly

---

17 A worker on a zero-hours contract is tied to an employer. There is no guaranteed work. In 2013 the British Labour Party claimed that zero-hours pay rates were 40% below average wage levels (Mason, 2013). European feudal societies of the High Middle Ages were characterised by serfdom. Under this system, peasants who occupied land were tied to the Lord of the Manor. Serfs engaged in subsistence farming and did whatever work the Lord of the Manor desired (general labouring, animal husbandry, arboriculture, etc.) in exchange for protection and justice.

being used to replace proper secure employment with its associated guaranteed level of paid work and other benefits. Even worse, it can be applied in such a way that a worker, in order to have any chance of getting paid work, is obliged to be available for work at the whim of the employer, and so cannot commit themselves to any other employment.

According to Pyper and McGuinness (2013), zero-hours contracts mean:

> [N]o certainty of earnings, a lack of employment rights and the potential disruption to family life caused by frequent short-notice requirements to attend work.

Nevertheless, a 2013 survey of attitudes towards post-downturn employment practices revealed a degree of resignation on the part of Britain's workers:

> British workers are bracing themselves for a 'new normal' in working conditions ... 22 percent believed that workplace conditions would 'never return' to what they were before the global economic crisis. More than half of those surveyed expected their jobs to change in the next year ... A post-downturn work environment would comprise more flexible working hours ... (Mostrous, 2013: 3).

Zero-hours contracts are especially contentious in aviation where unions claim that pilots employed on such contracts may be less inclined to report safety concerns and more inclined to report for duty when sick (so as to avoid losing income) (*The Guardian*, 2013; Wright, 2013). The (unrecognised) Ryanair Pilot Group (cited in Wright, 2013) claims:

> People are human and if you're not going to be paid [if you don't fly] you might think 'I can do this, I'm fine. I'll just get on with it'.

Flight International's safety editor comments:

> Ryanair are pushing their luck on human factors when they employ pilots like a warlord employs mercenaries. There is the worry that if they are self-employed that might place additional pressures on them to work even if, for any number of reasons, they might not feel entirely fit to do so (Learmount cited in Wright, 2013).

Not unexpectedly there is a reluctance on the part of the airlines to accept that safety is in any way linked to terms-and-conditions (like pilot compensation or the nature of a pilot's contract of employment). Pilots have a legal duty not to report if they believe themselves to be unfit to fly. Ryanair denies the possibility of a link between the nature of a pilot's contract of employment and this critical decision. The airline assumes such decisions are made without reference to contextual factors like terms-and-conditions (which have been described by the airline's Chief Pilot as 'non-safety issues') (Wright, 2013). As far as Ryanair is concerned, pilot decisionmaking happens in a social vacuum.

Dissociating employee perceptions and decisions from organisational politics (expressed, for example, in the type of contract offered flight-crew) denies the possibility of a link between organisational life or culture[18] and employee behaviour. This contradicts research that links organisational culture and employee behaviour (Fennell, 1988; Cullen, 1990; Vaughan, 1996; Reason, 1998, 2013; Cullen, 2001; Mason, 2004; Transport Canada, 2007; Steptoe and Bostock, 2011; Dekker, 2012; European Cockpit Association, 2013b; Chartered Institute of Personnel and Development, 2013a). As Mason (2004: 131) explains:

> Culture is ... a crucial determinant of human behaviour ... It forms the context for the decisions [employees] make and the actions they take.

Having the right culture is especially important in dynamic, risk-laden industries (like aviation):

> It has become clear that ... vulnerability does not originate from just 'human error', chance environmental factors or technological failures alone. Rather, it is the ingrained organisational polices and standards which have repeatedly been shown to predate ... catastrophe (Health and Safety Executive, 2002).

18 In 1966 Marvin Bower, Managing Director of McKinsey and Company, defined corporate culture as "the way we do things around here" (Denison, 2009). Talking about safety culture Uttal (1983) embellished Bower's definition: "[An organisation's safety culture consists of] shared values (what is important) and beliefs (how things work) that interact with an organization's structures and control systems to produce behavioural norms (the way we do things around here)".

In their survey of fatigue and well-being amongst commercial pilots, Steptoe and Bostock (2011: 35) noted a link between pilots' willingness to submit fatigue reports and their perceptions of management culture:

> Three quarters of pilots admitted not submitting fatigue report forms in situations where they should have done ... Key barriers were lack of motivation, fatigue and *concern over management reprimand* ... These issues must be addressed if the FRMS is to be effective [my emphasis].

Fatigue reports are the life-blood of an airline's fatigue risk management system (FRMS). Staunch the supply and the FRMS's functioning is impaired. Rosters that induce dangerous levels of acute or chronic fatigue may go unnoticed, creating resident pathogens – the preconditions for incident and accident.

Labour market duality is increasingly evident in airline employment practices, where there is a trend to hire pilots on zero-hours contracts. According to the chairman of the Ryanair Pilot Group (RPG), roughly 75% of the airline's pilots are employed through agencies and the majority of these are on zero-hours contracts. One fear about zero-hours contracts is that because work is not guaranteed, those subject to them feel inhibited about raising safety concerns. Put another way, there is a belief that such contracts are *tacitly* coercive. A contract that so significantly empowers the airline may dissuade pilots from speaking out, or persuade them to report for work when sick (and therefore, according to the rules, unfit to pilot a commercial aircraft). In a RPG survey of over 1,000 Ryanair pilots over 90% wanted an official inquiry:

> The RPG said 89% did not consider the airline had an open and transparent safety culture and two-thirds were not comfortable raising issues through an internal reporting system (*The Guardian*, 2013).

The exhaustive and timely reporting of errors is a prerequisite for safe operation. Anything that acts to inhibit error-reporting – like an employment contract drafted in such a way that it creates an affordance for coercion – is by definition a latent error or resident pathogen. Even if the contract is not used coercively, the perception that it might be is sufficient to influence employee behaviour. The RPG survey suggested significant mistrust amongst those polled.

Conclusion

Those who own, regulate and manage airlines respond to the world about them. They respond to shareholder demands, consumer preferences, fashionable employment practices, economic circumstance and a plethora of other social, economic and political conditions. The character and complexion of the industry is a reflection of wider social forces. For good or ill the industry's culture reflects these forces. Like all endeavours, the aviation industry reifies (expresses) society's values. The industry's *modus operandi* reflects *our* value system. The way the industry operates is an emergent property of its milieu.

CHAPTER THREE

Diarising Our Lives

Introduction

In 2010–2011 the author researched the pilot lifestyle using sleep/activity logs (SLOGs), an on-line questionnaire and interviews with pilots.[1] The SLOGs, questionnaire responses and interviews create an oral history of the modern pilot experience. The research follows in the tradition of Britain's pioneering Mass Observation project that recorded the British way of life before, during and after the Second World War. Mass Observation created an "anthropology of ourselves" (Mass Observation Archive, 2001). In the 1943 Publication *War Factory*, Mass Observation recorded, amongst other things, attitudes towards those who worked in a recently established factory employing nearly one thousand men and women:

> They ought to be shot, some of those fellows up there [in the new factory]. They've got nothing to do and they're just sitting tight there because they're frightened they'll have to join the Army (cited in Mass Observation, 2009: 16).

To the extent that it gives pilots the opportunity to tell their own story, the research emulates oral history projects like Ferdynand Zweig's (1948) *Men in the Pits*, Zweig's (1952) *Women's Life and Labour*,[2] and his influential account *The worker in an affluent society: family life and industry*[3]

---

1   The research was funded by the British Airline Pilots Association. Most participants were BALPA members.

2   The *New Statesman's* Giles Romilly said of Zweig's study: "It is Professor Zweig's achievement to have made ... the voice of millions – speak" (Romilly cited in Zweig, 1952: 2).

3   In his pioneering work on shifting social values, Zweig interviewed workers in five British firms, while his partner visited their homes. Zweig's ambitious methodology

(Zweig, 1961). The methodology used here emulates that used to produce the Centerprise Trust's (1977) *A People's Autobiography of Hackney*, Bill Couturié and Richard Dewhurst's (1987) made-for-television documentary *Dear America: Letters Home from Vietnam*,[4] the Greater Manchester Low Pay Unit's (1995) *Workers' Voices: Accounts of Working Life in Britain in the Nineties* and Simon Bennett's (2009) *Londonland: an Ethnography of Labour in a World City*.

There are lamentably few academically-significant oral histories or ethnographic studies of modern military or commercial flying. 'The few' include the United States Air Force's Lt. Col. Christian G. Watt's (2009) Air War College thesis that investigated fatigue "from an aircrew perspective", Ginnett's (1990) evocative *in vivo* study of a Boeing airliner crew's (pilots and cabin attendants) four-day duty, Alexandra Haertner's (2011) ethnography of female airline pilots (written in German) and several journal papers written by this author (Bennett, 2006, 2010a).

Reflections on the Research Methodology

Sample Size

There was a good response to the request for pilots to keep SLOGs. However, with a BALPA membership of over 10,000, the questionnaire response rate was disappointingly low. Despite publicising the questionnaire in BALPA journals, on the BALPA web-site and via e-mail (and

---

was informed by the assumption that "... industrial life enters family life on many counts, and equally family life crosses industrial life" (Zweig, 1961: ix). Zweig believed that social domains (home and factory, for example) interpenetrate and overlap. Such domains are *mutually affecting*.

4   Canby (1988) explains: "Bill Couturié's *Dear America: Letters Home From Vietnam* recalls the Vietnam War in the words of the men and women who fought it, in letters written in haste, without self-consciousness and, mostly, without pretence". The documentary's narrative is informed by a 'genuine voice'.

respondents being entered in a prize draw), less than 5% of the membership completed the questionnaire. It is not claimed that the views of a 5% self-selecting sample represent those of the general membership. Further, it is not claimed that the results have external validity (Cook and Campbell, 1979). Nevertheless the 433 questionnaires generated a significant volume of data that merits consideration.

Potential for Bias

Bias has the potential to undermine academic research. It may skew the construction, administration, scope, tenor and interpretation of research (Cook and Campbell, 1979; Burns, 2000; Gilbert, 2001; Lavrakas, 2008). The self-selecting nature of the questionnaire element of the research (and, indeed, of the sleep diary and interview elements) created a potential for bias. Olsen (2008: 809–811) explains:

> Self-selection bias is the problem that very often results when survey respondents are allowed to decide entirely for themselves whether or not they want to participate in a survey. To the extent that respondents' propensity for participating in the study is correlated with the substantive topic the researchers are trying to study, there will be self-selection bias in the resulting data. In most instances, self-selection will lead to biased data, as the respondents who choose to participate will not well-represent the entire target population.

The internal validity (Cook and Campbell, 1979) of the research was further jeopardized by the coterminous debate over flight and duty-time limitations. BALPA opposed the European Aviation Safety Agency's (EASA's) plan to liberalize flight and duty-time limitations on health and safety grounds (British Air Line Pilots Association, 2011). Members would have been mindful of this campaign, which included articles in *The Log* (BALPA's house journal), debate in the national press, television appearances by BALPA officers, BALPA officers testifying to Parliamentary Select Committees and the lobbying of MPs and MEPs.

Finally, the author is well-known to UK-based pilots for his work on flight-crew stress and fatigue (which spans fifteen years and has seen him observe several hundred flights from the jump-seat) and for publicly promoting the industry to politicians and civil servants. Perceptions of the author as 'pro-pilot' and 'pro-industry' had the potential to shape both the profile of the volunteers, and tenor of the questionnaire, sleep-diary and interview responses. These issues ask questions about the internal validity of the research.

Sleep Log Data

The ten sleep/activity logs (SLOGs) reproduced in this chapter are representative of the pilot experience in various sectors (scheduled long-haul, helicopter operations, freight, etc.). They provide a textured account of the pilot lifestyle. The diaries are reproduced verbatim (although information that could reveal the identity of the diarist – for example, the names of personnel or details of incidents – has been removed).

The following points should be noted:

1   All times are GMT/Zulu.
2   Where time asleep/time awake data was provided, the total amount of time asleep was calculated by the author and given in brackets. For example: "Slept from 22:00–06:00 (8hrs)".
3   Diaries (and accompanying e-mails) are reproduced verbatim (one aim of the study was to give pilots a voice).
4   The Analysis provided at the end of each diary was written by the author. Theory is used to interpret the data.
5   The diaries reproduced here are representative of the feedback provided from each sector (scheduled long haul, low-cost, charter, etc.). The data is typical. It was not possible to reproduce all 133 diaries.
6   The diarising commenced in the summer of 2010 (to ensure that the activities of the summer charter industry were accurately represented) and ended early in 2011. This was a turbulent period for the industry, with business affected by the global economic slump and opinion divided over EASA's proposed new FTL/FDP regulations.

7   One diary has been curtailed by the author, as the data recorded towards
    the end of the twenty-one day period did not reveal anything new.
8   The sectors are described in the following order: Charter; Helicopter;
    Freight; Low-cost short-haul; Full service long-haul.
9   The SLOGs contain much time-related information, as in the time a
    pilot went to bed, fell asleep, woke, rose, left for work, etc. If you do
    not want to wade through this detail, there is a helpful Analysis at the
    end of each SLOG written by the book's author that comments on
    the issues raised by the diarist.

Sleep Logs

Captain – charter (C1)[5]	
Day	Diary (All times Zulu)
1	Slept from 22:00–06:00 (8hrs). Felt refreshed. Set off for base at 07:00 to operate MAN–SFB (Manchester–Orlando). About a 30min drive from home to base. I had a 'good' First Officer. Not familiar with cabin crew. The Cabin Manager had her husband and daughter on board on Staff Travel. Against the rules. Didn't say anything to preserve the peace. Landed 18:35 (scheduled block time 09:30–18:50). Shopped in Florida Mall 20:00–02:00.
2	Single beer before retiring at 03:00. Woke at 10:30 (7hrs 30mins). I slept well but had a bit of a headache on waking which I attribute to dehydration. Socialised, ate at 22:00, drank two beers, then retired at midnight. Short sleep disturbance during the night.
3	Woke at 10:30 feeling fairly refreshed (9hrs 30mins). Return flight SFB–BHX (Birmingham) delayed by 1hr 30mins. Managed a one hour pre-flight sleep. Rotated at 21:00.

5   Diaries (SLOGs) are given sequential numbers. 'C1' = Case Study number one.

Captain – charter (C1)	
Day	Diary (All times Zulu)
4	Landed BHX 05:15. Transferred to HOTAC BHX. Got to bed at 06:30. Unable to get off to sleep. Woken by maid twice at 09:50. Unable to get back to sleep. Feel like shit. Got about two hours sleep. Dull headache. Got up. Sandwich at 14:00 before travelling to MAN. Home by 17:00. Watched T.V. Retired at 22:30.
5	Woke at 06:00 (7hrs 30mins). Slept OK. Got up at 08:00. Did chores. Feeling tired. Pub at 12:00. Supermarket at 15:00. Back to pub at 16:30. Retired at 23:00.
6	Woke 06:00. Feeling groggy. Fell asleep again, and woke at 09:30 (9hrs 30mins). Didn't feel too fresh. Gardened. Retired at 22:30 and watched TV until midnight.
7	Woke at 05:30 (5hrs 30mins). Got up at 10:30, unable to sleep. Drove to base to operate MAN–PVK–MAN (Manchester–Prevesa–Manchester). Drove home and asleep by midnight.
8	Woke at 05:00 (5hrs). Lay in bed until 09:00, unable to sleep. Drove to base to operate MAN–NAP–MAN (Manchester–Naples–Manchester). Drove home and asleep by 23:30.
9	Woken up at 06:00 (6hrs 30mins). Woken up by son going to work. Then a text to wife's telephone. Then the telephone rang. Prevented me from getting back to sleep. Drove to base to operate MAN–TCP–MAN (Manchester–Taba (Egypt)–Manchester). Flight delayed on stand for 15mins. A long duty day. Thirteen hours. 5hrs 30mins block time (times two). Got home at 01:30. In bed by 01:40. Asleep!
10	Woke at 09:00 (7hrs 30mins). Feel a little less than perfect. Bit of a dull headache. Domestic chores. In bed by 21:30.
11	Didn't get to sleep until 23:00. Woke at 01:00 and stayed awake until 04:00. Then slept until 08:00 (6hrs). In work by 09:00 to pick up taxi to LBA (Leeds–Bradford). Ninety-minute ride. Flight delayed one hour due to late inbound. Operated LBA–PMI–MAN (Leeds–Bradford–Palma–Manchester). Flight delayed PMI by one hour due to flow-control restrictions. No meal on return flight – oven unserviceable – so starving. Two hours late into MAN. Drove home. Quick chat to wife, then bed at 22:30 with sleeping tablet – I need to get some sleep.

Captain – charter (C1)	
Day	Diary (All times Zulu)
12	Woken at 06:40 by alarm (8hrs 10mins). I feel very tired. Errands in MAN. Returned home and in bed by 19:00. Unable to sleep. Rang in 'unfit' at 22:15. Fell asleep at 23:30.
13	Woke briefly at 06:30, slept on, and woke up at 09:00 (9hrs 15mins). Errands (bank, etc.). Rang Crewing and declared myself fit. Retired at 20:00 very tired. Did not get off to sleep until 23:00.
14	Woke at 07:15 (8hrs 15mins). Feeling a bit more rested. Crewing rang to ask if I would operate NCL–DLM–BHX (Newcastle–Dalaman (Turkey)–Birmingham). I agreed. Taxi to Newcastle, then HOTAC. Watched a film in bed until 09:30. Still awake at 02:30.
15	Woke at 05:20 (3hrs) feeling like ugh. Taxi to airport at 05:30. All flights on time. Back home by 19:40. Asleep by 21:30.
16	Woke at 08:00 (10hrs 30mins). Errands. My fatigue report has been rejected. The only way to do it is to go sick. It saves a call from the management. More stress and grief. In bed by 21:30. Asleep by 22:30.
17	Woke at 07:00 (8hrs 30mins). Good sleep, but still feel tired. Operating to MLE (Male) today. Forty minutes pre-flight sleep. Crew for MAN–MLE two Captains and a First Officer. Scheduled departure 17:20. Scheduled arrival 04:20. Wife had a confirmed seat. Didn't know the other Captain. Couldn't get paperwork, so rang Germany. No paperwork after 15mins, so I tried again. Captain entered. He had seen the planning at home on his computer. We are supposed to brief together. I went through the paperwork with the First Officer. I asked the Captain if he would like to take the flight out. 'Erm, no' was his reply. 'OK then, I'll take the flight out' said I. He seemed a bit of a dry bugger. My first impression proved correct. It was difficult to communicate with him. In-flight rest consisted of one hour each, then two hours each in the night. Arrived on schedule.
18	In bed by 06:00. Woke at 11:00 (5hrs). Went to beach, then hotel bar with wife. Had 3 or 4 beers. Bed at 21:00 feeling a bit drunk.
19	Woke at 05:00 with the light (8hrs). Wife got up and was sick. I didn't want to move my head. Hangover. Dehydrated. Slept for a further two hours. Got up at 08:00. Drank some water. Headache had gone. Felt hungry. Spent time by pool. Went sightseeing. Had a couple of beers before retiring early. Asleep by 20:00.

Captain – charter (C1)	
Day	Diary (All times Zulu)
20	Woke at 02:00 (6hrs). Felt refreshed on waking. Went sightseeing. Spent time by the pool. Asleep by 21:00.
21	Woke at 05:00 (8hrs). Eyes felt a bit sore/tired, but I decided to get up as waking up tomorrow would be even harder.
Analysis	

This Manchester-based Training Captain with over 16,000 hours (he started his career aged 21) flew for a passenger charter company. His diary covers the busy summer charter period.

According to the Federal Aviation Administration (FAA) (2010): "If a person has had significantly less than eight hours of sleep in the past twenty-four hours, he or she is more likely to be fatigued ... The average person requires in excess of nine hours of sleep a night to recover from a sleep debt". The diarist's pre MAN–SFB sleep of 8 hours would have generated 16 hours of productive wakefulness (8x2=16). (It is assumed that one hour of sleep generates double that amount in productive wakefulness (this can vary from person to person). Although "... it is not necessary to sleep for the exact number of hours to recover sleep debt" (Campbell and Bagshaw, 1999: 138) for the sake of simplicity a uniform 1:2 relationship is assumed here).

He appears not to have slept on the flight, and was active on arrival until his next major sleep from 03:00–10:30 on Day 2. The diarist's sleep credit of 16 hours would have been exhausted by 22:00 on Day 1, after which time he would have been in sleep debt. By the time he got to bed he would have been carrying 5 hours of sleep debt.

At the time he was flying the approach into SFB (at around 18:00) he would have been in sleep credit to the tune of 4 hours (approximately). As stated above, by the time he retired (at 03:00 on Day 2) he would have been in sleep debt to the tune of 5 hours (approx.) (16–21=–5). A Sleep Diary study conducted at a UK-registered freight airline (Bennett, 2010a) suggested that sleep debt was difficult to recover down-route (due to factors like hotel noise, telephone calls, the daylight zeitgeber, malfunctioning/noisy/uncontrollable air conditioning, etc.). The Federal Aviation Administration (2010: 55855) comments: "Sleep should not be fragmented with interruptions. In addition, environmental conditions, such as temperature, noise and turbulence, impact how beneficial sleep is, and how performance is restored".

The diarist obtained 7hrs 30mins sleep on Day 2, generating 10 hours of sleep credit ((7.5x2)–5=10). As he rose at 10:30, this credit would have been exhausted by 20:30.

On Day 3 the diarist slept from midnight to 10:30, with one hour awake because of a disturbance. This sleep would have generated 15.5 hours of sleep credit

Captain – charter (C1)
((9.5x2)–3.5=15.5). A one-hour pre-flight sleep boosted this credit to 17.5 hours ((1x2)+15.5=17.5). The return flight SFB–BHX rotated at 21:00, arriving at BHX 1.5 hours late. By the time he got to sleep in his BHX HOTAC (at 07:30) he would have been in sleep debt to the tune of 2.5 hours (17.5–20=–2.5). His two-hour HOTAC sleep (07:30–09:30) would have eliminated this sleep debt, leaving him with 1.5 hours of sleep credit ((2x2)–2.5=1.5). By the time he retired to bed at home (at 22:30) he would have been in sleep debt to the tune of 11.5 hours (1.5–13=–11.5). Here we have a good illustration of how a single bad sleep experience (in this case the BHX HOTAC) can generate significant sleep debt (of 11.5 hours).

That night the diarist got 7.5 hours sleep. This means that when he rose at home on Day 5 he had just 3.5 hours of sleep credit ((7.5x2)–11.5=3.5). It is unsurprising that he felt tired during Day 5, and that even after a substantial sleep that night (of 9.5 hours) he didn't feel too fresh on Day 6. The Federal Aviation Administration (2010: 55855) says: "The average person requires in excess of nine hours of sleep a night to recover from a sleep debt". This diary illustrates how a work-related stressor (sleep debt) can impinge on home life.

Prior to his NCL–DLM–BHX duty on Days 14/15 the diarist got at most three hours HOTAC sleep in NCL. One must question the wisdom of operating on just three hours sleep. The diarist's decision to operate may have been influenced by fear of victimisation (see his comments about fatigue reporting above, and below). Caldwell and Caldwell (2003: 95) say: "Insufficient sleep is an insidious threat to safety, performance and personal well-being ... [T]he greater the amount of sleep deprivation or restriction, the more the loss of performance, mental clarity, judgement and mood will be".

The airline's rejection of the diarist's fatigue report, and the diarist's reaction (see diarist's comments above, and below), give cause for concern. If fatigued pilots elect to go sick rather than file a fatigue report, then fatigue will be under-reported. Such 'masking' is a potential problem, especially in airlines that operate a fatigue risk management system (FRMS). FRMS requires full and accurate reporting of fatigue. Fear of victimisation (whether that fear is founded or unfounded) distorts reporting. For an FRMS to work there must be a just culture. A just culture encourages error-reporting by protecting those whose acts of omission or commission were the result not of wilful neglect, but of inadequate training, poor judgment (misreading a situation), fatigue, psychological pressure, insufficient information, etc. Punishing someone simply because they made the wrong decision serves no purpose other than to satisfy a base desire for retribution. Interventions should aim to establish *why* a particular decision was made with a view to learning lessons: "A just culture ... is

Captain – charter (C1)

particularly concerned with the sustainability of learning from failure through the reporting of errors, adverse events, incidents. If operators and others perceive that their reports are treated unfairly or lead to negative consequences, the willingness to report will decline (e.g. Ruitenberg 2002 cited a 50% drop in incident reports after the prosecution of air traffic controllers involved a near-miss). Writings about just culture over the past decade (e.g. Reason 1997; Marx 2001; Dekker 2008) acknowledge this central paradox of accountability and learning: various *stakeholders (e.g. employers, regulators) want to know everything that happened, but cannot accept everything that happened* and will want to advertise their position as such. Thus, rating certain behaviour as culpable is not just about that behaviour or its antecedent intentions, it performs a wider function of regulating a distinction between normal and abnormal, between order and disorder. 'A "no-blame" culture is neither feasible nor desirable. Most people desire some level of accountability when a mishap occurs' (Global Aviation Information Network 2004 p. viii). These are neo-Durkheimian ideas (see Durkheim 1950, 1895) about the boundary-maintaining function of ... organizational rituals [my emphasis] ..." (Dekker, 2008: 178).

Reason (cited in Global Aviation Information Network, 2004: vi) describes the purpose and boundaries of a just culture: "The term 'no-blame culture' flourished in the 1990s and still endures today. Compared to the largely punitive cultures that it sought to replace, it was clearly a step in the right direction. It acknowledged that a large proportion of unsafe acts were 'honest errors' (the kinds of slips, lapses and mistakes that even the best people can make) and were not truly blameworthy, nor was there much in the way of remedial or preventative benefit to be had by punishing their perpetrators. But the 'no-blame' concept had two serious weaknesses. First, it ignored – or, at least, failed to confront – those individuals who wilfully (and often repeatedly) engaged in dangerous behaviours that most observers would recognise as being likely to increase the risk of a bad outcome. Second, it did not properly address the crucial business of distinguishing between culpable and non-culpable unsafe acts. In my view, a safety culture depends critically upon first negotiating where the line should be drawn between unacceptable behaviour and blameless unsafe acts. There will always be a grey area between these two extremes where the issue has to be decided on a case by case basis ... A number of aviation organisations have embarked upon this process, and the general indications are that only around 10 per cent of actions contributing to bad events are judged as culpable. In principle, at least, this means that the large majority of unsafe acts can be reported without fear of sanction. Once this crucial trust has been established, the organisation begins to have a reporting culture, something that provides the system with an accessible memory, which, in turn, is the essential underpinning to a learning culture. There will, of course, be setbacks along the way. But engineering a just culture is the all-important early step; so much else depends upon it".

Captain – charter (C1)

In a survey of over 5,000 reports filed with NASA's Aviation Safety Reporting System (ASRS) the National Transportation Safety Board found some pilots reluctant to call in as fatigued: "Some of the air carrier pilots reported using [fatigue risk management programmes] successfully, whereas other pilots reported that they hesitated to use such programmes because of fear of retribution ... In addition, other pilots reported that they attempted to call in as fatigued but encountered company resistance. For example, a February 2006 ASRS report from a captain of a regional jet stated that she and the first officer 'were sort of robotic and tired' because of three consecutive early report times, and the first officer stated the following: 'I even called scheduling and spoke to a supervisor [twice] asking him to take me off the rest of the trip because I was so exhausted. He tried to work that out, but said we were short staffed ... I told him that I wouldn't call in fatigued because they didn't have the staffing ... [I]n hindsight, I feel that I should have called in fatigued instead of fighting the exhaustion'" (National Transportation Safety Board, 2008: 35–36).

The hangover episode on Day 19 evidences the acute health impacts of alcohol consumption. Drinking too little water when operating causes dehydration. Consuming alcohol when at the destination exacerbates the problem of dehydration. Alcohol may be seen as a means of countering stress and/or getting to sleep (Harris, 2005). Alcohol is a powerful drug, however, whose negative impacts should not be under-estimated. Rhodes and Gil (2002: 30) observe: "Avoid drinking alcohol before going to bed. Alcohol may help you fall asleep but it disturbs your sleep patterns. It will disrupt your sleep by causing early morning or even middle of the night awakening and prevent you from getting the proper amounts of slow wave and REM sleep you need to function properly".

The diarist responded pragmatically to the Cabin Manager incident on Day 1: "The Cabin Manager had her husband and daughter on board on Staff Travel. Against the rules. Didn't say anything to preserve the peace". In his seminal study of police work Bittner (1967: 715) differentiated between 'peace keeping' and 'law enforcement'. Peace keeping required officers to 'play it by ear'. Police officers' responses to tense situations were informed by pragmatism. Discretion worked in everyone's favour: "What the seasoned patrolman means ... in saying that he 'plays [it] by ear' is that he is making his decisions while being attuned to the realities of complex situations about which he has immensely detailed knowledge. This studied aspect of peace keeping generally is not made explicit ... [T]he ability to discharge the duties associated with keeping the peace is viewed as a reflection of an innate talent of 'getting along with people'". With over 16,000 hours this diarist was very much a 'seasoned commander'.

Additional information

The diarist appended a letter to his sleep log. Here are some selected paragraphs: "It probably appears we don't eat too well, that we don't sleep enough, that we drink

Captain – charter (C1)

too much and get little exercise – about right, really. There is little or no protection for us. There is a culture of 'bullying' by the management ('How dare you be tired') and no protection afforded by the Civil Aviation Authority (who are in bed with the company – the Flight Operations Inspector 'cherry-picks' a bullet Orlando trip once a month to stay current). The industry is an accident waiting to happen. It's just a shame somebody hasn't written off an aircraft and a couple of hundred people because it's the only way things will change. This might sound cynical, but that's thirty years in the business. With the introduction of EU-Ops in April 2011 it will get worse – two pilots will be able to do thirteen hours duty whatever time they start".

Regarding the reference to his airline's organisational culture, Glendon, Clarke and McKenna (2006: 233) posit management style as a potential stressor: "Sources of pressure are derived not only from inherent job factors, but also from the organisational context, such as the ... climate of the organisation (e.g. management style, level of consultation, communication and politics)".

Regarding the reference to alcohol consumption, it has been reported "that approximately 12% of professional pilots [drink] alcohol as a means of coping with stressful situations" (Harris, 2005: 206). Harris (2005: 206) explains: "[Three surveys] ... all reported that job-related stresses were frequently cited as a common cause of heavy drinking in professional pilots. These stressors included being away from home, job-related fatigue, long hours and boredom". Bor, Field and Scragg (2002: 244) say: "Stress, jet lag, fatigue, disrupted personal relationships, unusual routines ... may all take their toll on even the most resilient crew members. Recent changes in patterns of employment and piloting tasks may be an additional source of stress". Alcohol and stress are two of the risk factors associated with hypertension (King, 2011).

While cases of attempted 'drunk flying' create a serious risk and attract significant media attention, it is important to maintain a sense of perspective. The FAA, for example, administers more than 10,000 random alcohol tests each year (for blood-alcohol concentrations greater than 0.04%). In 2008 thirteen pilots tested positive. There are about 100,000 commercial pilots in the United States. The Human Intervention Motivation Study alcohol-intervention programme assists about 125 pilots a year (Levin, 2009).

First Officer – helicopter operations (North Sea) (C7)	
Day	Diary (All times Zulu)
1	Rostered non-flying day (it's the Sunday of my 2-off, roster-wise). Woke at 05:00 as girlfriend had to be in work. (She's a surgeon. As a good friend who's also a doctor said to me some years ago: 'People don't stop getting injured or dying just because it's the weekend or the middle of the night!'). Tired: got probably 5.5 hours of acceptable sleep. Breakfast of a pork pie and an apple while driving 2hrs to Aberdeen from her place. 12:00: ate 4 hot-cross buns with butter. Day spent online and doing paperwork-type stuff (non-work). Visited friends for Sunday dinner – roast chicken etc at 16:00. Received the following day's flying schedule at 17:00 as usual. Supper of a Tesco Egg/ Bacon sandwich with two bottles of beer at circa 19:00. Watched T.V., read a book, bed at 10:15. Asleep by about 10:20.
2	Rostered flying day (the first of my '7-on'). Woke at 06:00, though alarm set for 06:45. Pretty tired still, not a great night's sleep despite being almost 8hrs. Snoozed, got up and ate 3 slices of oatbread toast + fruit juice for breakfast at 07:15. Dressed in work uniform and left for work at 07:45. Arrived at 07:55 for a report time of 08:30. I always aim to be in half an hour before formal report time since if the weather is bad and the planning becomes complex it can take rather longer than just the allocated half hour (the other half hour of the allocated report time is for walking out and starting up). I'm also pretty new so allowing more time means I can learn more from taking my time over it all. Planned flight while Capt was still out on a previous flight, presented the planning to him when he got back, got changed etc (we fly in flying suits or immersion suits, not uniform). Flown with him before – nice guy, all very relaxed, no drama, plenty of time. Departed on time at 09:30, flying to a rig in the Beryl field (about 70mins flying time with today's winds). Good flight, no problems, decent weather. Ate a meal from the rig of roast pork, boiled potatoes and cabbage at 11:20. Returned on time at 12:30, completed post-flight paperwork, debriefed with Captain, and was released to go home by the Ops desk at 12:50. Home at 13:00. My journey to/from work is always 5–10mins by car, even with morning traffic, so extremely convenient. Spent afternoon going for a 4.2mile cross-country run, online, watching TV etc. Ate 2 rounds of sandwiches for dinner at 17:00, with a glass of milk and some vitamin pills. Received following day's flying schedule at 17:00 and saw that 1 of the next day's 2 flights will be my annual line check and I then have an hour's ground refresher training afterwards. Bed at 18:45 due early start tomorrow. Asleep by 19:00 (I was clearly very tired). Woken at 23:00 by a thunder storm so loud it woke me through my ear-plugs. Returned to sleep soon after.

First Officer – helicopter operations (North Sea) (C7)	
Day	Diary (All times Zulu)
3	Rostered flying day. Woken at 04:00 by the alarm. A good night's rest with at least 8.5hrs of good sleep but still felt somewhat tired after the last few days of limited sleep. Ate 2 buttered hot-cross buns for breakfast while driving to work, got to work at 04:55 after the usual 10min drive in. In half an hour early for 05:30 report time as it's my line check ride and also have to plan for both flights before the first, as it's likely to be a rotors-running changeover between flights. Both flights fine. Line Training Captain who I've flown with lots of times before. Line checks are essentially just a normal line flight, with the addition of some scenario-based questions, plus an airborne radar approach (ARA) at the rig (even if an ARA is not specifically required for the landing on the day). Departed slightly late for 1st flight at 06:40 (scheduled 06:30) due to late pax (passenger). Very short flight, just half an hour each way, which makes it fairly busy for both PF (Pilot Flying) and PNF (Pilot Non-Flying) as once in the cruise it's straight into preparation for the next approach and landing. As regards PF and PNF – at our company one pilot is PF outbound (usually whoever is making the first rig landing, based on helideck orientation and that day's wind direction). Then we swap roles for the inbound leg, irrespective of who is P1 (commander) or P2 (co-pilot). Nice visual flight rules (VFR) day helped make things easier. Managed to get a bacon roll from the 1st rig down my neck while doing the paperwork in the cruise back to Aberdeen, where we arrived on time. As anticipated/hoped we rotors-ran into the next flight as Ops and Security had got all the pax through in good time (we generally have a good working relationship with all areas of the company) and we got away early for the 2nd flight (scheduled 09:00, actual 08:45). Some trouble getting hold of the rig on the radio on the outbound leg, meaning it was rushed preparing the ARA and getting all the checks done in time since we can't set up the approach in the flight management computer (FMC) and brief it until we have the rig wx (weather) wind direction. All worked out fine in the end and all on time. Ate another of the bacon rolls and an apple at 11:30 in the cruise on the return leg. I am one of those people who needs to eat little and often. Back at Aberdeen on time 12:00. Straight into 1 hour of training 1-on-1 with the same Line Trainer I flew with. Just an annual recurrency on some of the emergency kit, no dramas. Post-flight paperwork done and debriefing etc., so that we left work after being released by Ops at 13:00. We always ask Ops if they're done with us once we've finished all our scheduled flying in case there are ground runs to be done for the engineers or extra flights that need covering. Home at 13:30 after doing some food shopping. Afternoon spent

First Officer – helicopter operations (North Sea) (C7)	
Day	Diary (All times Zulu)
	online, non-work paperwork, watching TV etc. Ate a microwave curry at 15:45. Received schedule for tomorrow; reporting at 11:00 tomorrow for a 12:00 flight. Ops then phoned at 18:30 to tell me there was a change of plan and I'm now on a 05:30 report for a 06:30 flight. Flight will be to the East Shetland Basin – an area with its own procedures, with which I'm not very familiar having only flown there once before. So I spent 20mins looking through some of our old line training docs to remind myself of the radio calls, handovers and QNH boundaries, etc. Phoned girlfriend, had a sandwich and glass of milk at 19:00 and bed at 20:00. Asleep shortly after.
4	Rostered flying day. Up once in the night to go to loo. Otherwise reasonable sleep but woken by the alarm at 04:00 (8hrs) and still quite tired as haven't caught up any sleep from the deficit after the weekend. In work just before 05:00 after usual 10min drive in. Report time 05:30. No problems planning/briefing. Flying with a Captain I've not flown with yet. Flight fine, plenty of time in the cruise with great weather, but deteriorating weather at both ends meant last minute changes from visual to instrument approaches both at the rig and at Aberdeen – required some quick rework but all fine and uneventful. We also changed our route outbound while in-flight to miss out the original intended refuel stop at Sumburgh as our burn rate was favourable and we ended up with enough fuel to go direct after all. Unusually long turnaround time at the rig due to problems with their fuelling system so we sat rotors-running for a good half hour (we don't shut down on the rigs for the refuel) instead of the usual 15–20mins. Ate a banana while waiting on the rig (circa 08:30) and 2 buttered hot cross buns during the return cruise (circa 09:30). 10 mins late returning to Aberdeen as a result of the rig fuel delay, landing at 11:10. Worked well with this Captain, nice guy (as are the vast majority of our Captains) and a good learning exercise on the East Shetland Basin operating procedures for me. Home at 12:00 after the usual paperwork, getting changed and 10min drive. Almost convinced myself to go for a run but still getting pain from shinsplints after Monday's run, so will leave another day and go on Thursday instead. Will also hopefully run Sunday – which'll be my target of 3 sessions for the week. Went to head-office at 13:00 to drop off a test paper I'd completed (part of another annual check). Thankfully passed the paper no problem. Got a MacDonalds on the way back and ate at circa 13:30. I allow myself one MacDonalds every 2–3 weeks. Afternoon spent doing my own thing at home, watching TV, online, reading, sorting a few things out for my girlfriend's visit this weekend, etc. Tomorrow's schedule received at 17:00 and I've a lie-in as report time is

First Officer – helicopter operations (North Sea) (C7)	
Day	Diary (All times Zulu)
	10:00. Will be flying to the same rig in East Shetland Basin as today but with a line trainer on a 'standards' flight. Standards flights are a customer (Oil and Gas Producers') requirement for every line pilot every couple of weeks and it just means flying with a line trainer who'll fill in a short report afterwards assessing us against set criteria. Be a good opportunity for me to consolidate today's learning. Later start also means I can allow myself a couple of bottles of beer (the odd drink the night before is fine as long as no alcohol is taken within 10 hours of report time. A tighter constraint for me personally is that I sleep very badly if I drink more than a couple of pints so no intention of doing that!). In bed at 20:30, read for a bit, asleep at 21:00.
5	Up once in the night for the loo, as usual. Rostered flying day. Awake at 06:00 but snoozed another half hour to 06:30 (9hrs 30mins). For the 1st time in a week I felt well rested and refreshed, having got a good 9+ hours sleep. Looked at the online departures board and saw my flight is now rescheduled to 17:00 so expecting a call from Ops shortly, either to say I'm on a different flight at original time or to delay reporting. Breakfast at 07:30 of 1.5 rounds of oatmeal bread sandwiches with fruit juice. Made up my 'emergency food supplies' for the day of some buttered hot cross buns and a banana – I always carry this along with numerous 'muesli bars' because delays, weather, etc., can mean long periods between meals and I do not operate well like that. Ops rang at 07:45 to advise I don't need to come in for the original flight, rather now doing a different flight, lifting at 14:45. It's with the same Line Training Captain as planned and still a 'Standards' flight but now out to the Atlantic West Of Shetland instead. Spent some morning time on my personal finances. I keep a close control on all my £ but am very lucky that I have no real financial worries. I own a house down south that pays for itself as it's rented out to good tenants. I live comfortably within my income (though as a junior F/O on a reduced salary to cover training costs this is much lower than it was 2 years ago in my previous career in banking) and really have no financial worries, other than how best to invest. However, I am very aware that, being 35, my financial situation is likely to change in the future when the whole 'family' thing happens, so I'm sensible with my money. But, for the time being life is very good. In Aberdeen I live in a shared house which is paid for by the week and I have 1 room that is my own with the rest of the place being shared. There are no communal rooms other than kitchen and bathroom, so often you never meet the other people coming through the house, particularly if they're only here a few weeks, working offshore, etc. It's extremely convenient – the weekly rate includes cleaning, bed linen

First Officer – helicopter operations (North Sea) (C7)	
Day	Diary (All times Zulu)
	and towels, so I have no cleaning to do. Ideal for a bachelor! Went for a 4.2 mile cross-country run before having a cooked lunch of 2 sausages, mash and peas (at 12:30) and getting ready for work. Reported at 13:15 for a 13:45 report. No problems with planning, though no fuel at the rig so we planned to go via Sumburgh for fuel on the way. Pleasant flight which all went to plan, departed on time at 14:45. Ate a very nice Chicken Tikka with rice and chips from the rig at circa 17:45. Returned at 19:00 and got home at 19:30 after debriefing and the 10 minute drive. Next day's schedule was waiting for me and I'm on standby tomorrow. This is the first time in a very long while for me to be on standby, but is perfect as my girlfriend is coming up from Edinburgh tomorrow. Spent the evening watching TV, phoned my girlfriend to finalise tomorrow, now the schedule's in, and ate my 2 hot X buns at 21:00 with a bottle of beer. In bed at 22:30, and asleep by 22:45.
6	Rostered flying day. Up once in night for loo, as usual. Woke at 07:00, feeling good (8hrs). Had 3 oatmeal bread sandwiches for breakfast with fruit juice. Felt good after another decent night's rest. Spent the morning cleaning my room for girlfriend's visit, doing washing, ironing, going to Tesco and filling in this log. Had 2 rounds of Tesco pre-packed sandwiches for lunch at 12:30. Girlfriend arrived about 14:00. Headed into Aberdeen at about 16:30, received tomorrow's schedule at 16:50, and saw I am on standby again: a real rarity to have 2 standby days in a row, particularly as I wasn't called in on Friday (I'd expect to be called in to do ground runs or cover a flight maybe 35% of standbys), but it's because the company's annual barbecue is tomorrow (a family event) and as someone without a family I volunteered to fly instead of going (I need hours, and am more than happy to fly). Hence the family guys were scheduled for the morning flights so they'd be released in time for the bbq, while those of us with no preference covered the bbq period as standbys. Spent evening in Aberdeen with my girlfriend, had 2 pints of beer at circa 18:00 and a Thai meal at 19:00. Asleep around 22:00.
7	Rostered flying day. Awake circa 08:00 (10hrs). Sleep not too bad, though broken due to my bed just being a double and so not great for 2 people (when one of us is well over 6 foot anyway). Breakfast of a Tesco pre-packed sandwich at 10:00. Went for a walk at Hazlehead Park and then on the beach. Had an ice-cream at circa 11:00. Called by Ops at 12:00 to say I had a flight with a 14:00 report, to go Atlantic West of Shetland again. Walked for another hour, came home and ate a small Tesco pre-packed Hoisin Duck Wrap for lunch at 13:00. Got changed for work, girlfriend set off for Edinburgh (actually at exactly the time she was going to anyway – the

First Officer – helicopter operations (North Sea) (C7)	
Day	Diary (All times Zulu)
	timings couldn't have worked out better this weekend!) and I departed for work at 13:30. Flight planning took some thought due to the timing of the flight meaning most of our usual alternates were closed, but planned out fine in the end by adding an extra refuel just before embarking pax. Lovely day, departed on time at 15:00: nice flight with no problems, flying with a Captain I know well and get on well with (which is the case with most of our Captains really). Ate my hot X buns at 16:00. My landing on the rig (i.e. wind direction and deck orientation dictated a left-seat landing, in helicopters the commander sits in the right-hand seat (RHS), the opposite to fixed wing) and it involved an interesting committal to the deck because the rig has obstacles in the approach on my side, necessitating that I fly forward of the rig (always facing into wind), then translate sideways in front of the rig (round in front of the obstacles), and then approach backwards to come to the hover over the deck still into wind before setting down. All absolutely within limits, trained for, safe and standard – but such a final approach is one of the more interesting bits of our flying! Good work by the deck crew and we were away within 20mins after the usual rotors-running refuel. Ate 2 meat salad rolls from the rig at 17:00. Nice journey back, ATC predictably quiet as so little traffic around. Back on the ground at 18:15 and got home at 18:45 after the usual bits and pieces, and quick drive home. Schedule waiting when I got back – flying at 15:30 tomorrow so can have a couple of beers tonight. Spent evening watching TV, ate some bread and pate at 21:00 with 4 cans of beer. The alcohol will be long gone from my system by 14:30 report time tomorrow. Bed at 22:30. Read for half an hour, and straight to sleep at 23:00.
8	Rostered flying day. Up once in the night for loo. Woke at 07:00 feeling good after 8 hours sleep. Ate 2 buns and fruit juice for breakfast at 08:00 and spent the morning catching up on this log, sorting out deposits/council tax changes etc., for the change of tenancy that went through yesterday at my house down south, and various other bits of admin and social catching up. Lunch of bread and pate/salami at 12:00. Got ready for work and went in early at 13:15 in order to do some Ops Manual amendments (one of my non-flying duties as a co-pilot). Flight planning all fine for a simple trip out to the East. Flying with a Captain I know well, one of the TRIs, no problems. Departed on time at 15:30 and returned at 17:55. Ate a small meal of pizza and chips from the rig at 16:50. Home by 18:15. Watched TV and had 2 double G&Ts and 2 beers. Ate a meal at 21:00. Asleep at 23:00.

First Officer – helicopter operations (North Sea) (C7)	
Day	Diary (All times Zulu)
9	Rostered non-flying day (the first of my '7-off'). Up once in the night for the loo and then lay awake for half an hour, due to the effect alcohol has on me, not good for my sleep. Awake at 07:00 feeling v mild effects of the alcohol and reasonably well rested. Edited some photos and uploaded some to Facebook. Breakfast of a sandwich and fruit juice at 09:15. Had a haircut, replied to some email, put on a couple of loads of washing/drying (including my flying suit – I made the mistake of opening a yoghurt at Flight Level 55 the other day, very amusing and it could have been a lot worse!) and went for a X-country run at 11:45. Ironed some shirts and got all my kit ready for next week's work, so I don't have to worry about it next Sunday. Ate a lunch of a microwave meal + peas at 12:30 and packed my things for a week down in Edinburgh with my girlfriend and seeing the fringe festival. Drove down to Edinburgh at 14:30, which took 2hrs 20mins. Had a pint at 17:30 in a bar with my girlfriend. Did some food shopping and ate a large chicken/cheese salad with bread at 19:00. Spent evening helping my girlfriend with a paper she's writing for work and then went to bed. Sleep at 23:45.
10	Rostered non-flying day. Woke at 05:20 (5hrs 30mins) with the alarm as my girlfriend is in theatre today. Felt shattered. I got up at the same time and moved my car out of the parking zone, ate a sausage bap (wholemeal, with lettuce – for all the good that was going to do to a sausage roll!) at 07:00. Spent the morning sorting out/setting up my new MacBook and downloading the developer suite of software for iPhone/iPad etc as I have written software before and am intending to convert one or two things into iPhone/iPad 'Apps'. Bought some tickets for a show at tonight's Edinburgh festival and then went for a swim at 12:30. Swam only a mile – I'd normally do twice that as I swim competitively for a club but haven't trained for a month and need to build up slowly again. Came back for a nap from 14:15 to 15:45. Not proper sleep at all as I rarely can sleep in the daytime but woke feeling better. Ate a snack of bread and cheese at 17:15. Went and saw a show at the festival with my girlfriend, which we both enjoyed very much. I love the fact most of the festival 'acts' are only one-hour long, as I can't sit still much longer than that, hence I actually enjoy going to most of the things at the festival. Went for dinner afterwards, eating a steak and chips at 20:00 with 2 glasses of wine and a bottle of beer. Asleep at 21:45.

First Officer – helicopter operations (North Sea) (C7)	
Day	Diary (All times Zulu)
11	Rostered non-flying day. Woke at 05:10 (girlfriend working all week). Didn't feel too bad. I always get up when she does as I can't get back to sleep after she's been doing her thing getting ready for work. Ate a MacDonalds breakfast (sausage/egg McMuffin meal w juice) at 09:15. Booked some more Fringe shows and went out into town to pick up the tickets in the morning. Grabbed a baguette with salami for lunch at 11:45 while walking to first show. Spent the afternoon seeing a couple of shows and then got the train up to Dundee to meet up with a friend for a few beers. 17:00 started drinking lager. 6 pints by 20:30, just catching up and bantering. Went for a Chinese at 20:45 with another pint. Got the 21:43 train back to Edinburgh, arriving 23:05. In bed by 23:30 (in the spare room! As pre-agreed because work is important to us both, and we both need sleep to do our jobs safely and well). Asleep immediately but, as always when I drink much: broken and not very good sleep.
12	Rostered non-flying day. Woke at 05:00 (5hrs 30mins), up at 06:00. Clearly tired though no real hangover so cracked on with catching up on this Log and doing some online admin-type stuff. Breakfast of 2 hot cross buns at 08:00. Swam 2000m at 12:00 and ate a baguette for lunch with a couple of bottles of Oasis on the walk back from the pool, at circa 13:00. Crashed out for a couple of hours 15:00–17:00. Up and showered for the evening. Girlfriend going to a big work dinner so I'm going to the Edinburgh Military Tattoo on my own (I've always been perfectly at ease with my own company). Quick pub meal of gammon steak and chips at 18:45 and then watched the tattoo from 20:00 to 22:00. Since my girlfriend was still at her dinner I found a local pub to grab a beer while looking through/editing the photos I'd taken at the tattoo. 2 pints until circa 23:00. Met up with girlfriend and met her work mates for the first time ... at least we'd all had a few and it was a good night, ending in a club at 01:30. (One more pint and I estimate 7 bottles of beer). Asleep at 02:30.
13	Rostered non-flying day. Woke at 05:30 feeling awful ... snoozed until 07:40 and then bit the bullet and got up (5hrs). 2 hot cross buns for breakfast at 09:00 was all I could manage at that point. Spent morning online, admin, paperwork, etc. Finally ventured to open the curtains at 12:30 (!) and grabbed a couple of sandwiches and a chocolate bar for lunch at 13:00. Did a couple of hours of shopping. Crashed out to sleep from 15:45–17:45. Up, showered and headed out for a drink (1 bottle beer at 19:00) before catching

First Officer – helicopter operations (North Sea) (C7)	
Day	Diary (All times Zulu)
	our first show of the evening. Very classy show, classical cellist playing her own work. Then had an Italian meal at 21:00 before heading to the 2nd show of the evening. 'Best of the Fest' is great stand-up that starts at 23:00 and hence has a fairly mashed-up audience! Great comedians and got home about 01:00. Asleep circa 02:00.
14	Rostered non-flying day. Woke at 07:00, then snoozed until 10:00. Felt pretty good. Brunch in 'Prêt-a-Manger' (sandwiches and a ginger beer) before getting the bus to pick up my girlfriend's car from her work. Spent the rest of the afternoon helping her with some data analysis for one of her research papers – in my previous life as a financial analyst I gained about 10 years experience using MS Excel and always think it's a waste of time seeing people struggle with manually analysing data when it can be done so much more effectively with some Excel models and code. At 16:00 drank coffee with my girlfriend and one of her friends. She turned out to be putting up one of the acts performing at the fringe (a couple of Doctors who do stand-up songs) so we got a couple of gratis tickets to see them and headed off to their show at 18:00. Dinner at 19:15 in the pouring rain of a pint, a burger and a crepe while waiting for the next show. Second show from 20:00–21:00. Then walked home. Ready for an early night and asleep by 22:45.
15	Rostered non-flying day. Woke at 08:00 (9hrs). Ate a banana in preparation for going running (as I can't do exercise without food in me), snoozed and finally got up at 09:30. At 10:00 went for a short 2mile run with my girlfriend – not exactly taxing but all worthwhile exercise. As we're generally limited on the time we can spend together due to geography, I'm happy to encourage her to do whatever she would normally do while I'm around and I'll just join in fine. In reality I have huge amounts of free time due to my job – as an NHS Dr she works in an environment that is more tiring, stressful and with far, far longer hours than most pilots will ever see. Hence her time off is rather more valuable (simply since there's so much less of it). 2 hot cross buns for breakfast at 11:00. Spent a couple of hours trying to match up our calendars/rosters to see when next to meet up, and when to go on holiday. Spending time together does require some planning and prior thought. At 13:30 had a cheese roll for lunch. Spent afternoon helping with Excel data analysis again. Received Monday's flying schedule at 16:30 and found I'm not flying until pm, so there was no rush to get back to Aberdeen early tonight. Left Edinburgh at 18:30 to drive to Aberdeen. Sandwich and a pasty for

First Officer – helicopter operations (North Sea) (C7)	
Day	Diary (All times Zulu)
	dinner en-route at circa 19:30. Was back in Aberdeen for 20:45. Cracked open a beer and spent a few hours editing some photos and a video and uploading to Facebook. Had another dinner of a few bowls of cereal at 23:00. Ended up drinking 6 cans of beer (stopped drinking at 23:00 ... 14rs before my report time). Asleep at 01:00 the second my head hit the pillow.
16	Rostered flying day (the 1st of my '5-on'). Woke at 04:00 feeling dehydrated and not good (predictably enough!). Back to sleep after half an hour or so and slept until 08:30 (7hrs). 09:30 had breakfast of a pasty and a sandwich from the local bakery. Did some food shopping and prepared a basic Excel budget for my girlfriend to complete before she sees her Financial Advisor next week. Dealt with a week's mail that'd built up while away last week and got ready for work. Left for work at 13:00 and after the usual 10 minute drive I reported at 13:10, which was a half hour early for my 13:45 time. Flying with the only Captain in the company who has a bad reputation with the co-pilots so I wanted to get everything squared away before he arrived to keep things as painless as possible. Weather not looking great but planned fine and we got away on time. Some fairly bumpy flying conditions on the outbound leg, which thankfully didn't have passengers aboard. As PF I had to monitor the aircraft closely, reduce power and manually help the autopilot deal with the up-draughting conditions. Popped out of the weather front into the clear and the rest of the flight was fine (we used the weather radar to skirt round the odd shower on the return leg). Actually started to get on with the Captain concerned and the flight was a lot better than it was the first time I flew with him. This is partly because I have gained in experience since I last flew with him and partly because I went into the flight with the attitude that I was absolutely not going to let a cockpit gradient develop. By the end of the flight we were getting on well and now I wouldn't have any concerns flying with him. On-time arrival and home at 17:30 after the usual short drive. Scheduled for an early flight on the 24th so aiming for an early night. Got to bed 21:20 and eventually to sleep at 22:45. I usually find it hard to get to sleep before my first 'early' as I'm simply not in sync with it yet. However I don't get worried by not being able to sleep as I know I can operate perfectly well on 4 hours when necessary and I also know that lying there waiting to get to sleep when relaxed is valid rest of a kind anyway.

First Officer – helicopter operations (North Sea) (C7)	
Day	Diary (All times Zulu)
17	Rostered flying day. Woke at 04:25 with the alarm (5hrs 45mins). Felt tired but fit to fly, particularly after a shower and some food. Breakfast of a sandwich and some juice while getting dressed. In work for 05:10 (report time 05:30). Planning all went fine. Flying with a Captain who only gained his command recently and similar age to myself. Like most of the guys he's a good bloke and I learn from him when I fly. Off-chocks on time at 06:30, but then held by ATC for 25minutes before departure, purely because of the volume of traffic trying to get out at that time of the morning at Aberdeen. Weather not great so we had to go instrument flight rules (IFR) (this particular trip is so short, at 60 miles, that it's usually done VFR if possible). Flight was very busy by virtue of its short sector time, but all fine and to plan. Managed to eat 2 bacon rolls from the rig at 07:45 while doing the paperwork and 1st-flight-of-the-day system power checks in the cruise. Weather still not good so had to do the ILS on return to Aberdeen, meaning I got both landings today (as we hand over control at the decision point at the bottom of all instrument approaches). Released by Ops at 08:45 and stayed to do 1.5hrs of paperwork amendments (my non-flying duty). Left work at 10:10 and home at 10:20. Went for a 4.2 mile run at 11:20. Big rice meal for lunch at 13:00. Showered and spent the afternoon trying to sort out a weekend away this weekend, a birthday present for my girlfriend and some paperwork that's been building up. Decided to get my girlfriend a fixed-wing trial flying lesson for her birthday, so she can see what it's like flying. Researched that and got it all booked and arranged for Saturday (weather-permitting). Following day's schedule through at 17:00 and I'm on another early Wednesday. At 17:15 had 2 rounds of sandwiches for dinner. Talked on the phone to girlfriend and watched a half hour's TV before going to bed at 20:00 with a book. Asleep by 21:00 (slowly getting into sync with the roster).
18	Rostered flying day. Woke at 03:35 (6hrs 30mins) with the alarm. Felt tired again but fit to fly. Ate a roll while dressing and left for work at 04:10, arriving at 04:20. Two flights today so planned both before the first, in case of any delays causing the two to bunch up together into a rotors-running changeover. Planning went fine, weather better than the last couple of days and we got away on time at 05:45 for the first trip. No problems, flying with an experience ex-RAF Captain who knows his stuff and is good for chat too. Back on time at 07:45 and plenty of time to re-plan the 2nd trip with the updated weathers while eating a couple of hot cross buns. Again away on time at 08:45 and another pleasant trip in reasonable weather, returning at

First Officer – helicopter operations (North Sea) (C7)	
Day	Diary (All times Zulu)
	11:10 on time. Ate a couple of rolls from the rig at 10:30 in the cruise. Shut down at 11:20 and finished off the paperwork etc., leaving work at 11:35, arrived home 11:45. Two hours spent catching up on filling this log in. Rest of the afternoon trying to make a start on the plethora of forms required to gain an airside pass from BAA and looking for somewhere to take my girlfriend for her birthday this weekend. Initially told (only unofficially) I'd be on the same 1st flight tomorrow as today with a similar 2nd flight but the schedule showed me on a 10:00 departure when it came out – a lie-in. Result! Had a curry and 3 cans of beer at 15:45. Had a call from my girlfriend, watched one hour of TV and was in bed by 20:45, asleep by 21:00 as very tired.
19	Rostered flying day. Woke at 06:00. Felt good after 9hrs sleep. Breakfast of toast and juice. In work for 08:30 (report time 09:00). Flying with a popular Captain; a line-trainer but one of those with whom the cockpit gradient tends to feel pleasantly minimal (although there's never any doubt who's in charge). Planning all fairly simple as the weather behaved. Good flight, via a refuel at Sumburgh. Ate a couple of hot cross buns at 11:15 in the cruise approaching Sumburgh. Ate a hot meal from the rig at 13:00 on the return leg. Arrived back at Aberdeen on time and got home at 16:00 after the usual 10 minute drive home. Ate a fish pie and peas at 16:30 in preparation for swimming training with my club at 19:30. Swam for an hour but binned the last half hour as not fit enough. Haven't managed to make a session with the club since 7 weeks ago (primarily due to work being either early or late ...). Bed at 22:25 and asleep circa 22:45.
20	Rostered flying day. Woke at 05:45 (7hrs), feeling not great due to a cold keeping me up half the night as every time I got to sleep I woke up unable to breather properly due streaming nose etc. *Compos-mentis* enough to be safe to fly and can clear my ears so got up then, though alarm set for 06:20, showered and got ready for work early. Flight was officially an assessed 'standards' flight but these don't really add any stress any more as they're just normal line flights about which the line trainer then ticks some boxes afterwards. In work at 07:25 (07:45 report time) and planning all went fine. Flying with the same Captain as yesterday so always going to be a good flight. Departed 25mins late due to late pax. Weather good and trip all went to plan. Returned to Aberdeen to shut down at 12:10. Good debrief with the

First Officer – helicopter operations (North Sea) (C7)	
Day	Diary (All times Zulu)
	Line Trainer after the standards flight with some positive feedback. Spent 2 hours doing Ops Amendments paperwork afterwards and left work at 14:10. Packed my stuff, showered, changed and grabbed a sandwich before starting the drive South to Edinburgh to see my girlfriend for the weekend. Journey took longer than usual due typically atrocious Aberdeen traffic. Got to Edinburgh 18:10 and went out for food. Ate a Chinese circa 20:30 with a couple of pints. Felt progressively more under the weather as the day wore on so not really the best conversationalist over dinner. Asleep at 23:00.
21	Rostered non-flying day. Woke at 06:20, not feeling too bad granted my cold, and got up to check weather reports. I had arranged my girlfriend's trial lesson for today and the weather was predicted to be iffy. Breakfast of a bacon sandwich at 09:00 and spent the morning shopping. Weather eventually looking good so drove to the airport at 11:30. Ate a sandwich at 12:00. 13:15–14:15 sat backseat on the trial flight (never turn down the offer of a jolly!) which we all enjoyed very much. It was good to be able to show my girlfriend a little of what we do – though the thing that surprised her the most was actually the multi-tasking required, particularly juggling radios, rather than the actual flying (well, aeroplanes are much easier to fly than helicopters so that's fair I guess!). Left and stopped at a petrol station for another sandwich at 16:00. Drove down to Hawick where I'd booked a B&B for the night – all part of the birthday thing for my girlfriend. Turned out to be a lovely place. Went out for dinner at 20:00, an Italian with wine and 2 beers. Bed circa 23:00.

Analysis

The diarist, a 35 year old helicopter pilot First Officer, sent this e-mail: "All line pilots with my company work the same roster of 5 days on, 2 days off, 7 days on, 7 days off. This 21-day cycle always starts on a Monday (i.e., the 1st week is a normal working week, the 2nd is a 7 day working week and the 3rd is completely off), hence we are all in 1 of 3 groups, so that 1/3rd of us are starting any 1 given Monday at each of the 3 different points in the 21 day rotation, and 1 group is 'on' for any given weekend ... We get 17 days leave which must be taken as 2 groups of 5 days and 1 of 7".

The diarist said this of the 5 on, 2 off, 7 on, 7 off pattern: "The roster pattern is extremely popular with all the pilots as, being fixed, we know exactly when we'll be on or off on any given date in the future". Despite the days being fixed, the duties could change, however: "Received schedule for tomorrow; reporting at 11:00 tomorrow for a 12:00 flight. Ops then phoned at 18:30 to tell me there was a change

First Officer – helicopter operations (North Sea) (C7)

of plan and I'm now on a 05:30 report for a 06:30 flight". In this case the notice given by Operations was sufficient for the diarist to adjust his sleeping plans. Bennett (2010a: 17) explains that night-freight pilots found short-notice roster changes problematic, as there was insufficient time to change sleeping times: "Late roster changes make it difficult to plan when to sleep, when to eat, when to drink coffee and tea, etc.".

Taken in the round, this diarist seemed both to enjoy his work and the company of those with whom he worked: "As anticipated/hoped we rotors-ran into the next flight as Ops and Security had got all the pax through in good time (we generally have a good working relationship with all areas of the company)". There was one mention of a 'difficult' Captain, but, on the day, the diarist found him less of a problem than anticipated: "This [was] partly because I have gained in experience since I last flew with him and partly because I went into the flight with the attitude that I was absolutely not going to let a cockpit gradient develop". Poor relationships with colleagues and dysfunctional organisational cultures act as stressors (Glendon, Clarke and McKenna, 2006). Working in a dysfunctional culture can be emotionally draining. Energies are dissipated in friction and dispute. The enterprise is less than it could be (Bennett, 2010a).

The diarist's commute to work took 10 minutes by car. This short commute can only have added to his enjoyment of work. Further, it would not have added to his fatigue: "[C]ontributors to fatigue [include] commuting time" (Rash and Manning, 2009: 40).

The diarist generally ate sensibly. He was careful not to over-indulge on poor-quality foods: "I allow myself one MacDonalds every 2–3 weeks". He ate healthily (bananas, milk, muesli bars, fruit juice) and made sure he did not go for long periods without food: "Made up my 'emergency food supplies' for the day of some buttered hot cross buns and a banana – I always carry this along with numerous 'muesli bars' because delays, weather etc., can mean long periods between meals and I do not operate well like that". He ate little and often. BALPA (1988: 23) says: "Aim for a well balanced diet; cut down ... on sugar and fats ... Provide roughage with fresh vegetables and fruit, or better still bran ... Eat little and often ... The stomach empties in two and one half hours ...". Bennett (2010a) found that night-freight pilots sometimes went for long periods without food. The diarist's day-flying routine, his 'emergency food supply' and access to canteen food (on the rigs) meant there was little risk of going without food. Rig food is generally good-quality (a means of keeping morale up).

Reflecting on his drinking habits the diarist concluded: "I sleep very badly if I drink more than a couple of pints". The evidence supports this conclusion. On Day 8 he wrote: "Watched TV and had 2 double G&Ts and 2 beers. Ate a meal at 21:00. Asleep at 23:00. Rostered non-flying day (the first of my '7-off'). Up once in the

First Officer – helicopter operations (North Sea) (C7)

night for the loo and then lay awake for half an hour, due to the effect alcohol has on me, not good for my sleep. Awake at 07:00 feeling v. mild effects of the alcohol". During the evening of Day 11 the diarist consumed 7 pints of lager. He wrote: "Asleep immediately but, as always when I drink much: broken and not very good sleep". During the evening of Day 12 the diarist consumed 3 pints and 7 bottles of beer. He wrote: "Woke at 05:30 feeling awful ... snoozed until 07:40 and then bit the bullet and got up (5 hrs). 2 hot cross buns for breakfast at 09:00 was all I could manage at that point". On the evening of Day 15 the diarist consumed 6 cans of beer: "Woke at 04:00 feeling dehydrated and not good (predictably enough!)". Even a moderate dose of alcohol affects sleep quality (Rhodes and Gil, 2002; Caldwell and Caldwell, 2003; Eurocontrol, 2005). Despite being aware of the impact of alcohol on sleep quality, the diarist persisted in consuming alcohol. The diarist had a full social life. Alcohol consumption was a feature of this social life.

The diarist exercised regularly. He set himself a target of three runs each week. He also swam: "I swim competitively for a club". The physically fit are less susceptible to fatigue and stress (BALPA, 1988; Swan, 1995; Campbell and Bagshaw, 1999; Rhodes and Gil, 2002). Sometimes, however, work made training difficult: "Swam for an hour but binned the last half hour as not fit enough. Haven't managed to make a session with the club since 7 weeks ago (primarily due to work being either early or late)".

Aviation was the diarist's second career. His first was as a financial analyst in London, where he purchased a house. His first career lasted ten years. He took a salary cut to become a pilot: "As a junior F/O on a reduced salary to cover training costs this is much lower than it was 2 years ago". He reflected that on his current salary, marriage and a family could be a test.

The diarist's sleeping habits were that he would normally get 8–9 hours each night, even when on duty. One night he got significantly less than his optimum: "Woke at 05:20 (5 hrs 30 mins) with the alarm as my girlfriend is in theatre today. Felt shattered". Later he claimed he could function on four hours sleep: "I don't get worried by not being able to sleep, as I know I can operate perfectly well on 4 hours when necessary and I also know that lying there waiting to get to sleep when relaxed is valid rest of a kind anyway". There is general agreement that most people require around eight hours of sleep each night (Battelle Memorial Institute, 1998; Goode, 2003; Federal Aviation Administration, 2010; Caruso and Hitchcock, 2010).

The diarist's relationship was asymmetrical in terms of time spent at work: "In reality I have huge amounts of free time due to my job – as an NHS Dr she [girlfriend] works in an environment that is more tiring, stressful and with far, far longer hours than most pilots will ever see. Hence her time off is rather more valuable (simply since there's so much less of it)". Asymmetry in a particular aspect of a relationship may cause stress. The diarist used some of his spare time to help his partner with her work (data analysis, for example).

Captain – helicopter operations (North Sea) (C11)	
Day	Diary (All times Zulu)
1	Woke at normal alarm time (04:45) and rose at 06:00 feeling great after a really good night's sleep. Breakfast coffee and yoghurt before rising. Devoted the day to scrubbing/washing paving slabs at entrances to (9) duck pens and washing and refilling all the feeders. Early frustration, a drain is blocked beside the domestic duck night pen. Lunch: coffee and apple 11:30, then to farm shop for another set of drain rods, layers pellets and rat poison. Back to scrubbing and digging afterwards. Quite weary by 17:00 when husband came home with fish and chips. 2 glasses of wine. Sent a few emails, on computer until 18:00, read for a while then watched T.V. Horlicks and biscuit at 20:00. Difficulty keeping eyes open so went to bed at 20:45. Slight frustration with our indoor plumbing – upstairs bathroom partly dismantled so teeth have to be done downstairs. Nevertheless asleep by 21:15.
2	Woke with alarm 04:45 but sleepy after waking up in the night. Far too hot. Dozed off again and rose just after 06:30 (9hrs 15mins) feeling fine. 15 mins exercise and went outside to empty duck pond. Today the last day of leave, been home 2 days after a week in Belgium visiting bird collections and birdwatching. Came in and cut husband's hair, sat down to leisurely cooked breakfast. Porridge, cranberry juice, grilled bacon, scrambled egg, tomato and coffee. Visitors arrived to buy ducks just as we were sitting down to eat. Made them coffee and rushed down food. Morning disappeared somehow, talking about birds but pleased to sell them an extra pair that they had not ordered. Coffee, mince pie and slice of cheese for lunch at 12:00. One of the last batch of eggs in the incubator pipped. Squeaking duckling lifted spirits. Started planned strimming at 13:00. Good steady exercise, slightly raised heartbeat throughout. Some elements of frustration: strimmer frequently clogged with wet grass. Repetitive task ideal to clear the mind and make a plan of future activities. Line ran out at 16:45, still feeling fine. Cleaned, refilled and put away machine. Husband helped me with evening bird rounds. Light supper: meatballs, tomato and cheese, fruit juice and a small sherry. Anticipated rostered early flight but cheered to learn was on 17:00 standby. Eyes tired after an hour on the computer. Horlicks and biscuit at 19:45, then bed with a good book at 20:00. Very weary climbing the stairs. Only a little conscience about not fixing the bathroom plumbing. Finished book and nodded off at 21:15.

Captain – helicopter operations (North Sea) (C11)	
Day	Diary (All times Zulu)
3	Woke up after midnight boiling hot but soon drifted off again, re-awoke with alarm 04:45. Dozed until 06:15 (9hrs), then breakfast: coffee and yoghurt, got up feeling reasonably chirpy. First call to incubator, assisted a duckling out of its shell. Not sure if it will survive, so don't want to get too attached to it. 3 more eggs have pipped. Did the rounds of the birds, one poorly duck needed to be put down. Sad but needed to be done. Then pottered in the garden cutting back an overgrown hawthorn hedge. Coffee 10:30 with mince pie. Very pleasant working in the sunshine, just a shame I could not hear the birdsong once I had on PPE and running a shredder. Husband came home at lunchtime, his activities at local helicopter training school (struggling financially) look set to continue, they have agreed to renew his FE, FIE, FI and FIC even though the company is to be sold at the end of the month. Brilliant news as he lives for flying (note; he is 71, goes in 3 days a week to help out and does it for free). Afternoon tea and biscuit at 14:30. More or less ran out of steam at 16:00. No problems with bird rounds and had a long leisurely soak in the bath before making supper. Pasta with bacon and tomato sauce, fresh parmesan and peas. Apple for pud and a pint of Innocent smoothie. Sat quiet for an hour or so and read aircraft notes. Horlicks, biscuit, piece of Toblerone then retired to watch Spooks in bed. Still no motivation for plumbing. Asleep by 21:00.
4	Terrible night. Kept waking up in a sweat – at least 3 times, then re-awoke 03:20 (6hrs), too late to sleep again. In consequence eyes really tired and dry. Coffee and yoghurt for breakfast. 15 mins back exercise, checked ducklings, took car to work 04:40 to arrive in good time. 06:00 departure: straightforward short flight to Captain WPP with experienced Captain. Second flight, 08:15 to Alba/FSU delayed due pax drug-testing. One pax bumped. Flights straightforward with easy conversation; fruit, coffee, cheese and tomato rolls provided. Latter inedible, picked out tomato and ate that. Called in at farm shop on way home for bag of duckling crumbs. Went to bed after opening mail, 12:30–13:30. Felt a little refreshed but still with muzzy head. Husband had 'uncertain' tum, accused breakfast egg. Afternoon tea with apple pie at 14:00, followed by bird rounds. Planned supper out at local bistro put on hold as both not feeling like it. Took solace by eating too many birthday chocolates. Leisurely bath followed by simple supper of beans on toast, left-over pasta and green salad with a glass of wine at 17:30. Sat for half hour or so at table until good friend from Canada phoned and we exchanged news. Watched a movie, Horlicks and biscuit then bed at 20:15 with a book. Asleep by 21:00.

Captain – helicopter operations (North Sea) (C11)	
Day	Diary (All times Zulu)
5	Slightly better night, though did wake once. Alarm was mis–set: woke at 03:29 (6hrs 30mins) and waited for it to go off but it didn't. Do not really get stressed about waking up as I always seem to. Thick head again but feeling reasonably cheerful: duckling hatch almost complete. Coffee and yoghurt b/fast. 15 mins back exercise, drove to work 04:40 arriving in good time. 06:00 to Armada/North Everest, departed on time with remarkably few ATC hold ups. Some thunderstorm activity to avoid, ADF range check for Armada less than satisfactory, they have it on maintenance. Communications very poor on N Everest. Clearances etc. only available at the very last minute. No drama as Wx good and no other local traffic. Full breakfast and coffee. A morale booster. Gap of 1 hour plus before second flight. Lay down in uncomfortable crew room intending to read flight manual but somehow only managed a few pages before closing eyes. Do not think I slept. Scheduled 10:45 departure to S704, got load and left early. Practised night deck approach and brief, as will need to regain currency before clocks change. Orange Juice and wonderful Chelsea bun off rig. Colleague (another experienced Capt.) had a good looking salad but I did not have mine as planning to eat supper. Home 13:45, cup of tea and biscuit then out to do birds. Quite a pleasant task in the sunshine, pottered with them until 16:30. Headache just about gone, wonder if it was the chocolate? Bath with G&T then curry, 17:30–17:50 ish. A bit of admin, a bit of book, Horlicks and biscuit then watched Grand Designs in bed. The Apprentice would be too exciting. Asleep by 21:00.
6	Another restless night. Woken by the alarm at 03:30 (6hrs 30mins). Would really rather have gone back to sleep. Coffee, yoghurt, rose 03:45. Fed ducklings and left 04:30 for work by car. Arrived earlier than necessary for 05:00 report but nice not to have to rush. Young but experienced Senior First Officer arrived same time. Fairly large load meant slight reduction in fuel qty, phoned to ramp. On arrival at a/c found it was full. Took gamble that there would be the usual queue at holding point but this time there was not. As no immediate landing traffic, requested backtrack and hold to allow 2 other helicopters to depart ahead. On Max Take Off Weight for departure and fully awake. North Everest/Lomond. Some turbulence, tried climb to FL 70 (7,000ft) but still in cloud and beyond icing clearance so descended. Breakfast and coffee supplied, but cold by the time we ate. I just had beans/coffee. Second rotation: 10:00 to Armada, rotors running away 5 mins early. Still turbulent. Ate small

Captain – helicopter operations (North Sea) (C11)	
Day	Diary (All times Zulu)
	amount of nice macaroni cheese and a few chips, plus shortbread and coffee. Both of us flagging on the inbound leg, almost to the point of wanting to shut eyes, but not quite. Got veg from farm shop for roasting tonight. Home 13:15, welcome cup of tea. Very lethargic. Pottered with ducklings, did bird rounds and a few emails. Bath with G&T then soup (veg roast held over for tomorrow), glass of wine and bowl of raspberries. Waded through some holiday photos then settled with book at 18:35. TV 19:30–21:30. Watched the news but drifted off with the local news/weather. Asleep by 21:00.
7	A brief wake up, but slept again soon. Woken by alarm at 04:45 (7hrs 45mins). Coffee and yoghurt. Revelled in being able to stay in comfy bed, did so until 06:20 listening to radio. Lovely. Fed and bathed ducklings, 15 mins back exercise. A little admin on computer then out to do bird rounds. Very chilly and wet. Prepared veg for supper and made out note for husband re times of cooking. Drove to work in good time for 10:00 report. 2 rotations, 11:00 S704, then 14:30 Captain/FPSO with experienced SFO I know reasonably well. Both on-time departures. Salad off first destination, cold drinks and stickies (cakes) off second. Various little hitches through the day; weather, freight, technical issues with refuelling. We both agreed that problem-solving on this level made the job more interesting. Crewing difficulties with sickness and roster changes means the Co. is short of pilots for the weekend. Volunteered one day, they accepted Sunday gratefully. A little bit weary on way home, annoyed to remember mobile phone left in flying suit, but cheered by fine smell from kitchen of roasting veg. They were enough for me but husband had 2 lamb chops with his. Poached pears and cream for pud. 2 large glasses of wine. Sat at table about 20 minutes. Admin, bath and time with ducklings. Still able to ignore lack of bathroom sink. Horlicks and biscuit 20:00 then bed with book. Asleep 21:30 ish.
8	Woke at 04:30 (7hrs), as if for an early. Resented the normal alarm when it came on. Still not really feeling rested but looking forward to the day's activities. Coffee and yoghurt, rose at 06:15. 15 mins back exercise, communed with ducklings. They are all feeding well, the first few days are critical. Job for the day; clean and refill bird feed stations, clean sheep drinker and unblock the drain to the duck night pen, has been backed up since returning from France. Coffee and mince pie 10:30. 2 sets of drain rods not quite enough to reach the blockage, had to go out for another

Captain – helicopter operations (North Sea) (C11)	
Day	Diary (All times Zulu)
	set. Very satisfying to dislodge a large gobbet of black gunge and drain the swamp that had formed. Fashioned a collar around the pipe union to stop soil going down again. Tea, biscuit, grapes and a handful of hazelnuts from the garden at 13:30. Between scrubbing slabs and pushing drain rods and sawing pipes all day, elbows are complaining. Husband similar with shoulders. Pair of old crocks. Evening bird rounds in a hailstorm, energy levels flagging with fading daylight, husband went out for fish and chips. 1 glass of wine, big glass fruit smoothie. Long soak in bath, sorely needed. Cleaned ducklings. Watched TV for an hour before retiring. Horlicks/biscuit at 20:00. Asleep by 21:00.
9	Woke a couple of times in the night again, enjoyed loafing in the bed after the alarm. Awake 04:30 (7hrs 30mins). Elbows still throbbing a bit. Rose 06:30, 15 mins back exercise, bathed and fed the ducklings. One of the six not eating as enthusiastically as I would like. On standby from 07:00. Had a leisurely breakfast; porridge, smoked salmon and scrambled egg and tomato. Plus fresh brewed coffee. Went out to do birds 08:15. Company called @ 09:00 requesting 12:00 report for ground runs/air tests. Pottered in shed until 11:15, had coffee and mince pie, changed and took car. Usual mix of leak checks, vibration runs, etc. shared between self and another Captain. Cup of tea and bacon roll shortly after arrival. Only air test; hover and (new) engine performance check. No significant weather and both enjoyed flying for 51 minutes. Enjoyed being released at 16:30 even more. Comforting to be re-united with phone. Bath, cleaned ducklings (one definitely fading away) then light supper of toast and pate, pepper stuffed with cream cheese followed by a plum. 1 small sherry and a large glass of fruit smoothie. Fairly tired eyes by 19:00. Read and watched T.V. until bed time. Horlicks and biscuit as usual 20:00. Asleep by 21:30.
10	Woke early (04:00) and did not really doze off again, too cold, too hot etc. Rose 06:00, did ducklings. Little one still hanging on – maybe eating? Feeling remarkably cheerful. Took a trailer-load of shed-building rubbish to the tip and collected tonne of sand on way home. Had a very productive morning doing more pruning and shredding. Coffee and mince pie at 10:00. Worked away until about 13:30. Lunch of apple, biscuit, slice of cheese and yoghurt. Did a few more odds and ends in the garden, then bird rounds. Unaccountably weary by 15:00, had bath at 15:45, loafed a good 45 mins. Supper: salad and stir fry, big glass of smoothie. Evening

Captain – helicopter operations (North Sea) (C11)	
Day	Diary (All times Zulu)
	Class (cabinet making 5th term) at Inverurie, 20 mins away by car, start at 18:00. Perked up considerably and lost myself in my woodwork. Making a fielded panel blanket chest from local hardwood and it is looking very handsome. Home 19:50, Horlicks, biscuit and bed at 20:00 to watch Spooks. Feeling pretty relaxed but sleepy.
11	Took a long time to nod off last night and woke with distinctly tired eyes. Pretty chirpy once up and about at 06:00. Coffee and yoghurt breakfast. 15 mins back exercise and gave the ducklings their swim. Fashioned a funnel to put sink unblocking stuff into the bathroom sink S-trap. Seems to be leaking from somewhere and cannot get access to tighten it up. Admin seemed to take up most of the morning and still there is a pile lurking. Doing bird rounds took more than an hour and then got called in early just as I came in to change. Drove to work arriving 11:30. Grabbed a mince pie and had coffee at work. First rotation (13:00) to Tartan had a Scott added first. Weather just above limits. With Training Captain and a pleasure just to get on with it – we are both the same vintage with a similar sense of humour. Salad and coffee provided second stop. Feeling a bit weary between flights, about 45 mins on ground so no time to rest. Second trip, 16:45 freight run to Fulmar and Clyde. My night line-check and night deck recurrency with same Captain. Felt fine once we were airborne again. Weather (Wx) not quite as bad as last time, able to complete task easily. Massive curry to eat on the way home. Far too much. Home by 20:45, raging thirst big glass of smoothie (it is always Innocent pineapple, banana and coconut). Belly feeling uncomfortably full going to bed at 21:15. Sad news from Canada, my friend's mum has died. It was expected as old and ill for some time but it will mean a big change for Tina who has cared for her for more than 10 years. Shoulders very tense.
Analysis	
The diarist, an EC225 (twin-engined passenger helicopter) Captain, sent the following e-mail with her diary: "I am 51, in general good health apart from a grumbly back which I manage with exercise and treatment with an osteopath every 6 weeks ... I consider myself to be a cheerful individual. You will see a constant reference to ducks. I have a wildfowl collection of some 400 birds. I am editor of ... the magazine of the British Waterfowl Association. I am on the Board of the International Wild Waterfowl Association. I deny being obsessed. My husband does not really share my enthusiasm, but is very supportive ... If you wish clarification on any points you are welcome to email or phone me. I look forward to reading your results".	

Captain – helicopter operations (North Sea) (C11)

This diarist's C.V. and diary suggest that the stereotyping of pilots as technophiles with little sympathy for the environment is unfair. Here was a pilot who understood the environment and gave much of her spare time to animal welfare.

The diarist worked on her wildfowl reserve every day. Some of the work could be considered heavy labour. For example, on Day 8 (an off-day), the diarist woke early and worked steadily: "Woke at 04:30, as if for an early ... Job for the day:- clean and refill bird feed stations, clean sheep drinker and unblock the drain to the duck night pen, has been backed up since returning from France ... Between scrubbing slabs and pushing drain rods and sawing pipes all day, elbows are complaining. Husband similar with shoulders. Pair of old crocks. Evening bird rounds in a hailstorm, energy levels flagging with fading daylight". The diarist found unblocking the drain "very satisfying".

Doing physical labour each day left the diarist feeling naturally tired by evening. For example, Day 1 (off-day): "Difficulty keeping eyes open so went to bed at 20:45". Day 2 (off-day): "Very weary climbing the stairs". Day 3 (Standby from 17:00): "More or less ran out of steam at 16:00".

While the diarist's devotion to the birds gave her great satisfaction, it required a significant time commitment. On occasion it was physically draining. The diarist woke early even on off-days (usually before 06:30). On duty-days, time permitting, the diarist did her bird rounds and administration before driving to work, then further bird-related chores after returning from work. Running a wildfowl reserve could be considered a seven-day-a-week commitment. Certainly, unlike other pastimes, it is not something that can be put to one side for a while. Regular exercise promotes physical and psychological health and enhances work performance (BALPA, 1988; Swan, 1995; Rhodes and Gil, 2002). It is important, however, to strike the right balance between work and non-work activities (like hobbies and sports). As Rhodes and Gil (2002: 31) put it: "Say no to ... activities that won't fit your time schedule or that will compromise your time for sleep".

The diarist's partner was a source of strength. He is described as being "very supportive". On Day 7 the diarist wrote: "Prepared veg for supper and made out note for husband re times of cooking". After her day's flying she wrote: "A little bit weary on way home, annoyed to remember mobile phone left in flying suit, but cheered by fine smell from kitchen of roasting veg". Having a supportive partner can help mitigate the physical and psychological impacts of work: "It has long been recognized that stable spouse and family relationships can act as a buffer against stress in the workplace; conversely, discord in close relationships may intensify stress, leading to impaired work performance" (Bor, Field and Scragg, 2002: 247). The Health and Safety Executive (2006) notes: "A happy social and domestic life is an important foundation for health and well-being" (Health and Safety Executive, 2006: 12). Rhodes and Gil (2002: 31) note: "Making time for sleep, family and friends will affect your sense of wellness". A happy relationship can boost resilience:

Captain – helicopter operations (North Sea) (C11)
"There is something about being in a high-quality marriage that seems to buffer a patient's emotional health" (Reese cited in *Daily Mail*, 2010).

When operating, the diarist seemed to be locked in to getting up at a certain time. On Day 5 she wrote: "Alarm was mis–set: woke at 03:29 and waited for it to go off but it didn't. Do not really get stressed about waking up as I always seem to".

On Day 5 the diarist got 6.5 hours sleep, which would have generated 13 hours of productive wakefulness (assuming no sleep debt or credit prior). This sleep credit would have expired by 16:30, well after her duty ended. Nevertheless, she remarked of the second rotation: "Both of us flagging on the inbound leg, almost to the point of wanting to shut eyes, but not quite". The diarist's short drive to work would not have added much to her fatigue level.

One of the advantages of servicing production platforms seemed to be easy access to good-quality food: "Orange Juice and wonderful Chelsea bun off rig"; "Salad off first destination, cold drinks and stickies (cakes) off second".

First Officer – night freight (C10)	
Day	Diary (All times Zulu)
1	CTC. Woke early at 07:30, slept well. Toast and Marmite for breakfast. Pottered about until 10:00 then DIY in house to 14:00. Ironed clothes and packed for next duty period and drove to girlfriend's house to help with her house move. Had a take-away for dinner. Went to bed at 23:30.
2	Woken up at 05:30 by girlfriend's 3 year old son. Dozed for another 2 hours and got up at 07:30 (8hrs). Toast and Marmite for breakfast. Helped with house move and drove car full of furniture to new house (1 hour away). Went for a brief walk around the new village and left for EMA at 12:00, arrived at 12:45; early for 15:30 jump-seat to BGY (Bergamo) (I am LEJ (Leipzig) based so am supposed to start/finish in LEJ. Jumpseats to work are a bonus and stop me having to self-position using commercial carrier), operating BGY–AOI (Bergamo–Ancona) at 23:05, as wanted to do admin and download hardcopy of this log! Flight delayed 1 hr at EMA due tech issue. Arrived BGY approx 18:30, went to restaurant with my Capt and another crew for dinner – Pizza. Back at BGY for 20:00 to wait for our departure – sat in Engineers hut watching TV and chatting to other crews as no nearby crew rest facilities at BGY. Hadn't flow for 11 days, due to leave, so elected to be PF on flight to AOI even though feeling a bit tired by the time we departed. Departed 15 mins late due to tech issue. Arrived AOI at 00:16.

First Officer – night freight (C10)	
Day	Diary (All times Zulu)
3	In hotel room by 01:00, read book for 15 mins and slept well until 07:30, considered going for breakfast but decided to go back to bed and slept again until 09:00 (8hrs). Missed breakfast entirely. Roster change; now operating BGY–LEJ instead of jumpseating – much better. 10:00 went and sat by pool in sunshine with Capt until 12:30 then gym/swim until 14:00. Dinner at 16:00 (tuna salad) then taxi to airport at 17:30 for 18:45 departure. Operating AOI–BGY–LEJ–CGN (Ancona–Bergamo–Leipzig–Cologne) with finish at 02:20. Another roster change now AOI–BGY–LEJ–CDG (Ancona–Bergamo–Leipzig–Charles de-Gaulle) with finish at 02:50 and earlier report tomorrow, so now slightly longer night tonight, followed by less rest tomorrow and subsequently longer night after the next – now a 9hr 20min duty. 30 mins from departure at AOI, crewing called Capt and advised we would now be jumpseating again from BGY to LEJ. Departed 10 mins late due to last minute reroute from ATC requiring reprogramming of FMC (flight management computer) (Ops pestering on ACARS (aircraft communication addressing and reporting system) as to why we departed late). Capt flying. On route to BGY, runway was changed to opposite end which has no instrument approach and requires a "circle to land". Caused utter chaos in the air (many Ryanair flights arriving). We had to enter 3 separate holds, reprogram the FMC numerous times and prepare for a rarely-used approach procedure. Many aircraft ahead had to divert due to landing delay and low fuel. We had 5 minutes hold fuel left, and were preparing to divert when the runway was changed again; fortunately, we were first in the queue at this time and landed at 20:04. A very busy and quite stressful flight. Rostered to jumpseat to LEJ at 21:25. On arrival at aircraft, found it to be tech. Waited 20 mins for it to be fixed, then advised crewing. Jumpseat changed to later flight departing at 22:10. Arrived at LEJ 00:00.
4	Due to operate to CDG at 01:15. No "snack packs" ordered (given to crews on short turnaround). Insufficient time to eat in canteen by the time we had got into the hub and collected our paperwork for the next flight (bought a sandwich but couldn't face eating it). Departed 10 mins late due to loading delays. Flight uneventful until approaching CDG. Requested "inner" runway – was refused so FMC reprogrammed for "outer" one. Approach re-briefed. When established on arrival procedure, "inner" runway offered! FMC reprogrammed again. Crew quite tired by now having left the hotel at 18:30. Landed at 02:55 and in hotel by 03:15.

First Officer – night freight (C10)	
Day (All times Zulu)	Diary
	Breakfast not available (despite it being set out, would not let us have any until 04:00) so went to bed without eating. Asleep by 04:00. Slept heavily, woke briefly at some point. Got up at 09:30 (5hrs 30mins); missed breakfast again, still feel tired. Pottered about hotel room doing admin/internet etc. Met Capt at 12:00 for lunch (salad and cake from shop in station eaten on a bench outside) and went for a walk. 14:30: went to gym; only managed 30 mins, as no energy. 15:15 went to bed, surprisingly managed to sleep for over an hour (1hr) and was woken 5 mins before my alarm by guests in the hotel room next door. Feel quite spaced-out even after a shower. Dinner with Capt at 17:00 (Salmon and veg). Pick up scheduled for 20:30 for departure at 21:45. Operating CDG–LEJ–VIT–LIS (Charles de Gaulle–Leipzig–Vittoria–Lisbon). Scheduled to arrive in LIS at 06:20. Uneventful flight to LEJ. Had about an hour in hub before next flight.
5	Departed LEJ 10 mins late due to loading. Very tired on leg to VIT, over 2.5 hrs flight time. I was pilot flying for the leg to VIT. Made a hash of the approach, too fast and late to descend. Very turbulent on final, with a tail wind which made my mistakes worse. Was unlikely we would be stabilised by 500 ft, so made a go-around. First one ever! Landed on second attempt. Been to VIT many times and never had a problem with the approach before. Was tired but all was going well and crew had discussed the arrival, which is tricky. I just didn't react quickly enough to events. Despite crew being tired, we made the correct decision to break off the approach. Had a sandwich from vending machine in hub. Final leg to LIS uneventful; very tired, flying in daylight with sun in our eyes. In hotel by 06:45: 10hrs 30 mins until pick up! Made breakfast for the first time this week. Had 3 glasses of Cava, slept really well from about 07:45 until 14:15 (6hrs 30mins). Met Capt. Lovely day, went for walk and had food (pasta). Pick up at 17:15. Flying LIS–BRU–LEJ (Lisbon–Brussels–Leipzig). Scheduled to finish in LEJ at 00:20. Have a jumpseat booked and approved to get back to EMA: hope I don't get bumped off. Pilot flying to BRU. Flight, nearly 3 hrs long, uneventful. Due to length of duty a snack pack is provided by hotel in LIS as there is no opportunity to get food in BRU. Ate it in BRU crew room (sandwich and cake). Have 3 jumpseat passengers for flight to LEJ. Departed BRU on time. Both crew members are LEJ-based and have jumpseat on same aircraft back to EMA, so very keen to get back and not miss flight. Worried that we might have been bumped but won't know until we arrive.

First Officer – night freight (C10)	
Day	Diary (All times Zulu)
6	Flight uneventful and arrived at LEJ early. First flight this week that had no delays or problems! Jumpseat confirmed – a big relief. Arrived at EMA slightly late. Drove home at 03:00 and in bed by 04:15. Had trouble sleeping as felt very cold. Woke at 10:00 (5hrs 45mins). Feel OK. Toast and Marmite for breakfast. Quiet day filled with domestic admin. Pasta for dinner. Went to bed at 20:30. Fully intended to sleep, but ironically watched a TV programme on how to get a good night's sleep. Slept heavily from 22:30.
7	Woke up initially at 05:30, still only managing 6 or 7 hrs total sleep and only 4 hours without waking. Went back to sleep and slept (intermittently) until 09:00. Very groggy when I woke so stayed in bed for another hour watching TV. Cornflakes for breakfast. Did some DIY, visited an Estate Agent to look for a new house and drove to collect teenage son for the weekend; haven't seen him for over a month so looking forward to the weekend. Back home with him by 17:30. Salad for dinner. October roster published, late again. Spent an hour on Internet trying to work out flights to get to work. Could only book one flight as the rest too expensive at the moment. Was feeling tired by 19:00. Went to bed at 21:30. Couldn't sleep, so watched TV until 23:30.
8	Woke briefly about 05:00 but went straight back to sleep, slept until 08:00 (8hrs 30mins). Felt good when I woke so got up straight way. Cornflakes for breakfast. Mowed lawn and did some DIY until 12:00. Sandwiches for lunch. Lazy afternoon with son, watched TV, went for a walk in the woods. Drove to cinema at 17:30. Ate snacks in cinema. Bed at 22:00.
9	Slept quite well. Woke up briefly at 05:00, but went back to sleep. Got up at 08:00 (10hrs). Pottered about doing domestic chores. Had late breakfast with son at 11:00 (fried egg sandwiches), then together we worked in the garden putting up a fence until 13:30. Cooked Sunday dinner and then drove him home at 15:30. Back home by 17:30. Watched TV and went to bed at 21:30. Fell asleep straight away. Back at work tomorrow night for only 2 days.
10	Slept well but woke briefly at 00:30 and 05:00. Woke up at 07:00 (9hrs). Always seems to be the same before work – never able to lie in when it's needed. Contemplated doing more work on the fence but decided not to as working until 01:50 in the morning. Spent some more time trying to

First Officer – night freight (C10)	
Day	Diary (All times Zulu)
	work out how to get to work next Sunday and in Oct, looks good for a jumpseat from LHR at the moment. Had a Ryanair flight booked today from EMA–SXF at 09:30 to get to work but got a jumpseat authorised (and put on roster). Saved an early start and hassle of train from Berlin to Leipzig. Late breakfast (toast and Marmite), packed for trip and left home at 14:00. Visited girlfriend on the way to work tonight for dinner (fish pie). Drove to EMA at 20:30, arrived at 21:15 horrible journey – very dark and wet. Jumpseat at 22:00 from EMA–LEJ, arrives at 00:05. Only passenger on flight so able to lie across all seats; managed to nap for at least an hour.
11	Landed in LEJ on time. Operating LEJ–BSL (Leipzig–Basle) at 01:50. Sat in hub chatting until time to depart to BSL. Feeling quite good. Pilot Flying to BSL, departed 10 mins late due to loading. Flight uneventful and in hotel by 03:45. Had breakfast and in bed by 04:45. Went to sleep easily and slept until 10:00, woke briefly and slept again until 11:30 when woken by cleaners outside room. Dozed off again only to be woken again by workman 'banging' somewhere in hotel, complained to reception! Dozed again until 13:30 (8hrs 30mins). Got up feeling good. Spent some time on Internet then went to gym at 15:30 for an hour. Met Capt for dinner at 17:30 (Chinese). Taxi at 19:30, operating BSL–LEJ–BLQ (Basle–Leipzig–Bologna) at 20:45. Have a 4.5 hour layover in LEJ. Scheduled to finish in BLQ at 04:05. Flight to LEJ uneventful, arrived 25 mins early. Had some chips in hub at 23:00 as breakfast not available in BLQ until after we are scheduled to arrive.
12	Sat around until 01:50. Went to collect paperwork for flight only to be told we had been taken off the flight and put on ASBY (airport standby) until 04:00! By 02:30 there were no spare aircraft left, but would not stand us down until 03:00. Scrounged a lift into town and went to flat. One of my room-mates was already there and asleep (three of us share a one-bed flat with separate beds). Talked with him to 05:00 and slept until 09:30 (4hrs 30mins). Spent the day in Leipzig. Had brunch in a café (scrambled eggs and smoked salmon). As I had finished early was able to get a jumpseat on an Aerologic 777 back to EMA at 17:30. Arrived on time. Decided to visit my girlfriend instead of drive home. Ate toast and Marmite for dinner. Went to bed at 22:30. Only managed to sleep for about an hour (1hr).

First Officer – night freight (C10)	
Day	Diary (All times Zulu)
13	Tried unsuccessfully to get back to sleep, so got up at 01:30 and drove home. In bed by 04:00 and slept, with frequent waking, until about 09:00 (4.5hrs). Felt tired all day with no motivation to go outside. Had limited food in house so had chips again as couldn't be bothered to shop/cook. Have to go to hospital in the morning for a small procedure so went to bed at 21:30.
14	Woke up at 01:30 and then slept on and off until 06:00 (8hrs 30mins). Skipped breakfast. Hospital went well and was back home by 13:00; just have some minor discomfort. Late lunch (sandwiches). Back at work on Sunday night so phoned crewing to arrange a seat in a taxi to LHR for a jumpseat to LEJ. Duty crewing officer unhelpful, even though his supervisor told me to do it. Have to 'call back' tomorrow to finalise arrangements. Have a Ryanair booked from STN to AOC (Stansted–Altenburg/Leipzig) on Sunday morning at 06:25 as a back-up; don't really want to drive to STN or pay for 5 days car parking when I can get it for free at EMA. Really sick of having to worry about travel arrangements and for living out of a suitcase in a shared house in LEJ. Veggie chilli and rice for dinner. Quite tired. In bed by 21:00, watch a film and asleep by 23:00.
15	Slept well, only woke up once I think. Woke up at 08:00 (9hrs). Felt quite good when I got up. Cornflakes for breakfast. More problems with travel to work tomorrow; taxi to LHR cancelled as other crew member now positioning from LTN. Spoke to crewing. There is one spare jumpseat on the aircraft but they will not guarantee it for me. Requested they cancel my LHR jumpseat and book it for me anyway and I'll take the risk. Packed for trip and left home at 11:00; drove to see girlfriend; arrived at 12:30. Had a day out at country fair. Pasta bake for dinner. Decided that I couldn't take the risk of not getting to work if I got bumped off jumpseat from LTN (Ryanair from STN departs at 05:25). Drove 2.5 hours to parents' house (25 miles from STN) in Essex at 18:00. Starting to feel the after-effects of the hospital procedure and am a little uncomfortable. Reluctant to go sick. Went to bed at 21:30.
16	Woke up at 03:15 (5hrs 45mins). Felt OK so drove to STN. Arrived at 04:00. Phoned crewing to check on LTN jumpseat and was assured that it was still available, so made the decision to drive from STN to EMA. Arrived at EMA at 06:15, had breakfast in service station. Whilst waiting in crew room, due to crews calling in sick, roster changed from jumpseat from LEJ–VIT (Leipzig–Vittoria) at 23:55, to operating LEJ–CIA

First Officer – night freight (C10)	
Day	Diary (All times Zulu)
	(Leipzig–Ciampino) at 18:30, as 'I was the only FO positioning to LEJ'. Despite the fact that I was travelling on my own time and without company support, crewing wouldn't even change the roster to put me 'on duty' until I reported for the CIA flight. 'Lost' the rest of my rostered flights from Monday night until Wednesday night, and now on SBY on my return from CIA. Fed up as I won't earn any duty pay and will have to spend 2 days in flat in LEJ; so much for helping out. Crewing agreed to find some work for me. Whilst waiting for the rest of the taxi passengers to arrive I was talking to the FO who would be operating the flight from LTN to LEJ. He lives in EDI and had been at EMA since Friday night waiting to operate this flight. On arrival in LEJ he had to wait for a return flight back to EMA and then a jumpseat to EDI at 04:00 before going on leave. I offered to operate for him (had no uniform with me as all left in LEJ to save Ryanair baggage charges) so he could get a train home a day early; crewing agreed and I was finally rostered for duty from 07:40. Taxi to LTN departed at 08:00. Journey to LTN and flight to LEJ both uneventful, arrived at 12:00. Captain elected to fly as he had been off sick. Got a lift from LEJ hub into town to meet up with other crew members and get some food (take-away kebab). 17:00 walked to hotel in LEJ and got a lift back to hub. Just before leaving flat in LEJ for journey back to hub I received a text from crewing requesting I call regarding changes. Expecting the worst and not having a company phone, I waited until I was in the hub before calling back. Was expecting to be put on SBY but was changed from 18:30 LEJ–CIA departure to 19:15 LEJ–STR (Stuttgart). Capt had positioned out from LTN with me but had been given a hotel during the day to rest so he elected to fly the leg. Good decision as weather at STR was very wet and windy and I had now been awake for over 16 hours. Flight went well but had strong fumes smell from one air conditioning pack so flew with it switched off. Approach into STR was very rough due to a fast approaching thunderstorm. Landed on time and was in hotel by 21:00. Have a 22-hour stop, so went to the bar.
17	Went to bed about 00:30. Slept well but was woken briefly by cleaners. Went to breakfast at 08:15 (7hrs 30mins). Nice day outside despite forecast bad weather. Met Captain at 10:00 and went for a walk/coffee in town. Found a nice park so made the most of the sunshine. Got back to hotel at 13:00 and went to bed. Slept for 2 hours. Met Captain at 17:00 for dinner (pizza). Taxi at 19:00. Flight scheduled to depart to LEJ at 20:35.

First Officer – night freight (C10)	
Day	Diary (All times Zulu)
	No call from crewing regarding further work tonight so I am resigned to being on SBY. Flight departed early and was uneventful. Arrived in LEJ at 21:30 and called crewing. Now operating LEJ–CDG (Leipzig–Charles de Gaulle) at 01:15 followed by jumpseat back to LEJ and ASBY until 04:00 on my return tomorrow. Sat around in hub talking; no spare bunks available to get any sleep.
18	Departed LEJ 15 mins late. Flight to CDG uneventful, was Capt's first night so he was PF. In hotel by 03:30, breakfast not available until 04:00 so went to bed, asleep by 04:00. Slept well, woken briefly by noise in corridor about 08:30 but went back to sleep, got up at 10:00 (6hrs). Met Capt at 10:30 and took train to Paris for lunch (very expensive 3 course meal). Lovely day so stayed in Paris all day. Got back to hotel at 17:30. Roster change; now operating LEJ–LYS (Leipzig–Lyon) at 01:45, followed by LYS–LEJ–MRS–VLC (Lyon–Leipzig–Marseilles–Valencia) on Thursday. Lost my last night LEJ–BSL: night extended by 3 hours and cannot now get a jumpseat on first flight back to EMA on Thursday night at 22:20. Next available jump seats are at 00:50 on 17th. Picked up at 20:15. Flight departed 15 mins late; arrived LEJ at 23:00. Hungry so ate some poor-quality food (can't even remember what it was) and then wished I hadn't. Sat about in hub waiting to depart to LYS.
19	French ATC are on strike and issuing slots to all flights. Told our aircraft had to depart on time. Ground crew didn't arrive to start loading until 20 mins prior to departure. Finally loaded by 02:00. Problems with the load sheet delayed us further and we missed our arrival slot. New departure slot 03:14. Flight departed 80 mins late. Arrived in LYS at 04:40, and had to wait for transport. Both crewmembers very tired. In hotel by 06:00. Late arrival at least meant we got breakfast. Asleep by 06:30. Slept well until 14:00; woken by hotel phone ringing briefly at 12:00, but went back to sleep. Met Capt at 15:00 to get some fresh air and food (falafel and salad). Phoned crewing and request I be taken off LEJ–MRS–VLC due to late finish; surprisingly they agreed and I'm now back on my original trip to BSL departing at 01:50. Should also now be able to get early jumpseat back to EMA tomorrow. Departed LYS on time and arrived in LEJ at 22:30. Flight uneventful. Sat around in hub until time to depart to BSL.

First Officer – night freight (C10)	
Day	Diary (All times Zulu)
20	Departed at 02:10; late again due to loading. Flight uneventful and arrived at 03:25, quite tired. Very glad did not go MRS–VLC and finish 3 hours later. Had breakfast and in bed by 05:00. Slept well, woken twice but went back to sleep. Woke up eventually at 14:00 (9hrs). Feeling better than I have all week so went to the gym for the first time in a long time. Spent 90 mins working out. Met Capt for food at 17:00 (Chinese). Taxi pick-up at 19:15. Flight uneventful, departed early and arrived at LEJ 40 mins early. Lost my jumpseat place on the early flight home and had to wait until 00:50. Ate some pasta to pass the time.
21	Flight 45 mins late departing due to technical problems. Very tired so slept on the floor as the seats are really uncomfortable. Arrived at EMA at 03:00. Drove home excessively fast and was in bed by 04:30. Struggled to sleep and woke up at 06:30 feeling very cold. Went back to sleep and woke at 09:30. Toast and marmalade for breakfast. Spent the rest of the day doing domestic admin/shopping etc. Drove to Sheffield at 15:30 to collect my son for the weekend. Got home at 17:30, feeling worn out couldn't be bothered to cook so went out and bought a take-away curry. Very glad that I do not have to go back at work until 23 Sept. Went to bed at 22:00. Slept well.
Analysis	

The diarist, a Boeing 757 First Officer at a U.K. registered freight airline, was based in Germany but lived in the U.K. In Germany he shared a one-bedroomed flat with two other pilots near his base. Each had a bed. He sent the following e-mail with his diary: "Hopefully attached you will find my completed sleep log for the past 3 weeks. I hope it's what you want – seems to read a bit like a Soap Opera! I will post you my roster as it was when I started work, and how it ended up at the finish just for comparison. I know that you are aware of [my airline's] operation, but over the past 12 months things have got steadily worse with longer nights, frequent changes, minimum days off and rosters with no fixed pattern or length leading to many [long] 'first' nights. The 3, 5, 7 finish pattern is virtually never adhered to. The removal of the hotel allowance means that we often miss breakfast and go for considerable lengths of time between meals. Food in LEJ hub is awful. As 'night' workers we need protection from long nights, and the FTL should recognise the nature of the work pattern we do and mandate more than 8 days off in 28. We need a separate FTL and not just a 'variation'. Very best wishes".

Food can be an issue for night-freight pilots (because many food outlets are closed). On Day 3 the diarist dined at 16:00. He arrived into Leipzig at midnight. He

First Officer – night freight (C10)

wrote: "Due to operate to CDG at 01:15. No 'snack packs' ordered (given to crews on short turnaround). Insufficient time to eat in canteen by the time we had got into the hub and collected our paperwork for the next flight (bought a sandwich but couldn't face eating it)". The diarist did not eat again until 12:00 on Day 4, some 20 hours after his last meal. Rhodes and Gil (2002: 50) say: "It is difficult to stay alert on the job, and function well when you are hungry. If you do not keep your blood sugars up and do not have adequate nutritional resources in your body you will not perform well. This means eating well all of the time ...". Eurocontrol (2005: 24) says: "Going to bed hungry can be as disruptive to sleep as going to bed too full".

Some time ago the diarist's airline removed the hotel allowance, which enabled the less well-paid pilots to eat reasonably well when down-route. One of the consequences has been that First Officers try to make breakfast – the only 'free' meal of the stay. If breakfast is missed, pilots not willing to spend their own money can go for a long time between meals: "The removal of the hotel allowance means that we often miss breakfast and go for considerable lengths of time between meals". Often, making breakfast means going to bed, then getting up, then returning to bed. Broken sleep is less restorative than continuous sleep (Federal Aviation Administration, 2010). On Day 4 the diarist wrote: "In hotel by 03:15. Breakfast not available (despite it being set out, would not let us have any until 04:00) so went to bed without eating. Slept heavily, woke briefly at some point. Got up at 09:30; missed breakfast again, still feel tired". Room service (if available) would have been charged.

Regarding his sleep on Day 7 (at home after returning from down-route) the diarist said: "Woke up initially at 05:30, still only managing 6 or 7 hrs total sleep and only 4 hours without waking. Went back to sleep and slept (intermittently) until 09:00. Very groggy when I woke". Further evidence that broken sleep is not as restorative as continuous sleep.

Night-freight flight crew tend to get shorter sleeps when down route (Bennett, 2010a). This diarist seemed to fit the pattern, getting relatively short sleeps when down-route, and longer, 'catch-up' sleeps when back home. For example:

Ancona HOTAC: 8hrs sleep
Paris HOTAC: 5.5hrs + 1hr = 6.5hrs
Lisbon HOTAC: 6.5hrs
Home U.K. night 1: 5hrs 45mins
Home U.K. night 2: 7hrs
Home U.K. night 3: 8.5hrs
Home U.K. night 4: 10hrs
Home U.K. night 5: 9hrs

First Officer – night freight (C10)

Caruso and Hitchcock (2010: 192) say: "A substantial number of studies found that workers on shift work and long hours frequently report short sleep duration and poorer sleep quality".

Regarding the diarist's sleeping pattern when at home, it seemed to take him a couple of nights to relax back into getting a full night's sleep. Of U.K. night 5 (his pre-report night) he wrote: "Always seems to be the same before work – never able to lie in when it's needed". Bennett (2010a) found that pilots tended not to be able to get pre-report sleep after settling back into a conventional night-sleep (domestic) routine. They reported that they would go to bed in the afternoon or evening, but would not fall asleep (because they were not tired). This could be a source of frustration (a stressor).

In his e-mail the diarist reported: "... frequent [roster] changes, minimum days off and rosters with no fixed pattern or length leading to many [long] 'first' nights". As evidenced by, for example, the several roster changes on Days 16 and 17, rosters are subject to frequent (short-notice) changes. While there are sound operational reasons for changes (sickness or weather, for example) they can leave crews short of sleep, short of food and full of caffeine at the wrong time (Bennett, 2010a). Airlines respond by saying that pilots should plan their sleep for the worst-case scenario (like a short first night becoming a deep (late-finish) first night). The *lived reality*, however, is that few pilots can 'sleep to order' (Bennett, 2010a). If a pilot is not tired (or is stressed) s/he will find it difficult to obtain top-up sleep. The result? Pilots may find themselves flying some 20 or more hours after their last sleep. As one of the pilots featured in *A longitudinal ethnographic study of night freight pilots* said: "I've been awake for almost twenty-four hours again. Original roster had me positioning to Leipzig for a hotel stand-by. On arrival this was changed to an airport stand-by. Then I was rostered to do a late departure to Warszawa. I went to the Crew Room to try to get some sleep ... I was almost asleep when I got a call from Crewing: flight cancelled. I was now on hotel stand-by. I arrived at the hotel and relaxed for 30 minutes. Went to sleep. Fifteen minutes later I got a call from Crewing. They told me a taxi would pick me up in 20 minutes to do a flight. I felt dead tired doing this sector at that time of the day" (Bennett, 2010: 17).

Workplace stress is a major problem in Britain: "[T]he incidence of work-stress has been steadily increasing in the U.K. since 1992 at a rate of about 0.5 to 1.0% each year" (United Kingdom National Work Stress Network, 2013: 14). Employees experience lack of control over their work as a stressor: "In workplaces where workers have little or no control over their work ... where demands placed upon them are beyond their (or anybody's) capacity; where there is little or no recognition of their efforts and where their voice is not heard, levels of damaging stress are likely to be high" (United Kingdom National Work Stress Network, 2013: 7). 'Low job-control'

First Officer – night freight (C10)

may generate a two-times higher risk for cardiovascular mortality (United Kingdom National Work Stress Network, 2013: 7).

The diarist's airline provided bunks at some of its hubs. Using the bunks could be problematic, however. At one base, getting to the landside bunks required a full security screening (faced with this hurdle, pilots sometimes slept in their seats while unloading/loading or congregated in the Engineers' Station). At another, all the bunks could be taken. The diarist records: "Sat around in [Leipzig] hub talking; no spare bunks available to get any sleep".

Based in Germany the diarist had to make his own way there to report. Sometimes he could jump-seat on a company aircraft. Sometimes he had to take a commercial flight (with, for example, Ryanair) to a proximate airport, then use public transport to get to his base (for example, by getting a train from Berlin to Leipzig). Flying scheduled air could be costly. Jump-seats could be in short supply. The diarist found the jump-seat 'gamble' stressful: "Really sick of having to worry about travel arrangements and for living out of a suitcase in a shared house in LEJ". Getting a jump-seat back to the U.K. could not be guaranteed: "Both crew members are LEJ-based and have jumpseat on same aircraft back to EMA, so very keen to get back and not miss flight. Worried that we might have been bumped, but won't know until we arrive".

While moving to Germany would eliminate such unknowns (and the resulting tensions), some pilots were reluctant to move away from family, friends and the familiar (as with this diarist). The Federal Aviation Administration (2010: 55874) acknowledges the role of family, income and job prospects in shaping pilots' domestic arrangements: "Commuting is common in the airline industry ... because of economic reasons associated with protecting seniority on particular aircraft, frequent changes in the ... flight crew member's home base, and low pay ... that may require a pilot to live someplace with a relatively low cost of living".

Millward (2010) makes a similar observation of the general U.K. workforce: "Internal migration in search of work was once common in this country ... Soaring house prices and the spiralling cost of moving has made the workforce far less mobile than it once was. Instead, many commute ridiculous distances every day, adding to the hideous congestion on the country's roads. Thirty years ago, somebody taking up a job fifty miles away would have moved house. Now, given the costs involved, few will take the risk".

In its research publication *The effects on families of job relocations*, the Joseph Rowntree Foundation (2003: 3) notes a predisposition to commute: "Some of the employees interviewed, faced with the option of relocation, chose ... to commute long distances. They thought this placed most of the costs of relocation on themselves, rather than on other family members. However, long distance commuting also has impacts on families, especially through separation for prolonged periods. Its sustainability in the long term is also questionable".

First Officer – night freight (C10)

Green and Canny (2003: 37) highlight the potential negative impacts on families of weekly commuting (where a family member rents a room or flat or shares a house close to their place of work): "[W]hen children were involved in such arrangements, the pressures on families were acknowledged more readily. In such circumstances the employee has two lives – a 'work life' and a 'home life' – with the former often being fulfilled at the expense of the latter ... A male employee with experience of long-distance commuting for over a year ... admitted that it was 'more difficult to live away from the family than I thought'. In this instance the commuting arrangement was not conducive to integration in the destination area and was also unsatisfactory from the employee's perspective for family life".

An employee who lives away from home is more likely to feel isolated. Relationships may come under pressure (Green and Canny, 2003). There may be an unpicking of the social fabric: "[There is a] potential of increasing individualism, as people become detached from traditional family and community networks ... [There is a] potential growth of 'second home' communities, populated by people who split their living locations between the week and the weekends" (Third Sector Foresight, 2010).

Airborne commuting can be uncomfortable: On Day 21 while returning to the U.K. the diarist slept on the vestibule floor. Freight aircraft floors are dirty (to the point of being sticky) and cold. The vestibule is noisy: "Very tired so slept on the floor as the seats are really uncomfortable".

The diarist no longer lived with his partner. The relationship had produced a child, now a teenager. The diarist was seeing a woman with a three year-old child. His bifurcated lifestyle (as between the U.K. and Germany) meant that family obligations were sometimes, of necessity, put on hold: "Collect teenage son for the weekend; haven't seen him for over a month so looking forward to the weekend". Cooper, Dewe and O'Driscoll (2001: 35) observe: "[T]here is now considerable evidence that shift-work can lead to a variety of difficulties for shift-workers and their families, primarily because of disturbances in circadian rhythms ... and disruptions to family and social life. In many cases these effects have been associated with a decline in physical health, satisfaction and overall subjective well-being".

On Day 4 the diarist got 6hrs 30mins sleep in Paris (in two attempts). He then operated three sectors (CDG–LEJ–VIT–LIS). He wrote: "Very tired on leg to VIT, over 2.5 hrs flight time. I was pilot flying for the leg to VIT. Made a hash of the approach, too fast and late to descend. Very turbulent on finals, with a tail wind which made my mistakes worse. Was unlikely we would be stabilised by 500 ft, so made a go-around"; "Was tired ... I just didn't react quickly enough to events". The approach was flown at 03:10, during the circadian low (which lasts from about 03:00 until 06:00). EASA/Moebus (2008: 39) say: "[F]atigue is increased by extended

First Officer – night freight (C10)

time awake, reduced prior sleep, the window of circadian low and task load". The Canadian Nuclear Safety Commission (2013: 2) says: "[Fatigue results] from sleep loss, extended wakefulness, phase of the circadian rhythm or workload. As fatigue increases, declines occur in many aspects of human performance, especially alertness. Alertness is fundamental to many cognitive tasks". The Federal Aviation Administration (2010: 55855) says: "If a person has had significantly less than eight hours of sleep in the past twenty-four hours, he or she is more likely to be fatigued". Campbell and Bagshaw (1999: 140–141) say: "Factors affecting sleepiness include: prior sleep and wakefulness; circadian phase leading to increased sleepiness in the early hours of the morning ... [and] decreased performance in the early hours of the morning".

Pilots' relationship with Crewing can be problematic. Crewing Officers' directive powers can be resented by pilots who are legally responsible for high-value capital and cargo, well trained and highly motivated (Bennett, 2010a). Lack of control over one's work-schedule is a stressor (United Kingdom National Work Stress Network, 2013). The relationship is not always problematic, however, especially when a Crewing Officer does a pilot a favour ... as happened on Day 19: "Phoned crewing and request I be taken off LEJ–MRS–VLC due to late finish; surprisingly they agreed and I'm now back on my original trip to BSL departing at 01:50". Discretion exercised in favour of pilots can generate good will.

Hotels can be noisy (Chittick, 1998; Bennett, 2003; Bennett, 2010a). Gander, Gregory, Connell, Graeber, Miller and Rosekind (1998: B26) say: "[D]aytime sleep is often compromised because [subjects] are trying to sleep when they are physiologically prepared for wakefulness, and when disturbances (noise, light, domestic or social demands) are maximal". While in the Basle HOTAC the diarist wrote: "Had breakfast and in bed by 04:45. Went to sleep easily and slept until 10:00, woke briefly and slept again until 11:30 when woken by cleaners outside room. Dozed off again only to be woken again by workman 'banging' somewhere in hotel, complained to reception!" Disturbed sleep is not as restorative as continuous sleep.

The demands of being down-route meant that exercise was sometimes not taken. On Day 20 he wrote: "Feeling better than I have all week so went to the gym for the first time in a long time [since Day 11]". Taking exercise evidences a *professional* attitude: "Pilots are required to maintain optimum physical and psychological fitness. High levels of responsibility for manoeuvring aircraft, transporting other crew and passengers, coping with demands and decisions, all require mental capability, excellent health, and emotional stability" (Bor, Field and Scragg, 2002: 244).

Captain – night freight (C14)	
Day	**Diary (All times Zulu)**
1	Awoke 06:00 in Belfast at Brother's house. Left for ferry at 07:30. 1.5 hours sleep in cabin after lunch. Arrived Birkenhead at 18:00. Then a 3-hour drive home. Bowl of pasta and pesto on arrival at 21:30. Bed at 22:30. Still fragile after clearing parents' house prior to its sale. But physically refreshed after ten days away from work – previous work detail had been cancelled by a dental abscess.
2	Awake 05:30. Usual cup of tea in bed with wife. Had slept soundly. Left house 06:15 for 07:50 report. Ate doughnut on the way. Report time delayed by ten minutes ... after I set out! Taxi to LTN, then position to LEJ. Drop operating crew to Globana hotel, then into town. Arrive hotel 13:30 ish for minimum rest. Depart at 22:40 for LEJ–BTS–SOF (Leipzig–Bratislava–Sofia), but will accept as hotels in town so much better than Globana at airport. Continental breakfast in room at 14:30. Read and was lazy. Tried to sleep, failed, so short walk. Back to bed at about 18:00, slept for about 3.5 hours. Woken by text. Change of roster. BTS–SOF cancelled. Hotel standby instead. Back to bed for fitful sleep. Dinner was to have been in LEJ hub, so a little hungry.
3	Awoke 06:30 for a leisurely but ample breakfast until 09:00. Read until 11:00. Fetched bike from Marriott hotel. Went to climbing wall 13:00–15:30. Crewing had texted. Agreed to operate LEJ–BGY–LEJ (Leipzig–Bergamo–Leipzig) at 18:00. Due back 22:00, then back to hotel for rest prior to LEJ–MRS–VLC (Leipzig–Marseilles–Valencia) on Wednesday a.m. So no rest required p.m., hence climbing wall. Left hotel 16:30. Quick meal in LEJ hub. Almost to BGY, when Operations asked us to divert to BRU. Ample fuel, so not a problem, except now we have 4 hours on the ground (instead of one) before returning to LEJ. New First Officer on board ten minutes before scheduled departure. He operated in from BGY. Departed only 2 minutes late. Easy flight back to LEJ. Off duty 01:13. Into hotel by 02:00. One very small whiskey, then bed.
4	Awoke 06:30. (4hrs 30mins) Feeling tired. No more sleep possible, so breakfast at 07:30. Not very hungry, but ate O.K. Out on bike 09:15–11:00. One beer at lunch time in sunshine between showers. Dozed for a few minutes by pool p.m. Ate soup and roll and had alcohol-free beer (tasted O.K.) at 17:00. In bed by 19:00. Good sleep. Awoke 23:00 (4hrs) for 23:40 depart from hotel. Text from Crewing. They had been trying to

Captain – night freight (C14)	
Day	Diary (All times Zulu)
	get hold of me at 17:00 for an earlier trip. I call Crewing. Am now doing LEJ–LYS–TLS (Leipzig–Lyon–Toulouse). I did not ask what trip I had missed earlier. Bowl of soup in hub before departure. I felt O.K. on both sectors, but flew an inefficient profile descent into TLS. Untidy.
5	Arrive TLS 30 minutes early. Easy transport to hotel. There at 05:45. Straight to breakfast with the new First Officer. Doing familiarisation flight as an observer. Ate a little, then went to bed by 07:00. Awake at 09:11 – not good (2hrs). Walked into Blagnac Village. Lovely warm sunshine. Bread and cheese for lunch. Too tired for gym/pool, so went back to bed at about 13:00. Read and slept from 14:00 for about an hour. Left hotel 17:30. Security easy despite new FO not yet having his company ID. Uneventful flight TLS–LYS–LEJ. Poor meal in hub on arrival. Not enough time for sleep.
6	Felt jaded on the flight LEJ–CDG. But luckily very simple. Arrived hotel 03:40, after dropping PAX at different security gate. Straight to bed. Awoke 07:30 (3hrs 45mins) (I never set my alarm, except for a report time). Breakfast and chat with other crew. First Officer awoke at 12-ish. Arranged trip to Roissy Village for coffee. Met up with other crew at 16:00 for pizza. Slept 17:00–19:00. Transport 19:45. Inbound aircraft was on-time, but its First Officer was unaware he was operating with me. He was very inexperienced and obviously underconfident. Departed early to try and make time up for very short turnaround (35mins) at LEJ. We made up nearly 20mins, so an easy transfer. Experienced First Officer LEJ–EMA (plus two passengers). Lots of chat en-route. Arrived 01:15. Into car by 01:45. Home by 03:05. Straight to bed in spare room, so as not to disturb wife.
7	Wife at work. Still awoke at 08:00. Leisurely morning, with some gardening and domestic chores. Still lots of unpacking of boxes from parents' house. Light lunch at 12:30. To horses at 17:00. Dinner 19:30. Bed 21:00.
8	Tea in bed 05:30. Light breakfast 07:00. Out of house at 07:30 to take son to do voluntary work at vets. Pottered around Lincoln until 12:00. Collected him and home by 13:30. Late light lunch. One hour nap in the afternoon. Dinner while wife fed the horses. Bed 22:00.

Captain – night freight (C14)	
Day	Diary (All times Zulu)
9	Slept like a log again until early-morning tea at 05:30. Made porridge while wife fed the horses. Caught up on e-mails. October's roster is now out. Out on bike and wife and son out on horseback 11:30–13:00. Light lunch, then a one hour nap. Unpacked more boxes. Dinner – salad in front of T.V. Bed 21:30.
10	Usual solid sleep until 05:30. Son's first day in Sixth Form, so I did the horses while the wife fussed over him. Both departed at 07:00. Domestic morning. Log book, lunch 12:30. Rested p.m. 14:15–15:30. Finished sorting parents' clobber. Ironing for one hour. Dinner in front of T.V. Bed 21:30.
11	Slightly restless night. Awake 04:00 (wife at 03:00). Tea in bed 04:30–05:15. E-mails and computer (looking for flights at Xmas) 05:30–06:45. Son to train 07:00. Breakfast 07:30. Into Lincoln. Blind from rental house to be re-altered, and meet other tenant re money shortfall. Some cash received. Made significant progress with tenant's financial problems in his bank. Lunch – bread and cheese, then tea at home 13:30–14:00. One hour rest 14:15–15:15. Son and two friends to kayaking at 16:10, back 19:35. I read while they were on the water. Thirty-minute drive each way. Dinner at 20:00–21:00. Bed 21:30.
12	Better night's sleep. Awake 05:15 (7hrs 45mins). Feeling good. Tea in bed 05:20–05:40. Breakfast 06:30. One hours ironing 06:30–07:30. To field to collect trailer 07:30 (Brother's piano arriving for safe-keeping about 17:00. Ours to rental house in Lincoln). Ready by 05:30. Into Lincoln. Re-erect blind in rental house. More money from bad tenant (not quite paid in full, but close). Coffee in café with wife at 10:00. To bed shop, buy new bed for good tenant. Home by 12:15. Standby 13:00–20:00. Changed into report at 21:00 for position EMA–BRU (East Midlands–Brussels). Operate BRU–LEJ 23:45–01:00. No notice of change. But now here for piano delivery. Tried to rest after lunch. In bed 13:30–14:45, but no sleep (unusual for me, but not feeling tired). Gardened 15:00–17:00. Piano arrived 17:30. Delivery completed 18:30. Dinner. Packed for 6 days/7 nights away. Left house 19:45. At work 22:00. Position EMA–BRU in A300. Twenty minutes on the ground, then operate BRU–LEJ. Arrive 01:00 in rain. Straight to the hotel. Two small beers in the hotel foyer 02:00–02:40, then bed.

Captain – night freight (C14)	
Day	Diary (All times Zulu)
13	Awoke 07:45 (4hrs 45mins). Read until 09:00. Had breakfast in room between 09:30 and 10:45. Cheese omelette, rolls, cheese, tea and orange juice. Read until 12:00. Tried to sleep. Failed. Short walk. Still not tired, so to climbing wall 14:30. Hard exercise until 17:30. Roll and bratwurst on way back to the hotel. Planned sleep 19:00 onwards. But roster changed. Now on airport standby (not hotel standby) at 22:00. To airport 21:30 and into bunk by 22:30. Text at 23:45 to operate LEJ–MAD 01:30–04:25. Trip uneventful. But made mistake whilst taxiing at MAD. Embarrassing but not serious. I just went the wrong way – fatigue! In hotel by 05:00, and went straight to breakfast. In bed by 06:15.
14	Woke up at 09:15 (3hrs). Tried to sleep on but failed. Slept 12:30–14:00 (90mins). Spent an hour by the pool in the sun. Dozed for 30 minutes. Roll and ham at 18:00. Left hotel at 18:30. To operate MAD–LEJ, 20:00–22:55. Toasted sandwich on aircraft (good!). Airport standby on arrival in LEJ. Got into bunk at 00:30, after bowl of soup (good) in canteen at 23:59.
15	Slept until 05:15 (4hrs 45mins) (standby ended at 04:00). Got taxi to the hotel at 05:45. Breakfast at 09:30, fruit, yoghurt, smoked salmon, roils, orange juice, one glass of fizzy wine and a tea. Chatted with four other DHL/EAT colleagues, then to climbing wall with them at 10:00. Stayed until 14:30. Half hour in sauna. Met at 17:00 for two beers and dinner – pork medallions German-style, croquette potato, veg, half a carafe of wine, two more beers. After dinner I walked back to the hotel. Colleague had Burger King as well ... how do they eat so much? Bed at about 00:30.
16	Woke at 07:30 (7hrs). Breakfast at 08:00. Joined by two others from last night. Breakfast until 09:00, then out for a bicycle ride to the lakes. Was out for 3.5 hours to do about 25 miles leisurely riding in the sunshine. It was very pleasant. Hot chocolate by the lake. Half an hour in the sauna, sandwich and juice, nectarine and kiwi. One hour's sleep, 14:30–15:30 (60mins). Woken by a text from Crewing: roster change, LEJ–STR 19:15–20:20 cancelled. Now doing a hotel standby (18:00–22:00). Meal of pasta carbonara at 19:00, and an alcohol-free beer. O.K. Watched some T.V., then bed at 22:00.
17	Slightly restless night. Awake three times, or so. Woke at about 06:00 (8hrs). Breakfast with colleague at 07:30–08:45. Omelette, sausage, bacon, roll, tea, fruit and cake! Hungry. Climbing wall by bike 09:30–13:00. Not

Captain – night freight (C14)	
Day	Diary (All times Zulu)
	sleepy, so went to pool for two hours. Bicycle 30mins each way. Back to hotel at 17:30. Bed at 18:00–21:45. Transport 21:55. Sleep (about 3hrs)? Felt O.K. when the alarm woke me up. Transport to hub. Bowl of soup – good. Ten minutes chat, then to aircraft. Minor tech issue. Departed 7mins late at 23:32 (23:25). Loading delay (not tech). Uneventful to EMA. Arrived 01:46.
18	Watched T.V. in EMA hub. Chatted with two Air Contractors colleagues until time to walk for EDI service. Loaded early and pushed early. Just about to taxi, then a tech fault re-occurred. More complex this time. Waited for Marshaller to return to stand. Spoke with engineer via headset while waiting. Appeared to clear problem, so started right engine again and taxied. The problem re-occurred while taxiing, but as we had been legally despatched we could use the Minimum Equipment List, and go. Long discussion as to what kit we had working. Uneventful flight to EDI. Arrived 14mins late. Taxi to hotel. Breakfast: fried eggs, haggis, toast and tea. Bed at 06:15. Woke at 09:25. Dozed for another 40mins (about 3hrs 45mins), then up to use computer e-mails/book transport for half-term and Xmas travel. Went walkabout with First Officer at 12:00. Two coffees in John Lewis. Nice view from rooftop café. Back to the hotel at 15:00. Haggis and chips from chip shop (very poor) and tea in room at 18:00. Transport 18:30 for 19:40 depart. Aircraft just as we left it this a.m. 13mins late loading. Uneventful but windy flight back to EMA. Off duty 21:13. Smooth drive home. Arrived 22:30. Bed by 22:50.
19	Wife awake at 04:55. Two cups of tea in bed. To field to finish off horses at 06:20, so she can go to work. Stay there until 08:20. Usual chores, but nice to be in fresh air. Cleaned and ironed at home until 11:30. Cleared some paperwork backlogs (letters, etc.). To EMA to collect 'middle son' at 13:20. He's coming in from Grenoble for a long weekend. He has just finished his masters, and has not been home for a long time). Ryanair flight in on time. Chatted all the way back home. Arrive 16:50. My back is now very sore and stiff (digging badly in the a.m., I think). Almost incapacitated. Take painkillers. Dinner at 18:30. Wife may be ill with 'flu. She is in bed by 19:30. I am in bed at 20:40 after slow clearing up downstairs.

Captain – night freight (C14)	
Day	Diary (All times Zulu)
20	Awake at the usual 04:55. Back is horrible. Wife is still ill, but she tends to the horses then goes to work. I take more painkillers. Supposed to be delivering piano today! Breakfast. My back slowly eased during the morning, so delivered the piano. Collected bed (in boxes). In town running errands until 15:00. Late lunch at 15:10. Dinner. Bed at 21:00.
21	Usual morning tea at 04:55. Back is stiff, but improving. Wife did the horses, I did the ironing. Domestic tidying. Then to EMA at 07:35 to meet my brother and his wife. Dropped brother and his partner at Newark rail station. She is lecturing in Bradford p.m. Bring brother home. One hours rest p.m. Prepared food. Back to Newark at 17:35 to collect brother's wife again. Dinner. Bed by 22:30.

Analysis

The diarist, who lived near Lincoln, was a Captain at a U.K.-registered night freight airline. The airline provided global air lift (using Boeing 757 and 767 aircraft) to a major German freight forwarder. He sent the following letter with his sleep/activity log: "All the sleep I get is good sleep. I always awake almost instantly, and feel alert immediately. I am physically very fit, but back pain has been a problem perhaps two times each year for the last four years. Each episode lasts 3–5 days, normally. I am emotionally still recovering after the deaths of my parents".

Night-freight operations can be volatile. Rosters are changed frequently, sometimes several times a day, depending on the circumstances (weather, sickness, network loads, aircraft technical problems, industrial action (by controllers, loaders, fuellers) etc.) (Bennett, 2010a). Consider, for example, Days 2 and 3: "Tried to sleep, failed, so short walk. Back to bed at about 18:00, slept for about 3.5 hours. Woken by text. Change of roster. BTS–SOF cancelled"; "Almost to BGY, when Operations asked us to divert to BRU. Ample fuel, so not a problem, except now we have 4 hours on the ground (instead of one) before returning to LEJ". Pilots are encouraged to plan for the worst-case scenario (a greatly extended night duty). While a sensible precaution, planning for the worst-case can be difficult. First, as indicated above, pilots can find it difficult to get pre-report top-up sleep. Few can sleep to order. A pilot who is not tired will not sleep. Secondly, most pilots try to relax when away from the flight-deck, by, for example, exercising or sightseeing. The perceived need for distraction eats into the time available for top-up sleep.

Crew resource management (CRM) promotes teamwork. Good teamwork makes operations safer (Wiener, Kanki and Helmreich, 1993; Krause, 1996; Bennett, 2010c). Short-notice crew changes inhibit CRM because pilots have less time to

Captain – night freight (C14)

interact and agree boundaries before push-back. As mentioned above, the airline's operating schedule could be somewhat chaotic. On Day 3 the diarist had to make the best he could of a short-notice crew change: "New First Officer on board ten minutes before scheduled departure. He operated in from BGY". Team membership volatility and/or insufficient time allowed to formate with colleagues inhibit cohesion and effectiveness: "With reference to Tuckman's (1965) work on team formation (forming, storming, norming, performing, adjourning) and Mathieu *et al.*'s (2000) work on shared mental models ... volatility [has] the potential to reduce ... effectiveness" (Bennett, 2010a). Speaking to the aviation experience, Hackman (1998: 250) writes: "Crews should be kept intact over time ... Yet in most airlines, crew composition is constantly changing because of the long-standing practice ... of assigning pilots to trips, positions, and aircraft as individuals".

Because roster changes interfere with pilots' sleeping plans, they pose a safety risk. On Day 13 a roster change foiled the diarist's attempt to sleep in the afternoon, resulting in a fatigue-induced error at MAD: "Planned sleep 19:00 onwards. But roster changed. Now on airport standby (not hotel standby) at 22:00. To airport 21:30 and into bunk by 22:30. No sleep. Text at 23:45 to operate LEJ–MAD 01:30–04:25. Trip uneventful. But made mistake whilst taxiing at MAD. Embarrassing but not serious. I just went the wrong way – fatigue!" The diarist had obtained less than five hours sleep the previous night. Assuming he was carrying no sleep debt or credit prior, this would have generated ten hours of productive wakefulness. As he woke at 07:45, this credit would have been exhausted by 17:45. This means that when he was taxiing to his stand at MAD (04:15) he would have been in sleep debt to the tune of 10hrs 30mins. Sleep debt degrades performance (Rhodes and Gil, 2002). Virgin Blue (2005) puts it this way: "[Sleep] debt may result in impaired performance, reduced alertness and higher levels of sleepiness and fatigue". Further, by 04:15 the diarist would have been continuously awake for 20.5 hours: "By the 18th hour [of wakefulness] the pilot will have great difficulty remembering things he has done or said a few moments ago (short-term memory) and his reaction time will have almost doubled in duration. By the 24th hour his ability to think creatively and make decisions will be dangerously low" (Rhodes and Gil, 2002: 15).

The diarist's sleeping patterns are worthy of note. When down-route he tended to get relatively short sleeps (sometimes two short sleeps per day). On Day 4, for example, he got four and a half hours sleep (although he did get a full four hours pre-report sleep later). On Day 5 he got just 3 hours sleep in TLS. He got a short sleep the next day, too. On Day 14 he got 4hrs 30mins sleep, then operated. On Day 15 he got 4hrs 45mins sleep. (There were exceptions, however: on Day 17 the diarist got 8hrs sleep, followed by 3 hours pre-report sleep). When at home the diarist tended to rise early (with his wife, who worked).

Captain – night freight (C14)

Regarding pre-report sleep, it is clear that when a pilot cannot get any top-up sleep, s/he may slide into sleep debt – sometimes when still operating. As mentioned above, sleep debt degrades cognitive skills. When at home on Day 12 the diarist obtained nearly 8hrs sleep. This would have generated 16 hours of productive wakefulness. The diarist then tried to get some pre-report sleep: "Tried to rest after lunch. In bed 13:30–14:45, but no sleep (unusual for me, but not feeling tired)". He positioned to BRU, then operated to LEJ. He was in bed by 03:00. Awake since 05:15 that morning, his 16 hours sleep credit would have expired by 21:15. This means that by the time he flew the approach into LEJ (at 00:45) he would have been carrying 3hrs 30mins sleep debt. Sleep debt can be difficult to recover when down-route (Bennett, 2010a). Hotel noise and other pressures impinge on sleep. The diarist's propensity to get relatively short sleeps when down-route would have made recovery of sleep debt even more difficult.
    The diarist made a determined effort to keep fit: "Out on bike 09:15–11:00". He was a frequent visitor to Leipzig's Climbing Wall. He also went walking and gardened. At home he helped keep the family's horses and looked after a rental property.
    The diarist could be critical of his own performance: "I felt O.K. on both sectors, but flew an inefficient profile descent into TLS. Untidy". Pilots have a tendency towards perfectionism: "[T]he preferred personality traits of pilots include a strong tendency towards being active, self-confident, and competitive, with a tendency towards perfectionism. These are in preference to a pilot exhibiting a lack of conscientiousness, assertiveness, arrogance, impatience or lacking interpersonal warmth and sensitivity" (Bor, Field and Scragg, 2002: 240–241).

First Officer – low-cost carrier (turboprop) (C5)	
Day	Diary (All times Zulu)
1	Off sick from work. Revisited the doctor today, virus now turned into an ear infection and signed off work until 20/09. Dreading telling work I'll be off sick for another week. The reaction from crewing is always one of disbelief. Emailed my base Captain and told him. Also asked if the airline has done a risk assessment on how filthy the flight decks are, as I'm convinced this contributes to getting illnesses. On the other hand I'm slightly relieved to have another week away from work and to be able to eat properly. The relentless roster has taken its toll on me in the last year. Went to the gym for an hour to try and sweat the virus out. First time I've had the time to go for about 3 weeks. It exhausted me. I may not go again until I'm better. However I feel it's a waste because once I'm back at work I won't have the time to go again. I ate at 02:00 and 19:00. In bed at 21:00.

First Officer – low-cost carrier (turboprop) (C5)	
Day	Diary (All times Zulu)
2	Up at 07:00 (10hrs). Feeling very tired. Broken sleep all night again, I can't seem to relax. I ate at 09:00 and 19:00. In bed just after midnight.
3	Up at about 07:30 (7hrs 30mins). Woke early … I can't sleep past about 07:00 because I've been mostly on early shifts for the last 3 months. Ear infection still hurting and still haven't told work that I'll be off sick for the next week too. I haven't thought about weather for nearly a week now. It's quite liberating. Weather dominates my thoughts usually because it affects how my working day will go. Bad weather = stress, and a tiring day at work. Ate at 10:00 and 18:00. In bed around midnight.
4	Woke early as usual (08:30) after another late night (8hrs 30mins). Feeling tired and ear and throat hurting more today. Start taking antibiotics … Finally called work and told them I would be off sick for the week. I'm glad to be able to relax at home tomorrow. I was meant to be teaching flying tomorrow at my local flying club, but I have cancelled. It's a pity because teaching flying in a light aircraft is now the only flying I actually enjoy. My airline has taken most of the enjoyment I had for my job away due to the pure intensity of it. Ate at 11:00 and 19:00. In bed at about 21:00.
5	Up at 09:00. Yet another night of broken sleep. I woke up every couple of hours. I have a very busy mind and contemplated getting up at 04:00 because I was just lying there wide awake thinking. It's so annoying being so tired but being unable to sleep. Luckily I managed to get back to sleep after about an hour and then woke up at 09:00. All this time at home is taking its toll on my waist line too! I really need to go to the gym but I'm not sure how I'll feel after last Thursday. I have lots to do also. My passport needs sorting out. I can't send it off because I need it for my job, so I have to arrange for a second passport. I'm not sure if I've got enough cash to pay for it this month, but it has to be done. I also need to study for my command simulator check … buy a new log book and sort my house out. I bought it 18 months ago with the help of the state. It's embarrassing that I'm a pilot and still don't earn enough to get a mortgage. The state lent me half the money to buy it. It's the only way I could afford a house of my own. Plus my ear is still hurting, I'm not sure the antibiotics are working yet. Ate at 18:00 only. In bed at around 23:30.
6	Went to bed quite late last night despite feeling tired earlier in the evening. Seemed to sleep a lot better, and despite waking at 06:00 for a bit, managed to sleep until 09:00 (9hrs). A lot to do today, I have to meet 2 friends. One is 8 months pregnant, one has just had her 3rd miscarriage this year. I haven't seen

First Officer – low-cost carrier (turboprop) (C5)	
Day	Diary (All times Zulu)
	my pregnant friend for 4 weeks, despite the fact she lives around the corner, simply due to my working life. I haven't seen the other for 3 weeks for the same reason. I also went to the gym and ran for a bit. I don't feel 100% but know that my return to work is imminent and won't get the chance soon, so I feel like I should make the effort. I managed a 3 mile run and just 10mins on the bike before I felt I should go home and get ready to see my friends. By the time I got back home after my visits it was 05:00 and I hadn't eaten all day. My fiancé calls me. He is ill. He lives in Bristol and we only see each other at weekends. He's coming over to be ill at my house, which makes 2 of us now. I ate at 11:00 and 19:00. Got to bed at about 22:00.
7	My fiancé woke me up at 04:30 this morning to make a phone call to his work to call in sick; it took me ages to get back to sleep afterwards, and then was woken at 07:00 (8hrs) by workmen in the car park. I got up at this point and felt ok, not too tired, but not 100% refreshed. Another busy day ahead of meeting with a friend for lunch so he can sign my passport form. Another trip to B&Q for more stuff for the house, then back to make dinner for me and the fiancé with man flu. There aren't enough hours in the day anymore. I've gone from being bored at home to being too busy. I still haven't started revising for my simulator assessment and I still need to buy and complete my log book. Went to bed at about 23:00.
8	Got up at about 07:00 (8hrs). I slept so much better last night and actually feel rested. I seem to have finally relaxed. I always find that when on holiday it takes me most of the holiday to relax and to be able to sleep, usually just in time to come home again! I went to the gym at 10:00 for an hour. It's the first time in about 2 years that I have been regularly and I love it. An action-packed day today. I went to see my diet counsellor first of all. Since starting work with the airline two and a half years ago, I put on a stone in weight and worked very hard last year to lose it, so want to keep it off. When you consider I have no time to go to the gym usually, losing the weight was no mean feat. They expect you to keep a decent body mass index, but feed you absolute crap crew food. Sandwiches, crisps and chocolate – if you're hungry you just eat it. I'd love management to eat what we have to and either survive or not get fat. I've had food poisoning from the crew food also. Anyway, after that I have to go wedding dress shopping, and then have to go back into town for a beautician appointment – all things I could never plan if I was working this week. Got to bed at about 23:00.

First Officer – low-cost carrier (turboprop) (C5)	
Day	Diary (All times Zulu)
9	Woke at about 07:00 (8hrs), feeling fairly refreshed again. I'm definitely back in the sleeping groove. I'm not looking forward to going back to work next week! My ear has been OK until today and is now hurting again, but not enough to warrant another trip to the doctor. More shopping for the house: I now have a total of 3 lamp shades to show for 18 months in my house. Thankfully the fiancé is starting to feel better and we go shopping together to Reading. A fairly relaxing evening, TV, film and food. So this is what it was like to have a normal life. My nails are even growing back! I ate at 09:00 and 18:30. Got to bed at about 23:00.
10	Woke again at a good time, around 08:00 (9hrs) to the sound of football practice in the field behind the house. As I draw the curtains I catch one of them parking in our private car park and climbing over the fence with a bag of footballs so shout at them because the fence is being destroyed by these people. I'm turning into a grumpy old sod and get them a parking ticket too. I hope it doesn't come back to bite me! Anyway, a lazy day of watching TV and finishing jobs. I was paid yesterday so can now afford to send off my passport application and buy my log book – that's £130 gone in minutes. It's also car insurance month. I hate asking my parents for money. You'd think a 33 year old airline pilot could afford to buy this stuff, but I barely break even each month. The thought of pensions and retirement scare the hell out of me: at this rate I'll have to work until I die. I so need my instructing job. Even though I'm not meant to get paid, I do. It means a tank of petrol each month – that's how tight cash is. Don't even talk about how we're going to afford to get married: it's one reason we've been engaged for 10 months and still have not set a date. Ate at 10:00 and 18:30.
11	Another good night of sleep. Woke at about 08:30 so a good 9hours+ and no rogue footballers to shout at this morning either. Went to the gym for an hour: I've managed to shed 5lb in weight in the last 5 days so feeling quite pleased with myself. My medical on Tuesday shouldn't be so painful after all! I'm doing a challenge at the gym, running a half marathon over the next four weeks – a challenge I could never have done in a normal roster month, but seeing as I'm now feeling better and off the antibiotics I'm keen to get it completed before I go back to work. A couple of years ago when I was at my last airline I had the time to train for an actual half marathon. I'd love to do another but know work commitments will not allow consistent training. I was meant to be teaching tomorrow but my student has just called and cancelled:

First Officer – low-cost carrier (turboprop) (C5)	
Day	Diary (All times Zulu)
	ill again. I'm ok with that, however. This total break from flying is doing me good. I'm actually looking forward to work on Thursday now. With this job you have to love what you do, like any vocational job, or it becomes like a living hell. The intense flying roster is just ridiculous and a reason everyone is starting to hate their job. Ate 09:00 and 15:00. In bed by 21:00.
12	Up at about 05:30 (8hrs 30mins). Back to broken sleep. I think it's the thought of my fiancé going back to Bristol today and the thought that I'll be back at work soon. A busy day of trying to sort out this parking issue. Emails back and forth to the management company, a trip to the police and conversation with the town council. Hopefully this will get the message through. Feeling a bit tired and in need of a decent sleep. In bed by 20:00.
13	Medical today, so up at 06:00 (10hrs). Drove to Birmingham. Went to the jeweller where my engagement ring was made to get the diamond reset, then off to the airport for the medical renewal. I felt tired – I haven't been up at this time for a couple of weeks. Got back home at 16:00 and started to get ready for the possibility of being called off standby at 05:00 in the morning. I felt quite refreshed still but dreaded going back to work. Early to bed at 20:30 just in case. Ate at 07:00 and 18:00.
14	I got woken by the phone at exactly 05:00 by Crewing to do a Glasgow and back (SOU–GLA–SOU). I had 1.5hrs to get to work. They told me to get there in 1hr 15mins. There was no chance as I live a 1hr drive away and I'm definitely not foregoing my shower. I text the Captain and he tells me not to rush because the aircraft is still stuck in Bournemouth and won't arrive for hours. Crewing always does this: get us to rush, rush, rush when there's no need whatsoever: it makes being called from sleep even more stressful. I felt absolutely knackered having been woken from deep sleep PLUS having woken several times during the night because I felt I was going to be called. There wasn't even time for a coffee before I left the house. I could barely keep my eyes open when driving down the M3. I felt sick and had a headache. Got to work at 06:30. Met the Captain in Costa for a coffee: it woke me up and our aircraft then arrived. We were 2hrs late and the passengers were kicking off [getting annoyed] in the terminal: at least I didn't have to deal with them in the cabin. I hadn't flown for 2.5 weeks and elected to do the first sector. I felt physically sick and dizzy the whole way to Glasgow. I didn't get to eat until I landed [on-blocks 09:30]. A twenty-five minute turnaround and off back to Southampton. I felt even worse and the cabin crew both felt sick too. On

First Officer – low-cost carrier (turboprop) (C5)	
Day	Diary (All times Zulu)
	landing we spoke to another Captain who has experienced something similar in the past. It was the noise and vibration of the aircraft that was making us feel so nauseous. I drove back home and after an hour felt OK again so decided to go to the gym and complete another 3 miles towards the half marathon challenge. Ate at 09:00 and 16:00.
15	Oh my god. I'm so tired as I write this at 04:00 after another night of difficulty getting to sleep and then what sleep I had was broken. After my Paul McKenna deep relaxation track I was feeling sleepy but despite going to bed at 19:15 the last time I looked at my clock it was 20:25 and I was still awake. My alarm was set for 03:10, and it was like a sledge hammer when it went off. The day turned into a testing day. It was a four sector day (SOU–LBA–SOU–AVN–SOU) (Southampton–Leeds/Bradford–Southampton–Avignon–Southampton) reporting at 05:20 and checking out at 14:20. The first two sectors went well. However due to French air traffic control going on strike we got a 3 hour slot delay leaving for Avignon. This meant that we weren't due to get to AVN until 14:15, and with a 2 hour flight back, this would have put us 35mins into discretion. However we had yet another departure slot at 15:26. With a 2 hour flight back, that would have put us 1.5hrs into discretion. Operations called. Unfortunately I picked up the call and told them we were too tired and were not going to go into discretion. He went mad at me, basically blaming me for not telling them we wouldn't BEFORE we left Southampton. I politely told them they had 3 hours to sort this out. We called them 3 times and told them we would be out of hours. The moment they told us to go we were always going to be out of hours. Plus discretion is exactly that, our decision not theirs. We'd all been up since 03:00 and were knackered. We hadn't eaten any proper food. Both cabin crew were out of base and were due to position back to their home bases. One of them would be going into a day off too, but all were happy to night-stop. I was livid and my Captain called the Fleet Manager to complain. He advised us to put in an Air Safety Report if we thought it was necessary. The airline has been taking too much from us for too long and we have no more to give. So we stayed in a hotel, as did our 74 passengers, at the airline's expense. Ate at 11:00 and 19:00. Got to bed at about 20:00.
16	Woke at 04:45, a lie in. People were shouting in the corridors until 21:00, but I still slept well (7hrs 30mins). No breakfast before leaving the hotel and no food or hot water on the aircraft. We arrived back at 08:30. Unfortunately the Captain got sent off to do another 2 sectors and I had to stay at the airport

First Officer – low-cost carrier (turboprop) (C5)	
Day	Diary (All times Zulu)
	on standby until 13:00 – still in the clothes we had come to work in the day before. I'm on 'days off' tomorrow, and there was no spare aircraft, cabin crew or Captain to accompany me, so I'm not sure why the hell they made me stay for another 4.5 hours for no reason other than revenge! The aircraft I flew 2 days ago (Day 14) had an oil leak in the propeller. The oil must have vaporised and entered the cabin as fumes. This was the reason we were feeling dizzy and sick. Ate at 10:00 and 20:00. In bed by 22:00.
17	Solid sleep all night until about 09:00 (11hrs). I'm feeling dizzy and sick for some reason when I lie down or get up. It's happened before and lasted for a few weeks. I'm wondering if it's to do with my low blood pressure or my diet, or maybe the oil fumes I've been inhaling for 3 days? I get up and study for my command simulator assessment until 10:30 and then get ready to meet up with friends to watch our beloved Manchester City beat Chelsea. I stay only for the match and stick to soft drinks, then go home and study more before meeting them again at 18:00 for dinner. I feel guilty because I haven't been to the gym today, but there aren't enough hours in the day. When I got back from the pub I noticed that the hire car that was delivered to me yesterday (for the simulator on Monday) has a flat tyre and I spend an hour trying to sort it out. I have left my fiancé with my friends drinking in the pub. They all think I'm pregnant because I'm not drinking. I may have a couple later to prove them wrong! Feeling tired again, I wish there was time for a nap before I go out. Ate at 10:00 and 18:30. In bed by 22:30.
18	I went to sleep at 23:00 and had a night of broken sleep. I woke at 07:00 and got out of bed only to fall into the wall with one of my dizzy spells – this is getting a bit strange. I feel very tired and also anxious. I'm not looking forward to my sim check tomorrow. I have no idea of what to expect and I feel very unprepared. I feel like I should go to the gym but I feel pretty awful and wonder if I would pass out on the treadmill. I go out and buy a nasal spray and menthol crystals to try and open my Eustachian tubes and drain the fluid from my ears. The lady in the pharmacy tells me she has the same problem and that it causes her dizziness. Perhaps my ears are the problem. I need to study before tomorrow. Work called again to try to sort out my transport to the sim: I can never escape work even on my days off. My dizziness feels like it's getting better until I lie down and all of a sudden the room spins. Ate at 15:00. In bed by about 20:30.

First Officer – low-cost carrier (turboprop) (C5)	
Day	Diary (All times Zulu)
19	Woke at 02:00 when my fiancé got up to drive back to Bristol. Managed to get back to sleep afterwards and woke to my alarm at 06:00 (9hrs 30mins). I feel like I've had enough sleep, but still feel like I could do with some more. It's the day of my simulator check and I have to be there at 08:30. I receive phone calls from work and the hire car company while I'm trying to get ready. Work want a receipt and the hire car people can deliver another car. More phone calls: do I get the new car or stick with the taxi? And I was hoping to get some last minute study in! I'm told to stick with the taxi: it's booked for 07:45 and it's late. The taxi driver on my road approaches my front door. He's my driver. However, his wife has accidentally taken his car keys to work. His colleague is on his way round and should be 10mins. This is cutting it too fine; I call work and explain I'm going to be late for my briefing. This is stress I really do not need today. My dizziness seems to have abated. I'm not 100% and decide to tell my sim instructor, even though I hate the thought of it sounding like an excuse, although if I'm suddenly sick due to the sim motion he'll need to know why. I manage to arrive at exactly 08:30 in the briefing room. My sim instructor got my message and is impressed I've made it. We have a 1.5hr briefing. This is the pre-command check and is kept a secret. There's no information on it anywhere so we're completely blind going in. I volunteer to go first and after 2 hours of passengers dying, bad weather, avoiding mid air collisions and executing diverts, my turn is over and it's time to swap. Another 2 hours and we're finished. Back to the classroom for an hour-long debrief. We've both passed. Another hour or so of paperwork filling-in and I get my taxi home. A long stressful day finally over. I feel so sick and drained – my ears really aren't right. I'm nearly sick in the taxi and I'm starving all at the same time. I haven't eaten since 07:30 and it's now 17:00. I'm on a late tomorrow – 4 sectors – so I have to try and stay up late tonight, so I can sleep in tomorrow. Ate at 07:30 and 17:30. In bed by about 22:00.
20	Back to the old routine of waking several times a night. I woke at 07:00 (9hrs) and just lay in bed for an hour trying to sleep again. I feel tired and have sore eyes. I have 4 sectors today with a 12:55 report time. Must leave the house by 11:30 as I have a one hour drive and it takes 20mins to get to the crew room and through security. I'm with a nice Captain so it should be an easy day (SOU–GLA–SOU–DUB–SOU) (Southampton–Glasgow–Southampton–Dublin–Southampton). The day goes without a hiccup and we finish 15mins early at 21:15, then my one hour drive home in the car, plus the daily call to the parking people because the automatic number plate recognition doesn't

First Officer – low-cost carrier (turboprop) (C5)	
Day	Diary (All times Zulu)
	recognise my car reg, it's so annoying. I get home starving hungry, have a bit of a snack and watch some TV: I'm totally shattered but can't motivate myself even to go up the stairs to bed. I finally go up at 24:00 and go straight to sleep. Ate at 10:00 and snacked at 18:00 and 23:00.
21	I wake at 07:00 after about 7 hours sleep. I'm still tired but can't get back to sleep. That's OK because I'm on an early tomorrow and always need to be tired so I can go to bed early at 19:00. I haven't been to the gym for a week because of work and my dizzy spells, but decide to go. I feel terrible on the treadmill and totally energy-sapped on the cross trainer. I'm meeting my best friend at 12:30, if I don't get called out, so decide to call it a day and head home before my standby starts. Usually when I make plans I get called! Ate at 08:00 and 17:00.
Analysis	

This diarist, a 33 year old First Officer, flew turboprops out of Southampton (SOU) for a UK-registered operator. Before commencing her diary she sent two e-mails:

"Dear Simon, I've just received an email from BALPA about pilot studies for fatigue and lifestyle. I believe quite strongly in getting this changed because at the moment I fly continually exhausted, therefore I am volunteering for the study. I fly short-haul turbo props, in case you need that information".

"Hi Simon, I'm actually off sick for the next week due to being overworked and finally succumbing to an ear infection! When I go back I'm only working for 9 days before being off for 2 weeks leave".

After completing her 21-day diary she sent the following e-mail:

"Hi Simon, I'm actually coming off a CAA grounding because that ear infection turned in to Labyrinthitis, which has put a medical restriction on my licence". (Labyrinthitis is an infection of the inner-ear. It causes a delicate structure deep inside the ear called the labyrinth to become inflamed. It affects balance and hearing).

The diarist believed her work to be a stressor. She attributed both her infection and erratic sleeping patterns to her roster: "The relentless roster has taken its toll on me in the last year". Locked into a routine of getting up early, the diarist found it difficult to 'lie in' during the early stages of her sick leave: "Yet another night of broken sleep. I woke up every couple of hours. I have a very busy mind and contemplated getting up at 04:00 because I was just lying there wide awake, thinking. It's so annoying being so tired but being unable to sleep".

First Officer – low-cost carrier (turboprop) (C5)
Gradually, however, her health and sleep improved. By Day 8 her optimism and humour had returned: "I slept so much better last night and actually feel rested. I seem to have finally relaxed. I always find that when on holiday it takes me most of the holiday to relax and to be able to sleep, usually just in time to come home again!" As her return to work approached, however, the problem of broken sleep returned: "Up at about 05:30 (8hrs 30mins). Back to broken sleep. I think it's the thought of my fiancé going back to Bristol today and the thought that I'll be back at work soon". Her first duty, a standby, seemed to affect her sleep: "I felt absolutely knackered having been woken from deep sleep PLUS having woken several times during the night because I felt I was going to be called". Campbell and Bagshaw (1999: 130) say: "Stress is the response to unfavourable environmental conditions [like a highly demanding work or home life] referred to as stressors, and describes how a body reacts to demands placed upon it ... [C]ontinued stress can create physical symptoms such as insomnia, loss of appetite, headache, irritability, etc. ... Each individual has a personal stress limit, and if this is exceeded, stress overload occurs, which can result in an inability to handle even moderate workload". Glendon, Clarke and McKenna (2006: 235) say: "[Workplace sources of strain include] ... working under time pressure ... work hours – number of hours worked and work schedules, for example, as in shiftwork".
The diarist said she struggled to live on her First Officer's salary. She said her second job (ad-hoc flying instruction) supplemented her wages and lifestyle: "I barely break even each month. The thought of pensions and retirement scare the hell out of me: at this rate I'll have to work until I die. I so need my instructing job. Even though I'm not meant to get paid, I do. It means a tank of petrol each month – that's how tight cash is. Don't even talk about how we're going to afford to get married: it's one reason we've been engaged for 10 months and still have not set a date". At the time of her death in the Buffalo air crash, First Officer Rebecca Shaw was earning around $23,900. To save money she and her husband lived in Seattle with her parents. This necessitated a trans-continental commute to get to work. In its accident report the National Transportation Safety Board (2010: 108) concluded: "[T]he pilots' performance was likely impaired because of fatigue ... ". Shaw said she felt unwell prior to the fateful sector. She failed to intervene when the Captain reacted inappropriately to activations of the stick-shaker. Is there a link between safety and remuneration? Low wages encourage junior Flightcrew to take second jobs (while employed by Colgan Air, Shaw had on occasion worked as a waitress). Second jobs sap physical and, sometimes, mental energies.
The possibility of a link between safety and remuneration has been acknowledged by the Federal Aviation Administration (2010: 55874): "Commuting [a potential stressor] is common in the airline industry, in part because ... of

First Officer – low-cost carrier (turboprop) (C5)

economic reasons associated with low pay and regular furloughs by some carriers that may require a pilot to live someplace with a relatively low cost of living". Bennett (2013a: 77) says: "Is pilot debt a safety issue? To the extent that it forces pilots to commute long distances, yes, it is. Is pilot remuneration a safety issue? To the extent that low salaries oblige pilots to live as cheaply as possible, yes, it is. Impoverished pilots cannot afford to buy or rent in airport catchments. Poor remuneration reduces geographical mobility. Are micro-economics and safety linked? Yes, they are. Are politicians, regulators and airlines in denial? Yes, they are. This can only end badly".

On Day 14 the diarist flew SOU–GLA–SOU. She wrote: "I felt physically sick and dizzy the whole way to Glasgow. I didn't get to eat until I landed [on-blocks 09:30]". She had not eaten since 18:00 on Day 13. Bennett (2010a) notes how night-freight pilots sometimes went for long periods without a sustaining meal. By the time she landed in GLA the diarist had not eaten for 15.5 hours. At various points the diarist talked about losing weight/keeping her weight down. Also she criticised the quality of the on-board food provided by her employer. Rhodes and Gil (2002: 50) say: "It is difficult to stay alert on the job, and function well when you are hungry. If you do not keep your blood sugars up and do not have adequate nutritional resources in your body you will not perform well. This means eating well all of the time ... Eating well includes ... paying attention to the type of meal that is appropriate for your body at any given time".

The diarist's forebodings about calling in sick ("Dreading telling work I'll be off sick for another week. The reaction from crewing is always one of disbelief") and falling-out with Crewing over going into discretion suggests she had a problematic relationship with management. Poor worker-management relations are a source of stress: "[Sources of stress in the workplace include] job insecurity; long work hours; control at work; and managerial style" (Glendon, Clarke and McKenna, 2006: 50).

The disagreement with Crewing on Day 15 over discretion suggests that the airline's duty Crewing Officer(s) assumed the pilots would be willing to go into discretion in order to fly their aircraft back from AVN: "The moment they told us to go, we were always going to be out of hours. Plus discretion is exactly that, our decision not theirs". The episode suggests that Crewing's understanding of discretion differed from that of the AVN-bound pilots. The episode demonstrates the importance of establishing and maintaining common understandings. Poor employee-management relations can generate stress on both sides. While a moderate level of stress helps maintain arousal and performance, a high level of stress may cause such an elevated level of arousal that performance degrades (Swan, 1995; Campbell and Bagshaw, 1999).

On her first day back at work (Day 14) the diarist had a dizzy spell: "I felt physically sick and dizzy the whole way to Glasgow". On Day 17 the diarist wrote: "I'm feeling dizzy and sick for some reason when I lie down or get up. It's happened

First Officer – low-cost carrier (turboprop) (C5)
before and lasted for a few weeks. I'm wondering if it's to do with my low blood pressure or my diet, or maybe the oil fumes I've been inhaling for 3 days?" On Day 18 she wrote: "I woke at 07:00 and got out of bed only to fall into the wall with one of my dizzy spells – this is getting a bit strange. I feel very tired and also anxious". The following day she took her pre-command simulator check. The day after she flew four sectors. It is troubling that the diarist reported fit for work when, manifestly, she had an unresolved health issue (the dizziness). (The Federal Aviation Administration's (2009) *I'm Safe* checklist reminds pilots to assess whether they are fit to fly. The first checklist question is: "Do I have symptoms of an illness?"). Given her earlier comments about the airline's culture, could it be that she decided not to mention the health problem for fear of victimisation? Unjust cultures may cause important safety-related information to be suppressed. (The mere *perception* of a culture as unjust may cause safety-related information to be suppressed by front-line employees).

First Officer – low-cost carrier (turbofan) (C4)	
Day	Diary (All times Zulu)
1	Went to bed last night at 21:30 but didn't sleep until after 23:30. Had a very disturbed sleep, kept waking every 30–60 mins or so. Got up at 05:30 with alarm (6hrs), had breakfast (cereals) and left for work at 06:15. Drove to work (back route to avoid M25). It took 50 mins. Arrived car park at 06:55 for a 0745 report. No issues on the drive to work. Roads were generally clear. Check-in OK. Had ATC slot which is 20 mins after Stated Time of Departure. Lunch on the ground in SAW (Istanbul) during turnaround (sandwiches) at 12:30. Had delays departing SAW due to slow passengers boarding – fairly normal for SAW. Dinner was fish pie in cruise at 16:30. Arrived back 20 mins late. Drove home (back route to avoid M25) in 50 mins. Got home at 19:50. Got to sleep at around 22:30.
2	Woke up at 05:20 as my young son woke (7hrs). Stayed in bed until 06:30 then played with son for 20 mins while my partner got ready to take son to Nursery (then on to work). 07:10 had breakfast (cereals). 07:50 took dogs out for a 35 min walk. Left for work at 09:45 for an 11:00 report. There was an accident on the M1, junction 6–8 due to an overturned car, so I re-routed via the A41, then through Hemel Hempstead. I took 48 mins to get to work, arriving at the car park at 10:35. Got into the crew room at 10:45. Have been changed to a longer 4 sector day, because the original F/O for this duty would end up going into his day off (as the aircraft was delayed inbound). As I am working tomorrow that would not affect me. My new rostered duty

First Officer – low-cost carrier (turbofan) (C4)	
Day	Diary (All times Zulu)
	(LTN–NCE–LTN–MXP–LTN) (Luton–Nice–Luton–Milan Malpensa–Luton) is to within 5 mins of discretion (given my original report time for original rostered duty). When aircraft arrived in LTN it was tech (re-occurring brake issue when aircraft landed). Aircraft change. Departed 48 mins late. Made up some time to depart NCE 38 mins late. Had lunch (own salad and grapes) at 13:30. On the LTN–NCE sector we were informed of an aircraft swap for the LTN–MXP–LTN sectors. Had dinner at 18:30 (own fish pie) and a bag of chocolate on last sector back into LTN. Arrived LTN 3 mins short of discretion. Have been changed tomorrow to a LTN–BCN–LTN (Luton–Barcelona–Luton) (originally I had been rostered to be in the sim for 2 days). Left car park at 23:16 for the 39 min journey home (motorway). Long day and very tired. In bed at 01:30.
3	Woke up at 07:00 (5hrs 30mins) to see my son before he went to Nursery. Had breakfast (cereals) at 07:30 and went back to bed. Didn't sleep and got up at 10:00 and took the dogs out for a walk at 10:30 (25 mins). Then I went for a run (3km) at 11:10. Showered, changed and had lunch (jacket potato with tuna) at 12:30. Cleared up and prepared my dinner to take to work. Partner got home at 14:45. Said 'Hi', then I left for work at 15:00. Its Friday rush so routed via Wendover, Dunstable and M1. Journey took 1:10, so I arrived at 16:10 for a 16:35 report (LTN–BCN–LTN) (Luton–Barcelona–Luton). Flight delayed by 35 mins at check-in. Captain had to make a two-taxi journey (he positioned from LGW, getting caught up in the M1 northbound delays). Then further delayed by STD + 1 hr (not related to Captain). While waiting I had a coffee in the terminal. Finally departed at 18:48 (over two hours after report). Had supper at 19:30 in cruise (own salad). On return into LTN we had an electrical burning smell in the F/D (Flight Director) while passing FL190 (descending through 19,000 feet). Captain continued a high speed approach into LTN, then had a 'master caution' ECAM (advisory) stating that the blower was faulty (the high powered fan that sucks air into the avionics bay to cool the electronics). The advisory may have been related to the 'electrical' burning smell that dissipated on switching the blower off. No emergency declared, but consideration was given to using oxygen masks to prevent incapacitation. We arrived back Stated Time of Arrival + 45 mins, arriving at 23:23. There were no steps so we had another 10 min delay whilst they were found and passengers could disembark. We discussed the flight tech. problems with the engineers when they came on board to do the daily inspection. Captain is on leave tomorrow.

First Officer – low-cost carrier (turbofan) (C4)	
Day	Diary (All times Zulu)
	He has done 893 flying hours (U.K. max legal hours is 900) in the past 365 days. He was utterly knackered and I felt I needed to be above my game to compensate – which is tough when I have been awake since 07:00. On checkout I learned that my standby for tomorrow has been changed to take account of the 12 hour minimum rest requirement. Was in my car at 00:10 for the 40 min drive home (motorway). Usual night roadworks – motorway down to single lane. Arrived home at 00:50 and in bed at 01:15.
4	Got up at 08:30 (7hrs 15mins) and had breakfast (cereals). Looked after my son for the morning until 11:30. Had a shower in preparation for my standby starting at 12:15. I was not called out, so I spent the day at home doing household chores and looking after son. Had lunch (baguette) at 12:30, and dinner at 16:00 with Lewis. Had a couple of glasses of wine while watching TV before going to bed at 09:30.
5	Woke up at 07:20 (10hrs). Had breakfast (cereals), shower, changed and left for work at 08:20 (it's a Sunday, so I routed via the M40–M25 and M1). The journey took 40 mins and there were no issues. Arrived at 09:00 for a 09:40 report. Nothing unusual during the day (LTN–AMS–LTN–ZRH–LTN) (Luton–Amsterdam–Luton–Zurich–Luton). Usual delays waiting for ambi-lift for wheelchair passengers. Had a new F/O on the jumpseat (observing). Lunch at 14:30 (salad). At 18:00 had fish pie. Left at 18:52 and arrived home at 19:40 (48 mins journey time) via Hemel Hempstead and Chesham, as the motorway is busy on Sunday evenings. Went to bed at 22:30.
6	Got up at 09:00 (10hrs 30mins) and had breakfast (cereals). Had a light lunch (crisp bread and salami) at 11:30. Left for work at 12:00 for a 13:00 report. Arrived at 13:00 due to an incident in the roadworks on the motorway. Good day with all flights on-time (LTN–HAM–LTN–ABZ–LTN) (Luton–Hamburg–Luton–Aberdeen–Luton). Had same new F/O on jumpseat again today. Had dinner in flight at 18:30 (fish pie). Left work at 21:50 and took 40 mins to drive home. Fairly tired now, but took 30 mins to go to sleep once I got into bed at 23:00.
7	Woke up with son at 05:30 (6hrs), but I stayed in bed until 07:00 (partner got son up at 06:00 and took him to Nursery at 07:00). Had breakfast at 08:00 (cereals) then a shower. I'm really tired today, but aware that I have only 2 days off before I have to get up very early on Day 9, so I have to get up early today so that I am able to sleep early tonight and get my body clock ready to get up at 03:15 on Day 9. I tidied up the house before doing some

First Officer – low-cost carrier (turbofan) (C4)	
Day	Diary (All times Zulu)
	admin (banking, etc.). Went for a short trip on our day boat on the Thames before it rains this afternoon! Had lunch (sandwiches) on the boat at about 11:00. Collected son from Nursery at 16:00, prepared dinner then did son's bedtime (bottle and bath). Finished at 18:00. I have felt shattered all day, not been able to concentrate/function. I've been agitated and short fused. Had a glass of wine and watched TV, although they were all repeats so I went to bed at 23:00.
8	Slept surprisingly well without waking during the night. Woke up at 05:30 (6hrs 30mins) with son. Got up at 06:00 and had breakfast (cereals). Played with son until he had his morning nap. Went for a run at 08:10 (3km), approx. 25 mins. Showered and changed and prepared swimming kit. Our neighbour came over for 30mins and had coffee. We chatted about him getting chickens which he'd like me to look after when he goes on holiday. Made lunch (baguette) at 11:00. Played with Lewis and then went swimming at 13:30–15:00. At 15:30 my mum came over to visit us, staying until 19:30. We had dinner at 16:30 (Mexican). Had a phone call with cousin Melissa about our weekend activities. Went to bed at 20:30 and read book until 21:30 when I dropped off to sleep.
9	Partner didn't sleep well last night, which meant I woke several times. So I woke up tired at 03:15 (5hrs 45mins). Left for work at 03:55. The commute took 45 mins in heavy rain. Arrived at 04:40, for a 05:00 report. I always have to leave a little bit of extra time, as there is heavy congestion on the approaches to the airport (LTN) between 04:15 and 05:45 every morning. All sectors went well (LTN–BHD–LTN–BOD–LTN) (Luton–Belfast City–Luton–Bordeaux–Luton) and on time (had cereals for breakfast at 06:00, and sandwiches for lunch at 12:00). We had poor weather in LTN (heavy rain, low visibility). Left for home at 13:45. The commute took 55mins (Hemel Hempstead and Chesham). There were lots of signal-controlled minor road-works, so it took longer than I had hoped to get home. A bit frustrated and tired. Had some toast as a snack when I arrived home. Looked after son in the afternoon. Had dinner at 16:30 – chicken, vegetables and chips. Went to bed at 20:00 and read a book. Slept at 21:00.
10	Woke at 02:15 (5hrs 15mins), left for work at 02:50 (via motorway). Arrived at 03:40 (50 mins). Both sectors were on-time (LTN–CDG–LTN) (Luton–Charles de Gaulle–Luton). Drove home (through Hemel Hempstead and Chesham) getting fuel (10 mins) on the way home (took 53 mins – driving time). Back home at 09:30. Went for a run 10:00–10:30 (3.5km). Had

First Officer – low-cost carrier (turbofan) (C4)	
Day	Diary (All times Zulu)
	shower and lunch (baguette and yoghurt) at 11:30. Went to bed 12:30–13:30, but felt very tired on waking – I probably should have had a 20 min powernap instead. Went to son's Nursery sports day at 14:00–15:00, then home and cooked his tea for 16:30. Played with him until 17:30. Then tidied and hovered the house. Cousin and partner arrived at 18:00. We had pizza and wine and plenty of chat. Went to bed at 09:30. I didn't expect to sleep (general noise and banter with guests) but even without earplugs I slept soundly.
11	I woke briefly at 04:00, and then got up 06:00, feeling surprisingly well rested. I got up with my son and had breakfast at 06:00. Packed the car with the picnic and headed out to the Inland Waterways Festival in Pangbourne (near Reading). We spent the day browsing boats and the trade fair. We had our picnic lunch by the lake (cold meats, cheese, quiche, sausage rolls and pasties). We also stopped for a coffee during the afternoon. Arrived home at 16:30 and prepared son's dinner. We ate at 19:00 (leftovers from the picnic). Watched the Grand Prix qualifying on TV followed by X-factor and drank wine. Went to bed at 23:00.
12	Woke in the night at about 04:00 then woke at 05:45 with son. I was tired after a long but enjoyable day yesterday. I got up at 06:00 and made breakfast for son, then played until his nap time. Showered. Made bacon sandwiches at 08:00. Packed an overnight bag and we (including dogs) drove over to parents' house at 10:30 and went straight out to the pub for Sunday lunch (roast). Went back to my parents' house for the afternoon – chatted and watched TV, then took dogs out for a walk (45 mins) and played with son. We had sandwiches for dinner and a couple of glasses of wine. In bed at 21:30.
13	(Today is a required day off as the duty tomorrow is a Level-2 Variation, which enables a 2-crew flight deck to operate up to 14 hours and 15 mins over 2 sectors the following day (needed to operate the Sharm El Sheik return flight), although this day off counts towards the minimum number of days off per 28 days). Woke at 05:40 with son, got up and prepared his breakfast for 06:00. Then had own breakfast at 07:30 (bacon sandwich). Drove home at 11:00. At 14:30 went for a walk to our local pub (2km) which had a 'Families Day' (bank holiday Monday). Met up with friends and walked home (2km) at 16:30. Went to bed at 21:30.

First Officer – low-cost carrier (turbofan) (C4)	
Day	Diary (All times Zulu)
14	I woke briefly at 03:00 for about 45 mins, then woke again at 06:00 (7hrs 45mins). Left home at 07:30 for a 09:05 report. Arrived at 08:25 (55 mins) via Hemel Hempstead and Chesham. A long day but no issues (LTN–SSH–LTN) (Luton–Sharm El Sheik–Luton). The Captain was friendly (the previous flight with him had been less friendly, so I felt a bit apprehensive about operating such a long flight with him. Might this explain my waking in the night?). I managed to catch up with updating my logbook with the last 1.5 months entries, which saves me using valuable time at home to do it. Had a snack at 13:30 (chocolate bar, crisps and biscuit), salad at 13:30 and dinner (fish pie) at 18:30. Left work at 22:50. Drove home via the motorway in 38 mins. Had some good news from husband on email – our application to have solar panels fitted to our house has been approved after being rejected initially. In bed at 00:00.
15	(This is a required rest day as part of the Level-2 Variation: it is not counted as a day off). Woke briefly at 06:00, but slept again until 07:30 (7hrs) when I woke feeling very tired, but by 08:30 I was more awake and had breakfast (cereals). Took the dogs for a walk at 11:00 (35 mins). Had lunch (cheese on toast). At 12:30 went to the pet shop (food) and guitar shop (to have guitar restrung) then met friends at the sports centre to go swimming with son 13:30–14:15. Had coffee in the café at the sports centre afterwards. Had a long chat with friends (who have a baby daughter) and make plans to book Center Parcs for October (I have 3 days leave in October. With my standard 4 days that gives me 7 days, so we plan to do a 4 night break). Back home, prepared dinner (pork and noodles), then played with son until bedtime. Did son's bottle and bath, finishing at 18:00. Had a glass of wine at 18:15. Checked out available holidays at Center Parcs, but it's quite expensive even for just 5 days. But we all need a break (my last holiday was just 2 days in June. It is now September) so we spend some time looking at other options before giving up for the evening. I logged into work to check for changes. Had changes for Day 17 – my standby is now a 3 sector day. So just 1 day off before 3 early starts. Went to bed at around 20:45.
16	Woke during the night at 04:00 but slept until 06:15 (9hrs 30mins) when I got up with son. Had a cup of tea and a Barroca (vitamin drink). Went for a run at 07:45, 3.6kms took 25 mins. Popped out at 09:00 to get some groceries. Had breakfast at 09:30 (cereals) and went to visit a friend (with baby boy same age as my son) for lunch (homemade soup). I was yawning quite a bit today which was a bit embarrassing; I may be more tired than I

First Officer – low-cost carrier (turbofan) (C4)	
Day	Diary (All times Zulu)
	think. Made son tea when I got back and had pizza (quick and easy) at 16:30. Did son's bottle and bath, finishing at 18:00. Got into the spa (at home) at 19:00 but son woke at 19:20. Once we'd sorted him out I spent an hour in the spa then watched TV. In bed at 21:30.
17	Woke at 04:15 but felt OK (6hrs 45mins). Left at 04:50. Drove to work in 40 mins arriving at 05:30 for a 05:55 report (LTN–MPL–LTN) (Luton–Montpellier–Luton). I had problems with my password to login to get the paperwork printed. In the end the Captain printed it all off. After 10 mins I managed to get it reset by contacting IT – not a great start to the day. Flight to MPL was OK. I was Pilot Flying and did a visual approach which I thought was fairly poorly executed. It was safely within SOP's but I felt a bit 'sloppy'. Left work at 12:00 to drive home. Roads were very busy. Got home at 13:00 (1 hour). Did some DIY and house work, then I walked the dogs at 15:00. I'm really tired now! I collected my son from Nursery at 16:30 and did his snack. Then we played until bottle and bath, finishing at 18:00. Partner went out to babysit for a friend at 17:30. I did some admin. in the evening (including emailing about work uniform and some logbook updating). I went to bed at 20:00 but didn't sleep until 22:00. Partner got back in at 22:30.
18	Woke briefly at 01:15. Got up at 02:00 (4hrs). Left for work (motorway) at 03:05 arriving 03:45 (40 mins) for a 04:15 report (LTN–AMS–GVA–LTN) (Luton–Amsterdam–Geneva–Luton). We were delayed because the Captain had been called on standby, so we (me and cabin crew) went out to aircraft and I prepared everything for departure. Aircraft departed at 05:31 (only 15 mins late). I had a really 'slow' day, lots of insignificant errors (missed radio calls, etc). Drove home (55 mins) via Hemel Hempstead and Chesham arriving at 12:45. I was very tired all afternoon. Made dinner at 16:00, then watched TV. Went to bed at 20:00 and was asleep by 20:30.
19	Woke just before my alarm at 05:30 (9hrs). I had slept solidly all night and felt much better. Drove to work in 40 mins (via motorway). Arrived at 07:15. Had Lunch (salad) at 11:30 and a jacket potato at 14:30. We had a nice day out with no issues (LTN–SAW–LTN). Drove home in 45 mins, leaving at 17:45 and arriving at 18:30 with no problems. Had a glass of wine and fell asleep on the sofa. Went to bed at 20:30 – quite tired.

First Officer – low-cost carrier (turbofan) (C4)	
Day	Diary (All times Zulu)
20	Slept well until about 02:30 when an alarm kept going off keeping me wake for 2 hours. Woke at 05:30 with son. Got up and gave him his breakfast, then went for a run at 07:30 (3.6 km in 25 mins). Had my breakfast at 08:15 followed by shower. Did some admin (banking) at 09:00. At 10:30 went to a 'bumps and babes' group to meet friends (with son and partner). I was very tired and not particularly sociable. We got back at 14:45 and prepared son's dinner. I had dinner at 16:00 (Bacon sandwich). Fell asleep on the sofa watching TV. Went to bed at 09:00.
21	Didn't have a very good night's sleep. Woke up at 02:30 then got up at 05:45 with son. Made him breakfast and got ready for Nursery. Spent the day doing chores/housework and some general admin. Walked the dogs (35mins at 14:00). Had baguette for lunch at 11:30 and pizza for dinner with son at 16:30. In bed by 20:00. I have another 4 days of earlies.

Analysis

Based at Luton Airport in Bedfordshire, this First Officer flew Airbus
319s/320s/321s (twin-jet short/medium haul passenger aircraft). There is further
evidence here of the constraints inherent in family life. The diarist's young son, who
was attending Nursery School at the time, woke relatively early most mornings,
requiring the attention of either the diarist or her partner. He also had to be delivered
to, and collected from Nursery School. Young children structure home life.
    The diarist accumulated sleep debt at various points during the twenty-one
day observation period. On Day 1 she woke at 05:30 having got six hours sleep. This
would have generated 12 hours of productive wakefulness (6x2=12) (assuming she
had no sleep debt or credit prior). She then operated a two sector day (to Istanbul).
Her sleep credit would have expired by 17:30. By the time she got to sleep at 22:30
she would have been in sleep debt to the tune of 5 hours.
    Because of this sleep debt, her seven-hour sleep would have generated 9 hours
of sleep credit ((7x2)–5=9). Awake at 05:20, this credit would have been exhausted
by 14:20. At the time she was flying the approach into LTN that night at 22:20 (her
fourth sector of the day) she would have been in sleep debt to the tune of 8 hours.
By the time she got to bed at 01:30 she would have been in sleep debt to the tune of
11 hours (approximately). Before retiring she wrote in her diary: "Long day and very
tired". She would have driven home while carrying a significant amount of sleep debt.
Driving while fatigued is risky. Eurocontrol (2005: 40) says: "If you are sleepy when
your shift is complete, try taking a nap before driving home. Remember that sleep can
quickly overcome you when you least expect or desire it to". The Health and Safety
Executive (2006: 35) says: "Driving to and from work can be risky, particularly

First Officer – low-cost carrier (turbofan) (C4)

after a long shift, a night shift or before an early start. The following strategies may make driving safer – consider using public transport or taxis rather than driving ...".
At the time she left the LTN staff car park (23:16) she would have been awake for 18 hours (05:20–23:16). The Federal Aviation Administration (2010: 55855) says: "A person who has been continually awake more than 17 hours since his or her last major sleep period is more likely to be fatigued". Rhodes and Gil (2002: 15) say: "By the 18th hour [of wakefulness] the pilot will have great difficulty remembering things he has done or said a few moments ago (short-term memory) and his reaction time will have almost doubled in duration".
    On Day 3 the diarist woke at 07:00, having slept for 5hrs 30mins. This sleep would have left her with no sleep credit ((5.5x2)–11=0). She then launched herself into a busy schedule of household chores, physical exercise, commuting and flying (two sectors). Technical faults occurred during operations. At the time she was on the approach into LTN (at around 23:00) she would have been in sleep debt to the tune of 16 hours. Sleep debt has cognitive impacts: "Lack of sleep, sleeping at different times of the day, mental stress, or high mental workload will quickly result in mental fatigue. You become increasingly inattentive while trying to concentrate on your tasks. As fatigue increases, your short-term memory becomes less effective and you may forget vital information. Your creativity and decision-making abilities start to wane and you have more difficulty dealing with novel situations. This means you have to work harder to avoid error" (Rhodes and Gil, 2002: 20).
    By 23:00 she would have been awake for 16 hours. Hersman (2009: 39) says: "Aviation accident data show that ... accidents are substantially more likely to happen when pilots work long days, shifts at unusual hours, or trips with a large number of takeoffs and landings. The National Transportation Safety Board's 1994 study of flight crew-related major aviation accidents found that Captains who had been awake for more than about 12 hours made significantly more errors than those who had been awake fewer than 12 hours". When she arrived home she would have been awake for almost 18 hours. Driving while fatigued is risky.
    On Day 16 the diarist went to bed at 21:30 and woke at 04:15. Assuming she had no sleep debt or credit prior, this sleep would have generated 13.5 hours sleep credit (6.75x2=13.5). This credit would have been exhausted by 17:45. By the time the diarist got to sleep (at 22:00) she would have been in sleep debt to the tune of 4hrs 15mins. On waking she would have generated 3hrs 45mins of sleep credit ((4x2)–4.25=3.75). This credit would have been exhausted by 05:45 (just after her aircraft rotated for Amsterdam on the first leg). This means she operated the whole day in sleep debt. She writes: "I had a really 'slow' day, lots of insignificant errors (missed radio calls, etc)". Battelle Memorial Institute (1998: 2–3) says: "[S]ymptoms that indicate the presence of fatigue [include] ... decreased short-term memory, slowed reaction time, decreased work efficiency ... decreased vigilance, increased

First Officer – low-cost carrier (turbofan) (C4)

variability in work performance [and] increased errors of omission which increase to commission when time-pressure is added to the task". Hersman (2009: 39) says: "Multiple small errors over a short period of time often indicate fatigue". The Health and Safety Executive (2006: 18) says: "Permanent night workers and early morning workers [like the diarist] run the risk of chronic sleep debt, fatigue ...".

At the time she started her drive home (11:50) she would have been in sleep debt to the tune of 6hrs (approximately). By the time she got to sleep (20:30) she would have been in sleep debt to the tune of 14hrs (approximately). Her nine-hour sleep would have left her with just 4hrs of sleep credit for the day's flying ((9x2)–14=4). The flying went well, however: "We had a nice day out with no issues".

This diarist used a number of strategies to improve her resilience to what was a potentially taxing operational schedule. She ate healthily (cereals, salads, baked potatoes, etc.). She tried not to skip meals. She exercised (she swam, walked, ran and went boating) and she planned her sleep to accommodate early starts (as on Day 7). Eating regular, healthy meals boosts resilience to stressors (like fatigue): "It is difficult to stay alert on the job, and function well when you are hungry. If you do not keep your blood sugars up and do not have adequate nutritional resources in your body you will not perform well. This means eating well all of the time ..." (Rhodes and Gil, 2002: 50). Fitness also boosts resilience: "Physical fitness enables toleration of greater physical stress, and reduces the effects of fatigue" (BALPA, 1988: 12); "Regular exercise will ... increase your ability to tolerate stress" (Rhodes and Gil, 2002: 29); "Physical fitness training has been demonstrated in shift workers to reduce general fatigue and sleepiness at work, increase sleep duration somewhat and decrease musculoskeletal symptoms" (Eurocontrol, 2005). Had the diarist not been fit she may have found it more difficult to tolerate sleep debt and long periods of wakefulness (see above).

Prior to her Sharm El Sheik duty the diarist had a waking episode during the night. She wrote: "The [Sharm El Sheik] Captain was friendly (the previous flight with him had been less friendly, so I felt a bit apprehensive about operating such a long flight with him. Might this explain my waking in the night?)". Workplace stressors can affect home life (and vice-versa). Cooper, Dewe and O'Driscoll (2001: 42) observe: "[T]he abrasive personality who is a peer is both difficult and stressful to deal with; when the abrasive personality is a superior, the consequences are potentially very damaging to interpersonal relationships and highly stressful for subordinates in the organisation". They define 'abrasive personalities' as persons who are "... achievement-oriented, hard-driving and intelligent". Such persons "... function less well at an emotional level. The ... critical style of the abrasive personality induce[s] feelings of inadequacy among other workers" (Cooper, Dewe and O'Driscoll, 2001: 42).

First Officer – low-cost carrier (turbofan) (C4)
For those who commute a reasonable distance to work, congestion can prove stressful: "The volume of traffic on motorways, unpredictability of journey times and fear of accidents, all [contribute] to the emotional stress" (Green and Canny, 2003: 38). The diarist commented: "I always have to leave a little bit of extra time, as there is heavy congestion on the approaches to the airport (LTN) between 04:15 and 05:45 every morning". Of one commute she wrote: "There were lots of signal-controlled minor road-works, so it took longer than I had hoped to get home. A bit frustrated and tired". This diary was kept during the late summer of 2010. In November 2010 the diarist's employer announced record profits (up from £55million to £154million) despite issues with on-time performance (less than 50% of the airline's Gatwick flights departed on time).

First Officer – scheduled long-haul (C3)	
Day	Diary (All times Zulu)
1	Rest day. Woke and got up at 05:30 by the kids (1 and 3 years old). Felt rested, but still a little tired. Got kids ready and prepared breakfast with wife. Went to church at 08:00 with the family. Afterwards chatted with friends. Went home for lunch, which we had at around 10:00. Wife brought little child to bed at 11:00. I played cards with the big one. Went to see friends at 13:30 and stayed there for tea; went to the playground. Went home at 16:00, bathed the kids, made dinner and got the kids to sleep at 17:30. Spent time with my wife afterwards and had a bottle of beer. Went to bed at 20:30 and read a book until 21:15. Fell asleep around 21:30–21:45. I fought an allergy throughout the day (except for the time on the playground). I spent a lot of time thinking about my job – I am new to long-haul flying and new on the aircraft I shall be flying, the Airbus A340–600.
2	Rest day. Awake at 00:20 for just a short while. Got up at 05:30 (8hrs) with the kids – felt rested. Got them ready, prepared breakfast. Wife took eldest to nursery, and left for sports afterwards taking the youngest with her. I went to the grocery store to buy lunch. Came home and just hung around a little and started to read some things concerning the flight next Wednesday. Prepared lunch at 09:30. Wife came home at around 09:45 and picked up daughter from day care. Had lunch together. I put youngest to sleep at around 11:30. Had a coffee and a cigarillo. Then did some gardening for about 30min. Woke the youngest from her nap at 13:30 then did some administration. Did some work around the house until about 16:00. Had dinner together. Put the kids to bed. Played an online computer game until 21:00 and went to bed. Allergy was better.

First Officer – scheduled long-haul (C3)	
Day	Diary (All times Zulu)
3	Leave day. Kids woke me up at 04:45. (7hrs 45mins) Felt alright. Usual morning tasks. Get kids ready, breakfast. Went to town. Packed suitcase and prepared for the trip until lunch-time. The wife was angry at me leaving – had a little fight about that. Family took me to the airport at 14:00. Flight from Dusseldorf (DUS) to Munich (MUC). Arrived 17:00. Rented a car and drove to the hotel. Arrived 18:15. Had dinner at 19:00. Did some preparation/reading for the trip (MUC–LAX–MUC) (Munich–Los Angeles–Munich). Went to bed at 20:45 and fell asleep at around 21:00.
4	Duty day. The hotel room was too hot. Air conditioning did not work properly. I woke up several times during the night. I wanted to sleep longer to make it through the flight. However I got up at 06:00 (9hrs). Got ready for work. I did not feel rested. Left at 08:00 and arrived at the airport at 08:30. I had breakfast and did some studying. Had lunch. Reported at 12:05 and met my colleagues. I had not worked with them before. Departed at 14:00 on my first A340 long-haul duty. Had dinner on the plane. The flight was uneventful – except that it was a training flight which is always a bit more challenging than a routine flight. Got some sleep at 22:00. I slept for around 2 hours.
5	I felt OK, but tired afterwards. We landed at 02:20. Went to bed in the hotel at 04:00. Got up at 09:30 (5hrs 30mins), again with a slight headache. Had a shower and sent some emails. Was a little disoriented until after breakfast. Went for 'breakfast' at around 14:00. Afterwards took a walk around town. Went to the beach and enjoyed the sun. Wanted to return to the hotel early to go to bed. Came back at about 19:00, drank a beer and read a book in the sun until 20:00. Went to bed at around 21:30 and fell asleep quickly.
6	Layover LAX. Woke up a couple of times at night, but fell asleep again. Woke and got up at 05:30 (8hrs). Got something to eat at the hotel bar. Had a coffee afterwards in the hotel room. Felt much better than the day before, even though it is night time in Los Angeles. Spent the local night surfing the Internet, watching TV and playing an online computer game. During the day I went shopping, packed my suitcase and had breakfast in the hotel. Because of the upcoming pickup I went to bed at 18:00 and fell asleep at 18:30.
7	Duty day LAX–MUC. Woke at 01:00 (6hrs 30mins). I got up and felt OK. Not a good night's rest, but better than nothing. Left the hotel and reported for the flight to MUC. It was scheduled to leave at 04:05, but actually left at 03:55. Took my in-flight rest between 11:00–14:00. I couldn't really sleep, because I was so excited about my first landing on the A340–600. I dozed a

First Officer – scheduled long-haul (C3)	
Day	Diary (All times Zulu)
	little. I made a good landing. Arrived MUC at 15:05 (30min early), but I still had to make my way home. My flight to DUS left at 17:30 (planned arrival 18:40 – actual arrival was 18:35). Fortunately I was upgraded to business class and could close my eyes for a while. I did not sleep, however. After arriving at DUS I still needed to take a train home. I was in bed at 21:00 and pretty much fell asleep instantly.
8	Rest day. Woke up at around 06:30 and got up (9hrs 30mins). I felt rested. We made it to church for 08:00. I still felt good. No jetlag. Had lunch together at 10:30. In the afternoon we went to my mother in law's house for her birthday. Stayed until 16:00. After putting the kids to bed I spent the evening with my wife. Went to bed at 21:00 and fell asleep shortly after that.
9	Woke at 05:30 (8hrs 30mins) Rest day. Had breakfast together. Then I did some house cleaning. We all had lunch at about 10:15. The food we were given by my mother-in-law tasted OK, but had some spices in it that we didn't really digest. We had digestive problems into the next day. Went to bed at 21:00.
10	Rest day. Woke and got up at 05:45 (8hrs 45mins). Felt OK. Had breakfast. Then took eldest to daycare. Spent the morning reading the newspaper. Did some studying for the next trip. After picking up daughter from daycare we had lunch. Went to bed at 21:00.
11	Rest day. Eldest daughter woke me up at 05:00 (8hrs). I have a headache and don't feel rested. Daughters need help getting dressed. My wife is feeling a little sick, so she wanted to stay in bed a little longer. I got the kids ready. Had breakfast together and then took the eldest to day care. Spent the morning shopping, getting clothes ready for work and doing minor repairs in the house. Had lunch at 10:30. Still have a headache. Wife got to sleep with the younger daughter. I enjoyed some silence. In the afternoon I did some gardening in the sun and went for a short run afterwards (just 20 minutes). I started to pack my suitcase for tomorrow's trip. At 16:00 we had dinner together. I spent the evening with my wife and went to bed at around 21:30 and fell asleep right away.
12	Leave day. Woke and got up at 06:00 (8hrs 30mins). I felt rested. Had breakfast with the family. Got my suitcase ready. Wife took me to DUS at 09:00 for a 10:30 flight to MUC. I had lunch at the airport. The flight left 30 minutes late, but I had plenty of time. Unfortunately I only got a

First Officer – scheduled long-haul (C3)	
Day	Diary (All times Zulu)
	jump-seat (which was very uncomfortable). We arrived at 12:00. As my report was not until 17:55, I tried to get a key for one of the three crew rest rooms. Fortunately a room was available. I slept from 13:30 to 14:30 (1hr), and stayed 'in bed' until 15:15 in preparation for my night-flight to GRU (Sao Paulo). Had dinner at 16:00, nothing much though. The flight left on time at 19:35. I flew the first 4 hours of the flight. I took my rest between 23:45–03:30.
13	I slept from 24:00 to 03:00 (3hrs). I felt tired afterwards – but well enough to fly the last 4 hours of the flight. I landed the aircraft. We landed well ahead of schedule and were on-blocks at 07:50. We drove to the hotel and I finally got to bed at 10:00. I slept until 12:00 (2hrs). I did not feel rested afterwards. However I walked to a nearby mall and had some 'breakfast' (bread, eggs and bacon) and a cup of coffee. Since we wanted to meet for dinner, I decided to take a nap from 18:00 to 20:00, and slept from 18:30 to 20:00 (1hr 30mins). I did not feel well afterwards. I went to the bar where we had arranged to meet and had my first drink of the evening, bought by my Captain – so I couldn't say no. I didn't really want to drink alcohol, though. We spent the rest of the evening (22:00–00:30) in a steak restaurant. I couldn't eat much because of the time of day (it was too late for me). Lots of excitement always affects my appetite.
14	I went to bed at 01:00. This was much too late for me. But I fell asleep quickly and slept until 08:30 (7hrs 30mins). I had a headache after getting up, but felt better after the first coffee. I met colleagues for breakfast at 12:30. I had some muesli and bread and lots of fruit. After I got back to my room, the headache returned. I also had some pain in my limbs that got worse throughout the day. In the evening I had intestinal cramps. I figured I must have been infected by a virus. I called my Captain to tell him about the situation. After having a club sandwich from room service at 19:00 I felt a little better, but still decided to go to sleep early. I had a bath and retired at 21:00. I fell asleep 30–45 min. later.
15	I woke up at 01:00 and was awake for 30–45 min. I finally slept until 08:30 and got up (10hrs). I felt a little better, but still believed that I had caught a virus. I called the Captain who expected me to be sick (and had planned accordingly). A First Officer staying at the hotel on a layover had been designated to take my place. I was to return home on the flight as a passenger. Had dinner on board the aircraft at around 21:00. I fell asleep at around 22:00.

First Officer – scheduled long-haul (C3)	
Day	Diary (All times Zulu)
16	Sick day. Woke up several times during the night but fell asleep again right away. Finally woke and got up at 05:00 (7hrs) feeling a little tired, but better. Had breakfast on the aircraft. We landed on time at 07:35. My flight home was scheduled for 08:30. It actually left at 09:20 and landed in DUS at 10:35. On the way home I had lunch (a burger). I got home at 13:00 after journeying by train and bus. I showered then went to the doctors. I was diagnosed with a virus – not serious. I spent the rest of the day with my family and went to bed at 21:00, falling asleep quickly.
17	Sick day. Woke and got up at around 05:15 (8hrs 15mins), feeling a little better than the day before. Had breakfast at 06:00. Spent the morning reading newspapers and unpacking my suitcase. Did some washing. Had lunch at 10:00. At 13:30 we went to a children's service in church. After that we had a meeting with parents and children until around 15:30. Had dinner at 16:00 at home. Put the kids to bed and spent the evening watching TV. Went to bed at 21:00 and fell asleep quickly. My infection has begun to go. I think there could have been a psychological aspect to my sickness: strange that it suddenly got better once I arrived home.
18	off-day. Woke and got up at the usual 05:00 (8hrs). Felt good. Had breakfast at 05:30 with the family. After that I did some cleaning. Had lunch at 10:30. I did some gardening. Had dinner together and spent the evening playing on the computer until 20:30. Read a book until 21:00 and went to bed – fell asleep a little later.
19	off-day. Pretty much like the previous day. Woke and got up at 05:30 (8hrs 30mins) and had breakfast together. Spent the day doing some work around the house and relaxing a little. In the evening I had a choir rehearsal. Came home and spent the evening from 18:00 till bedtime with my wife. Went to bed at 21:00 and fell asleep shortly after.
20	off-day. Woke and got up at 05:15 (8hrs 15mins). Felt OK. Had breakfast together and took the eldest to day care. I spent the morning preparing for my next flight. I did some revision, and other preparations like printing the chart, etc. Hopefully it will all become routine in a couple of months ... so the intensive preparation for each trip will reduce. We had lunch at 10:30. I went to bed at the usual 21:00 and fell asleep a little later.
21	off-day. Got up at 05:15 (8hrs 15mins) and had breakfast. Felt good. The youngest slept till 08:00, so we decided to skip the afternoon nap for her and go visit a children's fair in town. We had lunch there and stayed until 14:00. Came back at 14:30. After dinner at 16:00 we put the kids to bed and spent the evening together. I went to bed at 21:00 and fell asleep quickly.

First Officer – scheduled long-haul (C3)

Analysis

There is strong evidence here of how offspring impose routine on parents. The diarist (and his partner) were locked into a routine of going to bed at around 21:00 and getting up (or, more accurately, being got up) at between 05:00 and 06:00. There is also strong evidence of this being a tight-knit family unit with lots of time spent together (when the diarist was at home). Young families are demanding. Perhaps it was the prospect of having to cope alone that caused the minor spat prior to the MUC–LAX–MUC trip: "The wife was angry at me leaving – had a little fight about that". Absences can affect relationships (Beaty, 1969; Bor and Hubbard, 2006; Partridge and Goodman, 2007). Partridge and Goodman's (2007: 7) analysis of the cabin crew lifestyle is applicable to flight crew: "Realities such as a lack of control of lifestyle, being away from family and friends and the difficulties in planning ahead, could begin to deflate the glamour 'bubble'". Bor, Field and Scragg (2002: 244) observe: "[N]ot only do pilots have to deal with the unique pressures of flying aircraft, but also the daily, normal pressures of life". They also comment: "It has long been recognized that stable spouse and family relationships can act as a buffer against stress in the workplace; conversely, discord in close relationships may intensify stress, leading to impaired work performance" (Bor, Field and Scragg, 2002: 247). While flying long-haul exerted a centrifugal force on the relationship, the family's interactions when together exerted a (countervailing) centripetal force. This was a close-knit nuclear family.

The diarist had a time-consuming and potentially arduous commute to work. For example, his Day 3 commute to the pre-LAX HOTAC (by family car, aircraft and rented car) took over four hours (14:00–18:15). After returning from Sao Paulo (with a viral infection) the diarist spent five and a half hours commuting (by aircraft, train and bus) to his home (07:35–13:00). There are a number of issues with long-distance commutes that involve several transport modes. First, they are potentially fatiguing: "The impact of commuting to a duty station has been linked to increased fatigue, most recently in the crash in Buffalo, New York" (Federal Aviation Administration, 2010: 55874). The National Transportation Safety Board's (NTSB's) investigation into the February, 2009, fatal accident at Buffalo, New York State, revealed that both pilots commuted long distances to work: "The NTSB concludes that the pilots' performance was likely impaired because of fatigue, but the extent of their impairment and the degree to which it contributed to the performance deficiencies that occurred during the flight cannot be conclusively determined" (National Transportation Safety Board, 2010: 108). Secondly, the greater the number of transport interfaces (for example, as between an air service and a train or bus service) the greater the chance of missing a connection (and of being late for report). Short, single-mode commutes enhance operational resilience.

First Officer – scheduled long-haul (C3)

The diarist's viral infection (that prevented him operating the return flight from GRU to MUC) was relatively short-lived. The diarist writes: "I think there could have been a psychological aspect to my sickness: strange that it suddenly got better once I arrived home". Could it be that the home environment is more conducive to wellbeing than the work environment (with its associated stressors)? Could it be that a work regime that involves intercontinental travel and an itinerant lifestyle (regular hotel stays) is more physiologically and psychologically stressful than one that does not? Bennett (2010a: 12) observes: "Hotel life can be a lonely and isolating experience".

Taking regular exercise can help pilots cope with the stresses of commercial flying. Eurocontrol (2005: 28) says: "Exercise can be beneficial for good sleep ... If you don't exercise regularly, add good sleep to a long list of reasons why you should take up the practice". BALPA (1988: 12) says: "Physical fitness enables toleration of greater physical stress, and reduces the effects of fatigue". Swan (1995: 21) says: "A physically fit body ... reduces one's susceptibility to fatigue". Bor, Field and Scragg (2002: 244) say: "Pilots are required to maintain optimum physical and psychological fitness. High levels of responsibility for manoeuvring aircraft, transporting other crew and passengers, coping with demands and decisions, all require mental capability, excellent health, and emotional stability". This diarist gardened and took the occasional short run (twenty-minutes duration). He also went for walks when down-route. He did not, however, avail himself of hotel gymnasia. Physical fitness is best assured through regular bouts of vigorous exercise. In a survey of BALPA members working for a single airline, Steptoe and Bostock (2011: 35) noted: "Overall levels of physical activity ... were significantly below government guidelines for a healthy lifestyle. Occupational health could work with pilots to address workplace barriers to exercise and healthy work-day diets". Steptoe and Bostock (2011: 3) commented: "The survey generated 492 responses across four countries, an overall response rate of 47.1%. Response rates were highest in Germany, where 85% of BALPA members returned a questionnaire. Overall 70.8% of the sample was based in the UK. Almost two thirds of respondents were Captains. The mean age of respondents was 40.8 [years]".

When on stop-over in Sao Paulo the diarist wrote: "I went to the bar where we had arranged to meet and had my first drink for the evening, bought by my Captain – so I couldn't say no. I didn't really want to drink alcohol, though". In their paper *The mental health of pilots: an overview*, Bor, Field and Scragg (2002: 249–250) investigate the link between social or peer pressure and alcohol consumption amongst commercial pilots: "[P]ilots experience high levels of stress in their jobs, and have to endure considerable disruption to their personal lives. Intermittent absences from family and social support, periods of time relaxing and recuperating, sometimes accompanied by boredom and social pressure to consume alcohol with fellow crew members, may be the root cause of alcohol misuse and dependency".

First Officer – scheduled long-haul (C3)
Additional information
At the time he kept the SLOG the First Officer was undergoing training on the Airbus A340–600, a long-range, large capacity airliner. He wrote in a letter: "Please keep in mind that these [twenty-one days] were pilot training for me, so they do not fully represent a typical long-haul schedule. Usually I would have had more duties planned (about 5–6 rotations per month), so the rest times of about a week in-between are relatively long".

Senior First Officer – scheduled long-haul (C6)	
Day	Diary (All times Zulu)
1	Was woken up by the kids at 08:00. Husband had to go out so was fairly busy in the morning getting ready for work then dropping kids off with our neighbour as he wasn't going to be back until after I needed to leave. Traffic was very bad on the way to work – my journey is normally 1hr 45mins but today it took 3 hours. Had left extra time, so arrived just in time for report (LHR–LAS–LHR) (Heathrow–Las Vegas–Heathrow). I was the heavy pilot [augmented crew] for this sector (for flights long enough to require a third crew member (the 'heavy' pilot) normal operating practice is for the heavy to take the first break so most people try to report for work tired enough that they will sleep during this period) so had first break but was wide awake so didn't sleep. Feeling tired by the time we got to Las Vegas but went out for a drink as it was the Captain's birthday.
2	Very tired by the time I got to bed (06:30) so slept deeply, didn't wake up till 7am local (7 hours behind UK) (14:30) (8hrs). Spent the day hiking in the desert near the city, then met up with the other pilots for dinner and a show in the evening. Very tired during show, kept nodding off despite best efforts to stay awake.
3	Woke hungry after good sleep (07:30–17:30) (10hrs). Went for sightseeing flight over the Grand Canyon, back to hotel in the afternoon, tried to sleep before report but couldn't, so went to the gym instead.
4	Flight home. Busy for several hours avoiding storms over the USA so no chance for any controlled rest on the flight deck. P1 for the way home so was on last rest – very tired by the time it came round. Slept a bit in the bunk but still feeling jaded for landing and drive home (on-blocks 13:30). No chance to sleep once I got home as kids and husband wanted attention after I hadn't seen them for a few days. Felt like I always feel after night

Senior First Officer – scheduled long-haul (C6)	
Day	Diary (All times Zulu)
	flights – head heavy, feel distanced from everything going on around me, have to make an effort to keep listening to people, don't feel like I have energy for doing anything, hungry but usually can't think of anything I actually want to eat. In bed by 21:30.
5	Up at 07:30 (10hrs). Day at home. Woken up by kids as husband had left early for work. Busy for most of the day just doing washing/unpacking from trip, housework that had built up while I was away. Went to bed early (21:30) as still tired from trip.
6	Up at 08:00 (10hrs 30mins). Busy day getting ready for next trip. Husband away till Saturday night so have arranged for sister-in-law and family to come down and look after kids while we're both away. Made up beds, went shopping so there was plenty of food in the house for them, made time to take kids for a walk in the afternoon. In-laws arrived at 21:00, so spend some time catching up and getting them all settled in before bed. In bed by 23:30.
7	Up at 06:30. Didn't sleep well as was quite worried about leaving kids with the in-laws. Woke early so I could make breakfast for everybody before going to work (LHR–BLR–LHR) (Heathrow–Bangalore–Heathrow). Traffic awful on way in so only just made it in time for report (11:40) [report is 90mins prior stated time of departure]. P1 for the sector so on last rest – slept fitfully for 2 hours. New style bunks (777 Overhead Flight Crew Rest) which are bigger and more private than old style ones – much better and make it much easier to get some rest.
8	Long drive from the airport to the hotel in BLR – saw the sun coming up just as we got to our rooms to go to sleep. Slept deeply as was very tired by this time (01:00–09:00) (8hrs). Didn't set an alarm as felt that I needed to catch up on rest. Spent the day doing some admin on my laptop and went to the gym for 2 hours. Went to bed 4 hours before report to try to sleep but couldn't – dozed for about 40 mins at most. Ended up just reading my book as it was the middle of the night, everything closed.
9	Was the heavy pilot for the sector home – slept OK for 2 hours in the bunk. On-blocks 11:40. Got home feeling not too bad so stayed up to spend time with family as my husband was due to go back to work early the next day. Fell asleep on the sofa at 21:30.

Senior First Officer – scheduled long-haul (C6)	
Day	Diary (All times Zulu)
10	Woken up during the night by my eldest being sick – had to strip bed, give her a bath, put sheets in wash before getting back to bed. After that slept till nearly 10:00, which I needed. Kids were up and playing by the time I made it out of bed.
11	In bed by 01:00. Day spent with kids, playing at home, trip out to Swanage – town 5 miles away on the coast. Couldn't get to sleep till past midnight, but slept-in the next day (again). Up at 10:00.
12	Asleep by about 02:00. Up at about 05:30. (3hrs 30mins). I had a really bad night's sleep – husband is starting to get a cold so was snuffling and turning over a lot in bed. It kept me awake. About 3 hours before alarm went off, moved to bed in spare room desperate to get some sleep. Report time right at the end of rush hour – slow and frustrating drive in (LHR–BOM–LHR) (Heathrow–Mumbai–Heathrow). Luckily was heavy on the first sector so on first rest – slept in a Club seat from about 14:00 to about 17:00 (3hrs). Got to Mumbai feeling not too bad. Other pilots were nice, so went out for a drink on arrival.
13	Set alarm and got up so as not to miss breakfast (India is 5.5 hours ahead of UK), but still very tired. Slept from about 01:00 to 03:00 (2hrs). Feeling really bad by the time I got back to my room after breakfast – sick and exhausted. Had wanted to go out but just didn't feel up to it. I went back to bed instead, slept deeply and woke feeling much better (04:30–08:00) (3hrs 30mins). Went to gym/pool for 3.5 hours – first proper workout in ages: felt good afterwards. Had dinner in hotel then went to bed to try to sleep before pickup but it wasn't the right body clock time for sleep – dozed fitfully.
14	Uneventful flight – slept for about an hour in the bunk during my break. On-blocks 06:30. Drove home feeling weary but not too bad – once home got caught up as usual in catching up with kids and husband, doing washing, housework, etc. Had been invited round to friends' for dinner – enjoyed the evening but feeling a little dazed and heavy. Didn't get home until past midnight by which time I was exhausted.
15	In bed by 00:30. Up at 05:30 (5hrs). Set alarm to get up in time to go sailing in race at our local club – enjoyed the fresh air, exercise, being out on the water. I spent the rest of the day playing with the kids out round our local town on coast – by evening feeling tired so was nice to have a plain dinner at home and get an early night (21:30).

Senior First Officer – scheduled long-haul (C6)	
Day	Diary (All times Zulu)
16	Up at 08:00 with kids (10hrs 30mins) – husband having a diving lesson with a friend so had volunteered to look after friend's child as well. Took all the kids sailing – hard work with three in the boat but we all had fun. Dinner at home with family; once kids were in bed packed to take my girls away the next day. In bed 22:30.
17	Up early (05:30) (7hrs) to take girls to Exmoor for a short break – was feeling guilty that they hadn't been away anywhere all summer and I'd been working lots. Husband couldn't come as he was working – no time when we were both at home to all go away together. Had a good day – had a couple of good walks, dinner at our hotel – happy that girls were excited about being away and enjoying themselves. In bed 21:30.
18	Up 05:30 (8hrs). Good day out with kids – took them for a 10-mile walk, bribing with sweets and ice creams along the way. They both slept in the car as I drove home for them to start back at school the next morning (eldest into year 2, youngest starting in reception class). In bed 22:30.
19	Up at 04:30 (6hrs). First day at school went well – went for a 10 mile run then picked youngest up at lunchtime and was pleased that she had enjoyed it. Took her and her best friend out to lunch to celebrate the occasion. Feeling good after a few days off work – sleep patterns settling down, appetite better and no nausea, feeling more energetic. Starting a week's leave now which I feel like I need – kids have been complaining I'm away too much, several friends I've been meaning to catch up with for ages and haven't, several jobs around the house need doing. In bed by 22:00.
20	Up at 04:30 (6hrs 30mins). Settling back into the school routine. Went for a 2 hour bike while youngest was there in the morning, then ran with her while she biked in the afternoon. Last few days have been eating salads for both lunch and dinner as have been craving vegetables – difficult to eat healthily while away, and when I'm tired (especially on night flights) all I want to eat is carbohydrates and chocolate. Now I'm at home for a while I want to get back into a healthier routine. After school, pack up and take kids down to a local campsite where friends are holding their wedding over the weekend.
21	Didn't sleep that well in the tent, but have a good day at the wedding – watching what I eat and drink as am racing in a half marathon the next morning. Have fun anyway – wedding v relaxed and informal. Not too late getting to bed.

Senior First Officer – scheduled long-haul (C6)

Analysis

The diarist, a Boeing 777 (long-range widebody airliner) Senior First Officer e-mailed the following background information: "I have two children aged 4 and 6, on their summer holidays during the period of this diary, with the youngest starting school this September (2010). My husband also flies for British Airways; we are normally both part-time and manage our rosters so that there is always one of us at home, but during my conversion onto the 777 (which I started in April and will complete at the end of September) I have been full-time which has made organising childcare quite challenging. I exercise a lot (I have run 3 ultramarathons this year) which I find helps to regulate my sleep – if I exercise during the day I'm nearly always tired enough to sleep well. I can generally sleep anywhere, anytime as I never get enough sleep, but have found the change to longhaul has messed up my body's routine quite a lot, so now I sometimes struggle to get to sleep, and experience nausea/lack of appetite".

Regarding the diarist's point about exercise and the regulation of sleep, Caldwell and Caldwell (2003: 78) comment: "[A]erobic exercise 3–4 hours before bed-time ... has been shown to improve the onset and quality of sleep ... So, if psychological stress is producing transient sleeping problems ... aerobic exercise ... may offer a solution".

From getting up at home on Day 1 to getting to sleep in Las Vegas the diarist was awake for around 22 hours. She tried to sleep on the aircraft, but was unable to do so. Hence the long period of wakefulness. (Her in-flight bunk sleep on Days 4 and 7 was of a poor quality). On Day 3 the diarist wrote: "Tried to sleep before report but couldn't". On Day 8 (while on stop-over in BLR) the diarist wrote: "Went to bed 4 hours before report to try to sleep but couldn't – dozed about 40 mins at most. Ended up just reading my book as it was the middle of the night". On Day 13 (while on stop-over in BOM) the diarist wrote: "Had dinner in hotel then went to bed to try to sleep before pickup, but it wasn't the right body-clock time for sleep – dozed fitfully". Bennett (2010a) notes how flight crew can find it difficult to 'sleep to order'. They understand the need for pre-report or in-flight sleep. They go to bed with the intention of sleeping. But fail to sleep (or sleep fitfully). This is a 'lived reality' for pilots.

The diarist flew her last sector on Day 14. On Day 19 she wrote: "Feeling good after a few days off work – sleep patterns settling down, appetite better and no nausea, feeling more energetic". Inevitably, perhaps, the diarist's sleeping patterns while at work, or during the short periods between trips, were somewhat erratic (see above). After a few days at home, however, a more settled sleep/wake pattern was evident. Bennett (2010a: 12) observes of night-freight pilots: "If a pilot got to bed at, say, 08:00, s/he might sleep for five or six hours (few pilots managed seven or eight hours continuous sleep)".

Senior First Officer – scheduled long-haul (C6)
Reflecting on her eating habits she wrote (on Day 20): "Last few days have been eating salads for both lunch and dinner as have been craving vegetables – difficult to eat healthily while away, and when I'm tired (especially on night flights) all I want to eat is carbohydrates and chocolate. Now I'm at home for a while I want to get back into a healthier routine". Bennett (2010a: 10) notes night-freight pilots' unease at the non-availability of quality food. One pilot said: "Not having good, healthy food available makes a big difference to how I feel. If I eat the rubbish in the [food] box I feel worse". The food box usually contained a mix of salty snacks, chocolate and energy bars. On Day 4 the diarist wrote: "No chance to sleep once I got home as kids and husband wanted attention after I hadn't seen them for a few days. Felt like I always feel after night flights – head heavy, feel distanced from everything going on around me, have to make an effort to keep listening to people, don't feel like I have energy for doing anything". On Day 7 the diarist wrote: "Didn't sleep well, as was quite worried about leaving kids with the in-laws". On Day 19 the diarist wrote: "Starting a week's leave now which I feel like I need – kids have been complaining I'm away too much". Getting the work-life balance right is difficult. Strained relationships with family members and friends (psychosocial stressors) and/or feelings of guilt (however unjustified) may impact physical and mental health: "Stress, jet lag, fatigue, disrupted personal relationships, unusual routines ... may all take their toll on even the most resilient crew members" (Bor, Field and Scragg, 2002: 244). Partridge and Goodman (2007: 7) say of the cabin crew lifestyle: "Realities such as a lack of control of lifestyle, being away from family and friends and the difficulties in planning ahead, could begin to deflate the glamour 'bubble'". This diarist made a determined effort to bond with family members during her time at home (as evidenced by the walks, bike rides, days out, short-breaks, etc.).

Captain – scheduled long-haul (C2)	
Day	Diary (All times Zulu)
1	Woke at 06:10. Pre-flight sleep 11:30–12:45 (1hr 15mins). Felt well-rested. Departed by car for base at 14:00. Arrived 16:30. (Drive-to-work took 2.5 hours). Pushed 19:30 for LHR–EWR (Heathrow–Newark). In-seat sleep for 45mins.
2	Pilot Flying (PF) for arrival. On-blocks 03:30. Felt absolutely whacked by the time I boarded the crew bus. Crew bus to Manhattan hotel accommodation (HOTAC). Checked-in by 05:30. Asleep by 06:30. Slept until 10:25, then restless sleep until 13:30 (7hrs). Ate breakfast. Took a walk around Manhattan. Pre-flight sleep 19:30–23:00 (3hrs 30mins). I slept pretty well for the last hour.

Captain – scheduled long-haul (C2)	
Day	Diary (All times Zulu)
3	Crew bus to JFK 00:20. Rotate 02:45 for LHR. In-seat sleep 05:45–06:30 (45 mins). On-blocks 09:15. Drove home, arriving 12:15. Slept in bed 12:30–14:30 (2 hrs). On waking I felt, as usual, like death warmed up. I came around gradually. Was in bed by 21:45.
4	Woke at 07:30 after a good night's sleep (9 hrs 45 mins). Did some odd jobs then played squash. After attending a committee meeting returned home to take partner out for dinner. Night caps. In bed by 22:00.
5	I slept well until 02:30, then got up for a drink of water. Although I felt quite tired my sleep was rather restless after that. I could not get the desired deep sleep. I rose at 06:30 (8 hrs 30 mins). Went to Flying Club, arriving home at 16:00. In bed by 22:00.
6	Slept until 07:30 (9 hrs 30 mins). Pre-flight sleep 12:30–13:30 (1 hr). Departed by car for base at 16:00. Arrived 18:30. Pushed 21:30 for LHR–HKG (Heathrow–Hong Kong).
7	No Upper Class seat available for in-flight sleep, so resorted to bunk. Three and a half hour rest break. There was an extra duvet available, so I slept unusually well. On-blocks 09:45. Checked-in by 11:00. Retired at 20:00 after going out with crew.
8	Slept until 07:00 (11 hrs). Went out with crew. Retired at 17:00.
9	Woke at 03:30 (10 hrs 30 mins). Breakfast and sauna in an effort to relax into a pre-flight sleep. Pre-flight sleep 06:00–07:30 (90 mins). Pushed 11:30 for HGK–SYD (Hong Kong–Sydney). Two and a half hour rest break taken in Upper Class seat. The Flight Service Manager warned me she would need the seat if we hit turbulence as one of the passenger seat belts was defective. Aware of this prospect I never slept at all really. I kept waking when we hit turbulence anticipating a seat-swap. My eyes were stinging as the sun started to come up during our approach into Sydney. On-blocks 20:15. In bed by 22:30.
10	Intermittent sleep until 03:00 (4 hrs 30 mins). Socialised, then retired at 14:00. Woke at 21:00 (7 hrs). Met relative in hotel, then returned to bed at 22:30.
11	Intermittent sleep until 01:00 wake-up call (2 hrs 30 mins). Pushed 04:30 for HKG. Pilot Flying (PF) for sector. In-flight sleep taken in Upper Class seat between 10:00–12:30 (2 hrs 30 mins). I was flagging by the time I took my in-flight sleep. I was fairly relaxed and dozed. On-blocks 14:00. Checked-in by 15:30. Went out for some drinks. In bed by 21:00.

Captain – scheduled long-haul (C2)	
Day	Diary (All times Zulu)
12	Woke at 05:00 after a good sleep (8hrs). Socialised, then retired at 18:30. I slept well at first, but an incoming crew decided to hold a room party in the room above mine.
13	I slept off and on until 03:00 in an effort to put some sleep 'in the bank' for tonight's return flight to LHR. Sight-seeing then back to HOTAC for pre-flight sleep. In bed between 08:45 and 10:00, but unable to sleep. Departed HKG for LHR. Commenced in-flight rest at 20:30.
14	Slept erratically due to turbulence. Woke at 01:30 (5hrs). Landed 05:45. Home by 08:30. In bed by 09:30. I felt very tired initially. Then I got the 'wake-up buzz' as I reflected on chores that needed doing after being away for so long. Rose at 11:00 for some food (1hr 30mins). Took two relaxant pills (herbal variety) then returned to bed. Slept 11:45–13:00 (1hr 15mins). Gardened, ate, watched television. Felt extremely fatigued, so I went to bed at 21:00.
15	Made some tea at 03:00 (6hrs). I felt very tired but could not sleep. Did some admin work, then returned to bed at 04:30, to be woken by partner going to work at 06:30 (2hrs). In bed by 22:00.
16	Woke at 07:00 (9hs). In bed by 22:00 after taking a couple of sleeping tablets in an effort to get a full night's sleep.
17	Woke at 06:30 (8hrs 30mins). The tablets worked well. Chores in town and at home. Played squash for an hour. In bed by 22:00 after taking a single sleeping tablet.
18	Slept soundly until 03:00. Toilet break. Slept until 06:00 (8hrs). Travelled to London to stay at hotel. Journey into London made by public transport. Tortuous. In bed by 23:00.
19	Woke at 06:30 (7hrs 30mins). Watched offspring run half-marathon, then returned home. Journey out of London made by public transport: Another transport fiasco. Eventually got to the North London car park 3–4 hours later. In bed by 21:30.
20	Rose at 03:30 (6hrs). Restless sleep as I knew I had to get up early. Made LHR in two and a quarter hours. Worth the extra early departure, as I avoided most of the traffic build-up. Pushed for MIA at 10:15. Tried unsuccessfully to get some in-seat sleep. On arrival MIA socialised with the crew.

Captain – scheduled long-haul (C2)	
Day	Diary (All times Zulu)
21	Asleep by 06:00. Woke at 13:30 (7hrs 30mins). I woke every 2–3 hours. Dreamed and slept well in-between. Walked on sea-front. Pre-flight sleep 16:00–20:30 (4hrs 30mins). Pushed 23:30 for LHR.

Analysis

Flying scheduled long-haul passenger services this Captain had a stable roster (in contrast to, say, night-freight pilots whose rosters are characterised by instability (Bennett, 2010a)).

Pre-flight and in-flight sleeps broke up long periods of wakefulness. For example, during the LHR–EWR–LHR trip the diarist would have been awake for over 24 hours (06:10 on day 1 to 06:30 day 2) had he not obtained some pre-flight sleep (1hr 15mins duration) and an in-flight sleep (45mins). Despite these 'sleep oases', the diarist, who was PF, "felt absolutely whacked by the time I boarded the crew bus [in EWR]".

Stress can affect sleep duration and quality. On returning from HKG on Day 14 the diarist went to bed, but, finding himself reflecting on the chores he had to do, woke early. He had obtained 1hr 30mins sleep. Later he got 1hr 15mins sleep. His inability to sleep may have been a stress-reaction. By 21:00 he "felt extremely fatigued". On Day 20, aware he had to get up early to make his MIA report, the diarist slept restlessly. Stress may have affected the quality of his sleep.

After dining out the diarist had a night cap at home on Day 4. He then experienced restless sleep during the second half of the night. This is what Eurocontrol (2005: 22) says on the subject of alcohol consumption and sleep quality: "Studies show that a moderate dose of alcohol consumed as much as 6 hours before bedtime can increase wakefulness during the second half of sleep. The subject may sleep fitfully during the second half of sleep, awake from dreams and return to sleep with difficulty. This sleep disruption may lead to daytime fatigue and sleepiness". This is what Rhodes and Gil (2002: 24) say on the subject of alcohol and sleep: "Avoid having any alcohol before going to bed. Alcohol may help you fall asleep but it actually disturbs your sleep patterns. It will disrupt your sleep by causing early morning or even middle-of-the-night awakening and prevent you from getting the proper amounts of slow-wave and REM sleep that you need to function properly".

The diarist seems to have benefited from quiet and relaxing HOTAC, with the exception of the room party incident in HKG. In his study of a European night-freight operator, Bennett (2010a: 12) notes: "Hotel life had its irritations. Hotels can be noisy during the day: rooms are cleaned, goods are delivered, guests are dispatched and maintenance is done. Unfortunately, the noise starts just when the pilots are getting

Captain – scheduled long-haul (C2)

ready for bed. Sometimes pilots kept awake by intrusive noise would ask to be moved to another room or floor. *In extremis* a pilot would ask to be moved to another hotel". The diarist lived roughly a two and a half hour drive from LHR, his base. On landing he would drive home. Eurocontrol (2005: 40) says this about driving home after work: "If you are sleepy when your shift is complete, try taking a nap before driving home. Remember that sleep can quickly overcome you when you least expect or desire it to". The Health and Safety Executive (2006: 35) says: "Driving to and from work can be risky, particularly after a long shift, a night shift or before an early start. The following strategies may make driving safer – consider using public transport or taxis rather than driving ...". Transport Canada (2008: 5) says: "Driving fatigued impairs your performance in a similar way that driving drunk does. Even if you think you're okay, bear in mind that sleep can come when you're not expecting it. You are not always able to accurately judge just how sleepy you really are". (According to the Trades Union Congress (TUC) (2010): "£339 million-worth of working time is spent travelling to and from work every day". Some twenty-five million U.K. workers commute. Nevertheless, average daily commute times have fallen from 52 minutes in 2005 to 48 minutes in 2008 (despite an increase in the number of people in work). Factors like homeworking, flexitime and "better traffic management" have helped reduce commute times in the U.K. (TUC, 2010)).
 	
    During a short stay in London to watch his daughter compete in a race the diarist wrote of the capital's strained transport system. It goes without saying that the quality of the transport infrastructure impacts both work and leisure activities. It is possible that investment in infrastructure would help this diarist get to work more quickly. Some pilots locate themselves an equal distance from several large airports in the hope of accommodating redeployments/job moves. Downturns reduce job security.
 	
    Generally the diarist seemed able to obtain pre-flight and in-flight sleep. The Upper Class seat episode on Day 9 illustrates the importance of undisturbed, stress-free sleep opportunities. This was manifestly not a stress-free sleep opportunity. Hence the diarist's inability to get to sleep. The Federal Aviation Administration (2010: 55855) comments: "Sleep should not be fragmented with interruptions. In addition, environmental conditions, such as temperature, noise and turbulence, impact how beneficial sleep is, and how performance is restored".

Conclusion

Keeping a diary for three weeks while holding down a busy and stressful job takes a great deal of commitment. The author is grateful to each
diarist. In the author's opinion the flying public should also be grateful to
the diarists for recording their hectic lifestyles in such detail. It is not easy
to construct a blow-by-blow account of your day when hungry, tired and
dirty. Several themes emerged from the diaries. Diarists spoke about long
periods of wakefulness, fatigue, pressure, fitness, food, the down-route
lifestyle, commuting, health issues, domestic issues, etc. These themes are
expanded upon in the next chapter and analysed in Chapter 5.

Quantitative and Qualitative

Introduction

The author researched the pilot lifestyle using sleep/activity logs (SLOGs), an on-line questionnaire and interviews with pilots. The questionnaire closed at the end of January 2011. The fifty-four question on-line questionnaire produced 433 responses. Because many of the questions allowed free-text answers, the questionnaire survey produced a large volume of qualitative data. This data broadened and deepened the ethnographic dimension of the research. The interviews added further texture.

Many questions permitted a narrative (free text) response. Because it would be impractical to reproduce every narrative response (the narrative responses to Question 8 alone totalled over 11,500 words), a few *typical* responses are reproduced. Further, some questions that are not directly concerned with the pilot-lifestyle have been omitted. For example: "Q4. What type(s) of aircraft are you flying at the moment?" The question numbers that appeared on the questionnaire have been retained. Responses have not been edited. Pilots describe the industry *in their own words*. Like the previous chapter, this one presents an oral history.

Questionnaire Responses

8. Please describe (with dates) the most intense period of commercial flying you have done (for example, a busy summer charter period).

"August 2010 saw me flying 6 day-weeks of 4 sector-days solid from the beginning until the end of the month. There was so much tension on crew numbers that I had no option but to go back to work less than 24hrs after the birth of my first child. How can an employer expect one of his pilots not to be distracted to say the least?"

"[Flying with a UK-registered low-cost carrier] 2003 to 2006. 750–800 hours per year. LGW. During the whole of this period I was chronically fatigued. It is only with hindsight that I realise this. The fatigue was also cumulative over this time. The company became more ambitious with their rostering. Due to FTL alleviation on early duties on returning to LGW I would basically be asleep or nodding off between the Isle of Wight and 1,000ft on approach. After two days 'off' (read sleeping and ironing) I would do 5 days on, each of approximately 12 duty hours. With my drive to work, and a 30 minute bus drive from the car park to the crew centre, I would be out of my house for at least 15 hours a day (nine hours for dinner, breakfast and sleep). On one occasion, after 5 days of lates, approximately 60 hours duty, 18 sectors and the last day running into a day off, I spun my car into the central reservation of the M25 at about 80mph. In my fatigued state I was completely unable to assess the risk of driving at this speed on a waterlogged motorway".

"I used to work for a shorthaul operator flying turboprops between Scotland and London. I would regularly be doing 98 hrs in 28 days and would total 890–900 hours a year. The airline was used by business people and the timetable was fixed. There was no flying on a Saturday as London City Airport was closed, and the roster was never disrupted. Even though you would work to the maximum limits I did not find that fatigue was an issue because I could plan my life around the stable roster".

"A period in 1999 on the long-haul Boeing 777 when I just did 3-day transatlantics, with 2 days off between on a constant basis for several months. My life was a blur. Eventually I turned up on the wrong day for a duty which mystified me in my 'zombified' state".

"Before T5 opened at LHR, we had operational chaos at LHR (2006–2008). [My carrier] had resourced the ground staff for T5 for all areas so we were short of operational support (tugs, dispatchers, buses etc.). Equally, our pilot numbers had been reduced from roughly 3500 to around

3000 which stretched our scheduling agreements to breaking point. This resulted in a lot of 'forced drafting', leading to roster instability on top of a lot of operational stress. I was flying upwards of 750 hours annually even on a 75% contract for parts of those years. When I look back not only was I knackered (we all were) but I was psychologically fragile from the constant chaos-induced stress".

"Thirteen transatlantic crossings in one month. This was on the Boeing 747-100/200".

"17/12/10–23/12/10. I turned up to work at 11:10z on the 17th, did a Manchester – Jersey – Manchester pair of sectors, sat in the crew room on airport standby for 5 hours, flew Manchester to Southampton, got stuck in Southampton and Bournemouth (unscheduled nightstops) for 2 days. Got home at 16:00 on the 19th. Had the 20th off as a rest day, came in early on the 21st and 22nd for 3 hours of airport standby and 2 x 1 hour sectors and 3 hours of airport standby respectively. Called off home standby at 09:00 on the 23rd to fly a Manchester – Paris – Manchester. An hour and a half late leaving for Paris due to an air traffic slot. Stuck in Paris due to snow for around 5 hours. Landed at 21:30. Home by 22:45".

"Summer seasons, 2004–2007, LGW 737. 400 hrs+ each summer (6 months). I have flown more hours per season on long-haul since then, but that was the most tiring period. I would often fly 4-sector, 12-hr days finishing at 23:00–01:00 with 12 hrs off in between. So I'd have 9 hrs at home taking account of travelling time, plus M25 flex. I often used to have to get out of my car on the way home in the early hours to walk up and down the hard shoulder to stay awake".

"April 2004 to November 2007 on the B737 with [a UK-registered carrier] at Gatwick immediately after the introduction of the 'High Utilisation Schedule'. The whole operation was under-resourced with both pilots and ground resources and, consequently, the schedule ran up to two hours late day after day after day. It wore me down so much after the first 2 years of it (and I loved short-haul up until 2004) that I had to bid to give up my command and become a long-haul first officer just to get some work-life balance back".

"During my time in Shorthaul I did sequences of 6 days, 1 day at home, followed by another 6 day flying period. All the days had very early starts, sometimes 03:00z, and then long days. Often extended due to standard delays and disruptions at the busy European hubs. I found the repeated early starts very tiring. On longhaul the tiredness is different. Repeated insomnia due to jetlag, and never seeming to get enough time in one time-zone, including at home, to recover. I remember doing a London–Tokyo–London 4 day trip, followed next day by a London–Los Angeles–London 4 day trip, followed next day by another London–Tokyo–London trip. 12 consecutive days, crossing 48 timezones!"

10.a. Are you a Cadet/New Entrant; First Officer; Senior First Officer; Captain?

Cadet/New Entrant:	1.2%	5
First Officer:	8.5%	37
Senior First Officer:	45.0%	195
Captain:	45.3%	196

13.a. Have you refused any duties in the last 12 months because of fatigue?

Yes:	13.2%	57
No:	86.8%	376

13.b. How many have you refused?

1–5:	96.5%	55
6–10:	1.8%	1
11–15:	1.8%	1
16–20:	0.0%	0
21 or more:	0.0%	0

Please describe the circumstances of as many of these refusals as possible (even the briefest details would be helpful).

"On the back of two days off, living in a hotel as part of a secondment with another airline, I had a 02:30 get-up for a 04:15 report. Hotel had a wedding function that evening which got going around 22:00. I struggled to sleep due to the noise, and eventually realised that at 01:30, still wide awake, it would not be safe to operate an 05:30 flight when my get-up would have meant, perhaps, 1 hours sleep. Crewing were understanding and immediately removed me from the flight duty".

"Long days with heavy delays, only to find next day's duty has just become even longer and now with minimum rest. Any call to Crewing asking for a shorter day is bluntly ignored, and so there is no option but to file a Fatigue Report to maintain the safety of aviation".

"1 – just too exhausted, couldn't operate safely. 2 – after days off, had a bad night's sleep due to next-door's baby crying all night, was too fatigued to report for work. Was running at a rolling 800+ hours for the year's duty. It was the end of the summer and I'd had no leave since January. Had I not been so overworked, I might have been more able to absorb the bad night's sleep, but under the actual circumstances, it was not possible. 3 – Had a 2 night 'unscheduled' night-stop with bad weather. Results in 10 hours in the hotel each night only, and upon returning to the UK was given 'minimum rest' for what was to be day 5 of the 5 day block, and a change to do a long 4-sector day. I told the company I would have to see if I was fit to fly before the duty (i.e. regarding my fatigue level). Eventually I spotted that the duty was illegal in many ways (including breaching the 95 duty hours limit in 14 days), so as a result, the duty was scrapped anyway, but the company did have several chances to change it and only agreed when I told them it was illegal. I would definitely have called in fatigued otherwise".

"Disturbed rest down-route, a 6 day trip with consecutive minimum rest periods (11 hours at the hotel) with 4 sectors on each day, except the last".

"My mother had a heart attack on the first day of her chemotherapy. The in-laws had used my house for a large party through the weekend. I had two days of the simulator with a CAA inspector in the right seat who told me I looked absolutely exhausted and that I should go sick for my next trip! It took someone that senior to tell me to do it or I might still have gone to work (stupid I know!)".

"Only once when due to do a 4 sector day starting at 06:15. I had trouble sleeping and was still wide awake at 03:00. It was recorded by the company as sickness".

"As per usual, had a week with a transition from earlies to lates, then discretion two days in a row and then called fatigued on my last day. Another time I had a poor night's sleep (2 hours) before an early 4 sector day, which would have lasted around 11 hours. I called in fatigued. In all honesty, I think we fly fatigued regularly and have just accepted it as the norm, which of course is a huge safety factor. I would be interested to know if there is a link between flying hours flown in a short haul outfit and the number of air safety reports".

"Younger child teething during night resulting in 1.5 hours of sleep. At 4.00am I called in to inform Ops that I would not be operating the first two sectors (alarm set for 4.45am)".

"We start the week on early shifts and end the week on late shifts, so it's difficult to change your body clock that quickly. It results in difficulty going to sleep early before the first early shifts, so I'm often fatigued at the start of the week when we have the longest shifts in Glasgow. Call in 'sick' the night before because I couldn't get enough rest for the next day's work. The Dash 8 has a lot of technical problems which can cause stress during work. These lead to delays and late nights so I get less sleep than needed. We're given poor quality crew food (sandwiches as there are no ovens on the turboprop) so I often get a hot meal when I return from work at 22:30, which then leads to a poor night's sleep".

"Too little sleep due to noise from neighbours. Transitioning from late duty to early duty, was not able to sleep".

"Recently operated in poor weather conditions resulting in night stops away from home. Company offered 'Company Day Off' (CDO) downroute to allow me to operate on my planned day off. But CDO consisted of full day's work contacting Operations and Crewing to arrange duties for all the crew after 3 days of disruption with days of up to 16 hours duty. Company rosters 'Lates to Earlies' (i.e. 22:30 finish and 06:00 start) around days off as a matter of course. Required to operate onto six day's duty after single day off as it was 'legal'. Operated first day's service but felt totally fatigued during flights. Unable to concentrate. Declined to operate for the next 48 hours. Previous companies had low crew retention leading to poor roster fatigue-management. Had my CAA licence temporarily suspended for exhaustion and stress".

14. Have you ever commenced a duty knowing you were fatigued?

Yes:	74.4%	322
No:	25.6%	111

15. Have you ever flown a sector knowing you were fatigued?

Yes:	86.1%	373
No:	13.9%	60

16. What is the longest period of continuous wakefulness (in hours, from waking up to setting the brakes at the end of the last sector) you have experienced at work?

Up to 17:	13.9%	60
18–22:	32.6%	141
23–27:	33.3%	144
28 or more:	20.3%	88

Please describe how you felt when you set the brakes on your final sector.

Up to 17 hrs: "Utterly drained, very slow to think and process information. My brain hurt (headaches) and the greatest worry was that we had minimum legal rest (10 hours in a hotel) before reporting again – hence the worry that the clock was ticking and I needed to get rest as soon as possible".

Up to 17 hrs: "Felt drowsy, but confident I could drive home safely and not much more".

Up to 17 hrs: "Ill. Found it difficult to concentrate, or engage in any meaningful conversation".

18–22 hrs: "Tired but alert".

18–22 hrs: "At shutdown, quite alert. However, approximately 1 hour before landing and 1 hour after shutdown I felt tired, with 'itchy leg' feelings".

18–22 hrs: "Relieved, physically sick, dreading what the company had in store for me the next day".

18–22 hrs: "Appalling! I should have binned it at a few times during the flight. We pushed back, had a massive delay due to weather at night, and we considered turning back, but as we were under-way, this was very difficult. Commercial pressure".

18–22 hrs: "(Ironically) not too bad, as the duty, assigned off standby, started late and involved a long turnaround in Madrid. Although we finished at 4am having been up since 8am the previous day, it was manageable AS A ONE-OFF. Had I undertaken a series of duties in the build-up, it would have been very different, and I would have been significantly more tired".

18–22 hrs: "I could not even string a sentence together. Could not do basic maths. Could not make any decisions. But I have done many long periods at work. Sometimes back-to-back with minimum rest. I personally think the only thing that will prevent this type of rostering is an incident, and thereafter the CAA putting pressure on airlines to change their rostering practices".

23–27 hrs: "Was missing radio frequencies".

23–27 hrs: "Adrenaline keeps you awake. However, there is a great relief after the parking brake is set. I find it amazing how you can maintain alertness until the end of the sector, but then tiredness is very evident, the drive home being very challenging indeed".

23–27 hrs: "Completely exhausted, and 'punch drunk'".

23–27 hrs: "Physically and mentally shattered. The interesting thing is that I didn't actually realise how bad I was until after the flight (which concluded with a bad approach and a bad go-around)".

23–27 hrs: "Extremely tired, after the effects of adrenaline and caffeine rapidly wear off. Occasionally feel light-headed (spinning sensation) and nauseous".

23–27: "Like death! I was aware that, whilst perfectly legal, what I had done was unsafe and I resolved never to be coaxed into doing it again".

28 hrs, or more: "'Drunk' with tiredness. Unable to carrying out any task that required any form of mental agility".

28 hrs, or more: "Punch drunk. Utterly exhausted. Incapacitated. Checked straight into a hotel and didn't even drive home. The trouble with long-haul flying is you simply cannot predict how tired you will be at the end of a flight, because you have no way of knowing whether you will be able to sleep during any planned bunk rest".

28 hrs, or more: "I felt psychologically and emotionally irritable. I was unable to complete routine post-flight procedure without error or omission. I felt that I was prone to cognitive and tactical error during the flight, but was lucky that the operation had turned out to be closer to 'routine'".

28 hrs, or more: "I felt relieved the day was done. It was a constant battle against complacency. This occurrence was due to a sleepless night spent in a noisy (60dB on average, with 73dB peaks) hotel room. After that day, I seriously considered writing an ASR on the HOTAC, but did not do it".

28 hrs, or more: "The circumstances were entirely company induced ... I felt overwhelmingly tired, and angry with myself. But most of all I felt like an irresponsible fool/criminal for not having the balls to say 'I was too fatigued to do the duty'. I should have done that, of course, before the duty commenced. But the truth is, I felt more afraid of my employer than I did of doing the responsible thing!"

28 hrs, or more: "Relieved that I'd got through the sector without an incident. For all the modern safety hardware airlines seem keen to invest in (EGPWS, TCAS, Runway Incursion Monitors) I am absolutely certain that the fatigue level of myself and my colleagues on the flight is the most important influence on the safety of the flight".

17. Stress is said to have physical, emotional, psychological and behavioural impacts. For example: Physical: sleeplessness; headaches; muscular tension; elevated pulse. Emotional: low self-esteem; depression; apathy; irritability. Psychological (cognitive): poor concentration; forgetfulness; more error-prone. Behavioural: lethargy; increased use of alcohol/nicotine; refusal to take orders; alienation.

What do you understand by the term 'stress'?

"Having suffered long term stress in a previous job, there is very little of this in aviation. Stress in aviation to me is very short-term in nature and primarily generated by tiredness and fatigue, and can be accentuated by unserviceabilities".

"I recognise all of the above symptoms as being typical of the professional life I lead".

"I have personally experienced all of the above and was divorced last year as a direct consequence".

"I decided not to become stressed in my life. I took frequent days off whilst working for a low-cost airline, refused to answer my phone on standby at unsocial hours (3am), refused duties I considered unreasonable, etc".

"I like the 'stress bucket' analogy. Such that when I'm stressed I cannot take on any more information and I feel like a computer that freezes. Only when something is removed from the 'bucket' can I start to function again".

"I agree with the above definitions of stress. It definitely impacts on my ability to perform, both mentally and physically, and if the stress continues then it has a noticeable effect on my health".

"I can associate stress with these above factors: sleeplessness, muscular tension, depression, irritability, poor concentration, forgetfulness and error proneness, alienation (self-induced). I would say that stress can also be a feeling of helplessness or inability to do something which you feel needs putting right. For example, going through security is often stressful, especially when running late, and the procedures seem irrelevant; or feeling like you HAVE to go to work even when you might be better off not going (e.g. to pay the bills or because of the threat of being put down as a no-show)".

"Encompassed by all of the above, compounded by an inability to find someone to talk things over with, pressures to 'get on with it', worries that if you make this public at work then it could damage your health record/ worries about being certified medically unfit, etc".

"For me, stress is about a lack of control. Usually as a result of others letting you down. This can mean 'subordinates' not doing their job properly, or 'superiors' not giving enough support. This increases workload and distraction which erodes capacity, which leads to less control of a situation and hence, stress".

"[Stress is] forgetfulness and a pissed-off wife".

"All of the above. It is physically and mentally draining, to the point where you do not care about anything, except getting away".

"All of the above (they are very familiar!). I have experienced all of these impacts at some time, and they seem to feed/develop from one another. A conscious effort is required to keep them at bay".

"All of the above define Stress quite well. It manifests itself very differently in different people, but essentially it can be described as a response to environmental factors experienced in day-to-day life. It can have dramatic effects that would adversely affect one's capability to carry out normal activities both at home and at work".

"As above. Also – pressure on me to do what other people want (family/ close friends rely on me to function on a daily basis). Much worse when you are tired. Putting the needs of others before mine, and hence missing out on my needs. Financial pressures".

"'Stress' is being pushed mentally and physically to a 'level'. The level is different for different people. However I believe there is an optimum stress level where performance can be heightened and maintained for extended periods. It's when the stress level goes beyond this level that you become 'maxed out' and performance degrades quite significantly. The right amount of stress is good, too much is negative, and in this job, dangerous".

"An increase in perceived pressure upon the individual concerned. It can be caused by many things, such as family, financial and work pressures, etc., as well as lack of rest time".

"'The difference between perceived task and perceived ability'. One real example at my airline is struggling to carry out the SOPs in accordance with the Ops manuals during a 25 minute turnaround – it is the briefing that regularly suffers. Also trying to stay alert and assertive for an 11:30 hr, 4 sector duty day. With 4 approaches, landings and departures, with 4 stressful short turnarounds. Winter Operations make this all the worse. In conclusion, it is the unrealistic commercial targets imposed by my airline – simply not a sufficient amount of time on turnarounds".

"A feeling of being wound up like a spring and every problem is another twist. No capacity left to deal with issues, and a general feeling of 'edginess'. Up until recently I considered someone who said 'I'm stressed' to be some- one just whinging. I now realise it can be a genuine medical problem which needs resolving and can lead to major illness if not identified and dealt with".

"I certainly recognise all of the above symptoms as indicators of stress. Stress, to me, is any kind of event/ action/situation that you have limited influence over that produces the above reactions. It could be trying to sleep when there is incessant (road) noise from a poorly located crew hotel, or it could be financial, matrimonial or other worries".

"I think the body requires a certain background level of stress. At low levels or for occasional peaks it is a thoroughly good thing. However I think under certain circumstances stress can build up. Being constantly tired, exhausted due to overwork, combined with being away from home and family for long periods can push people to braking point".

"Most of the above but for me, the most stressful period of my flying career resulted in extreme irritability (to the point of significant anger at anything to do with the company) and frustration with my life in general as I didn't have enough time off to manage my life successfully. With hindsight, I was probably socially drinking too much, and doing less of that would have enabled me to be more productive in my private life, but I felt that I needed to wind-down after working so hard, so it was a bit like 'Hobson's Choice'".

"Poor terms and conditions, being underpaid, undervalued and disrespected by Crewing and Operations departments, aircraft with lots of defects and poor reliability record combine to form a worrying day at work. 25-minute turnarounds don't give you time to have a cup of tea and collect yourself before you have to rush to keep to the commercial schedule".

18. Have you ever felt unduly stressed at home?

| Yes: | 79.9% | 346 |
| No: | 20.1% | 87 |

How did the stress manifest itself, why do you think you felt stressed and how did you resolve the matter?

"Irritable over usually trivial matters, not concentrating fully on tasks, very lethargic, low self-esteem. I suspect the symptoms were related to feeling over-tired, and concern that I could not continue working at that pace safely. Short-term solutions included putting home life on hold to ensure as much rest as possible. However, over time this introduced additional pressures".

"Anger towards children who were taking lots of attention though I was tired. Had to leave room to calm down".

"Apathy and withdrawal from loved ones. Luckily I have an understanding wife – many of my friends are divorced. Resolution: heavy and exhausting physical activity".

"Anger, frustration, depression. Onset of marriage break up".

"A form of panic that I was missing my life, and a feeling of always being in the wrong place at the wrong time. Solved only by having more than several days break at home after a flight, or some holiday".

"Apathy, alcohol, sleeplessness, indifference ... Resolved by professional help ... Coping mechanism improved, but situation is still existent.

A long-term break from flying with a clear or realistic view on the horizon on how to re-engage should be ideal".

"Breakdown of relationship causing severe anxiety. Resolved by divorce".

"Arguing with my wife over very minor issues. The stress was caused by too much pressure at work. I resolved the matter by taking my GP's advice and had a week off sick. This gave me a break and 7 nights of quality sleep".

"I had my elderly mum with severe Alzheimer's disease, Parkinson's disease and Macular Degeneration (partial sight) living in a Granny Annexe at home. She used a lot of my time and resources making sure her basic needs were met and hospital appointments were attended. I also spend a lot of time 'managing' the carers who were coming in to help out 3 times per day. When I eventually realised that my work-life balance had become so bad that I couldn't self-deny the amount of stress I was under any longer, I wrote to my chief pilot explaining the situation and requesting that he try to expedite my transfer to long-haul ASAP. He couldn't do that but he did give me a free reign to drop trips that were particularly difficult for me during my last 3–5 months of short-haul flying. The extra flexibility (as opposed to just 11 days off month after month) did help a bit".

"Chest pain, breathlessness, irritability. Resolved by (eventual) realisation that I could not cope and needed to shed non-essential 'stressors'".

"I have 3 indicators [for stress] – I become very pessimistic, I don't sleep well and I drive like a mad thing. I am very lucky to have a very understanding wife and she flags it up and we do something about it. We go off and do things, we chill out, we go out for a family day out. We manage it all at home. [My airline] is useless and do not understand, so I never bother them with it".

"I often suffer from insomnia and irritability. I get a build up of tension leading to a feeling that I am unable to meet all of the demands on my time. This includes 'being myself' when with family and friends, and coping with the minutiae of daily life. I know I'm stressed when organisation of bills, bank accounts, meetings etc seem like difficult things. They are not difficult and ordinarily they don't bother or worry me. I often suffer from insomnia, forgetfulness and lethargy. I believe the prime source of stress in my life is a lack of sleep. I find it very difficult to deal with extremely unsociable hours

(05:00 check in – 03:00 wake-up) most especially when I have compounded jet lag. I have spent no more than a couple of weeks in the same time zone for four years, and normally I change time zones 8 times a month. I resolve stress by exercising. I have taken up running, and when I don't exercise I feel a marked rise in stress levels and deterioration in sleep quality".

"Nasty divorce meant I was regularly stressed. It hasn't been fully resolved with constant issues over contact with my children".

19. Have you ever felt unduly stressed at work?

Yes:	73.4%	318
No:	26.6%	115

How did the stress manifest itself, why do you think you felt stressed and how did you resolve the matter?

"Eventually collapsed leading to loss of medical. Time off solved problem".

"Felt it difficult to contribute effectively on the flight deck. It becomes harder to project ahead and think about all the possible threats to safety, and risks associated with a flight. I felt stressed due to tiredness and working through the night".

"At work stress manifests itself in a different way, as the cause is generally different. Work stress manifests itself when I realise that I am loosing capacity, and I can feel myself 'getting behind the aircraft,' and that I am unable to assimilate new information. It can be brought on in several scenarios, including intense weather activity and weather avoidance, especially when combined with high ATC work load; during very technical abnormal/emergency situations; or for example when working hard to manage the aircraft's energy (speed, altitude and configuration), which most often happens on intermediate/final approach; and also if you are uncomfortable with the way a colleague is flying the aircraft (generally in terms of energy management, or not complying with SOPs). When/if it becomes apparent that I am experiencing such stress, my first course of action is to share my mental model and difficulty with the other pilot. If it is something they are doing, I explain why I disagree with their course of action, or think we could do something better/differently".

"Complete bewilderment. Lack of confidence in decision-making skills". "Again, more irritability and angriness (occasionally). This is usually due to delays and technical challenges, particularly when a solution is obvious but you can't get agreement or resources to resolve the problem. The occasional CRM issue is also a problem when conflicting personalities on the flight deck occur. Lastly, being force-drafted when not expected, resulting in working across family events. The consequence of my experience was to end up in front of the director of flight operations and being told that I was EXPECTED to go into discretion if I report for work – this was following my extra trip and having stated to the Capt that I wasn't fit to go into discretion (the following day after returning from my rostered trip of 2 consecutive night sectors). I have never really got over that particular experience. Otherwise, I normally deal with other issues by thinking them through and accepting the fact that resources are limited, or by talking to my colleagues about it, which normally brings back the emotional response".

"Being very direct/short with colleagues. Ranting at my management".

"Came back from a Phoenix route check to be met on the flight deck by a manager saying that I was being drafted to go to Boston the following day. I had childcare issues as my wife would be working the following day and the children were too young to be left alone. I had an argument with the manager and refused to do the trip, as I didn't see why my wife should have to miss work because of my company's crewing problems. I got on the crew transport telling the manager that I wouldn't be reporting the following day. I guess somebody else did the trip".

"Difficulty in thinking logically. Too many problems at once, and battling against crew maximum hours to get pax to destination. Just buggered on through!"

"Frustration at a Captain who didn't operate the aircraft correctly. It wasn't that he wasn't following SOP's, but his understanding of the autopilot system and displays on the FMA left me feeling very frustrated. He was pressing buttons he shouldn't have been. A simple non-precision approach became a very dramatic and frustrating event. Unfortunately, the stress seemed to manifest itself in me 'not really caring' about what he was doing. The aircraft was still operating safely, it just explored the boundaries of that safety area".

"Six-monthly simulator-check pressure. Sleepless nights and irritability seemed to [accompany] being anxious about failing the simulator check and hence losing one's career. How do I resolve the issue? Live with it; it's a consequence of the job!"

"A number of issues arose at 'top-of-descent' which, given that I had just woken up from my bunk rest during the cruise, increased my workload. As I was fatigued and was suffering from 'sleep-inertia', my stress level increased resulting in errors being made and a rushed approach, which, with the benefit of hindsight, was thoroughly unprofessional".

"Became withdrawn and uncommunicative. Recognised this behaviour due to CRM training and personality typing, so was able to consciously mitigate the effects".

"During a flight in severe turbulence and hail stones – the physical characteristics of the aircraft motion and vibration coupled with the intense noise level prevented me hearing anyone or anything at the time whilst flying the aircraft and ensuring it remained in reasonably controlled flight! I recall the intense concentration [needed] to deal with what was happening, and trying to assimilate what was happening so quickly. I believe that due to, I suppose, a survival instinct to make sure events did not get out of hand, I was not overtly aware of stress. A few hours later I felt some of the shock symptoms taking effect e.g. I noticed my hands shaking slightly".

"I always feel quite stressed at work. Due to the disciplinary hearing I had I feel very vulnerable and I feel the management are not behind me, and cabin crew cannot be trusted".

"Feeling angry, annoyed, frustrated. Due to employer under-resourcing of staff transport from aircraft-side at end of duty ... we were frequently kept waiting for over an hour before we could get to our cars to return home. Resolved stress (only partially) by filing endless reports to BALPA and company, which ultimately got us nowhere".

"Going through stupid security. I just bit my lip".

"How does stress manifest? – An inability to sleep properly, a constantly repeating 'mental loop' of the situation, difficult to think of anything else – a constant nagging voice! Why? Triggered by a highly derogatory 'Line check' report, where I was significantly – and in my view, very unfairly – criticised, including some matters which were either factually wrong or were vastly over-inflated in importance. The Check Pilot seemed to 'Have it in for me', a situation which had been commented on previously by others. The Squadron (I was in the RAF at the time) took his report at face value and started serious administrative action. How resolved? By my formal written, point by point, rebuttal of the critical report to my superiors. After investigation of my rebuttal, another line check operation was flown with one of the senior training pilots. This showed no significant faults or serious observations. The critical report was removed from my record, and the original Check Pilot was so advised".

20. If you felt stressed and/or fatigued, who would you talk to?

Family G.P.:	97
Authorised Medical Examiner:	59
Partner:	336
Offspring:	13
Trusted (non-work) friend:	162
Trusted colleague:	219
Chief Executive Officer:	1
Personnel Director:	1
Operations Director:	2
Chief Pilot:	23
Fleet Manager:	62
Rostering Manager:	8
Crewing Officer:	14
Other:	52

What outcome(s) would you seek, and what outcomes do you think you would achieve?

"A different perspective on a problem which would enable me to rationalise, come to terms with and resolve the situation I was in".

"For acute stress/fatigue I would try to tell Crewing I was unfit to operate (although when away from home the pressure to get home, 'keep the show on the road,' not let down fellow crewmembers and passengers is compelling). My partner is generally sympathetic and understanding of the stresses, although I often do not have time to follow solutions or remedies she suggests!"

"I feel that most people either don't understand or don't want to sympathise, so I don't raise it with anyone".

"I would seek some reassurance, but would be more interested to hear of any different strategies they may have for tackling my issues. Talking, I am sure, would help to achieve a more favourable outcome. The best outcome I could realistically achieve with reference to fatigue is reassurance that I am not alone".

"I would look for help with any commitments that could be done by another person. I would look for advice on lifestyle issues. Any natural cures/remedies which would be acceptable without issue to flying medical. I think most GPs would not be able to do much as they would want to issue pills that pilots would not be able to go to work with. The GP would be a last resort if I was really unable to cope any more".

"A bit of sympathy. Rarely get any. People just see the glamour!!"

"From the GP, advice and some sleeping tablets as a last resort. From my family, more rest when at home, and to expect less of me until I have had a chance to recover. In terms of myself, I would try for less tiring trips. More time at home in terms of numbers of days off, and, importantly, in blocks of at least 2 to 3 days".

"A sympathetic ear! Hopefully some of the issues would be fed back informally/formally (if requested) – in particular from AMEs. From partners/colleagues, a different viewpoint and interpretation of the situation is always invaluable".

"A chat is a good start. In my company the Chief Pilot would probably swap a roster day or two to lance the boil".

"From the GP I would seek confirmation about the symptoms, and advice on how I might deal with them. There is not much I can get from my partner, except sympathy (with work-related stress and fatigue) as I am the only bread-winner. If I got to talking to the Chief Pilot about it, it would have to be really serious (i.e. at the point where I felt I could be on the verge of endangering myself and others by flying), because I wouldn't really expect him to be able to effect an outcome suitable for me".

"I do actually believe that I would get a sympathetic hearing from the company but suspect that no stone would be left unturned in my personal life, which in my view would be a step too far".

"I'd want help in sorting myself out. I would never talk to a manager or anyone in work about it, as they have an unbelievable skill of not being able to listen, and point out that it's all my fault, and that not performing properly in work is a disciplinary offence".

"I would like to see changes to duties that are fatiguing, and to route combinations that always suffer delays. I would like to have the option to refuse more than two duties a year without getting into trouble over it. It would be nice if Crewing Officers would be more understanding and polite (on average I find them friendly). Some will push the problem back to you saying the flight is now cancelled, and that you were the last one that could have done this duty. This makes people feel bad about the situation. Now you get stressed-out, and in the long run you might end up getting chronic fatigue".

"I could not possibly contemplate talking to anyone in authority within my employer: I have utterly no confidence that the matter would be dealt with properly. My poor wife bears the brunt of things. Her support is sometimes all that keeps me going".[1]

21. How many miles away from your designated base is your permanent residence? (If you usually use kilometers, please multiply your answer by 0.62)

50 miles or less:	51.0%	221
51–100:	22.9%	99
101–150:	6.7%	29
151–200:	3.2%	14
201–250:	1.6%	7
251–300:	2.1%	9
301–350:	1.4%	6
351–400:	2.1%	9

1   Family members can provide invaluable emotional support. Unfortunately, for the increasing number of pilots who work away from home, perhaps residing in a bed and breakfast for several days each week, such support is no longer available (although many pilots in this situation telephone home or use e-mail each day to communicate with partners/offspring).

401–450:	1.6%	7
451–500:	0.9%	4
501–550:	0.5%	2
551–600:	0.9%	4
601–650:	0.2%	1
651–700:	0.2%	1
701 miles or more:	4.6%	20

23.a. Do you use temporary accommodation close to your designated base?

Yes:	29.6%	128
No:	70.4%	305

23.d. Please explain why you use temporary accommodation.

"I use temporary accommodation because I have to be within 1hr 30mins of the airport".

"Because I can't commute 2,000 km on a daily basis".

"Aircraft removed from my home base to a new base 130 miles away. Still trying to sell my old house in order to complete move to new base".

"I commute from abroad in order to afford a better standard of living".

"I commute from Scotland, as my family is based there. [My airline] closed its Glasgow pilot base and could not move family to LHR".

"Because I am commuting to work – 2,000 miles".

"I use temporary accommodation because I have a young family. I don't want to disturb my sleeping wife and baby when I would have to get up before 6am".

"When you have a tour finishing one day and starting the next, it's a 180 mile round trip. It's just too far".

"I use temporary accommodation (Hotels) near my base for standby duties, training days and early starts, and generally for all duties where I think it would be unreasonable and I'd start my work-day tired if I did not sleep near my base".

"I use it because my wife and I do not want to live where my base airport is".

"My company, as a general rule, bases command upgrades away from their current base. Therefore when I got promoted 20 months ago I was moved from my base in STN (I live in London) to EMA, 140 miles away (so a daily commute is not reasonable). This is usually a 1 or 2 year situation, and generally people get moved back after 2 years. I tried renting, but that was not flexible, and running two houses with bills was extra work, as well as being a useless expense when I am not there half the time. With special rates and deals I can manage my hotel stays and save money, while also doing away with the worry of the upkeep of my accommodation".

"I use temporary accommodation because I don't consider myself appropriately rested if I have to get up before 3am. Also, I find the drive to work scary before 4am, with the problem of falling asleep and concentrating".

"I use temporary accommodation between back to back trips/simulator duties and before early reports".

"My commute is 90 miles, and approximately 1hr 30mins. Because my rosters involve very few night stops, if I didn't have the rented room I would be adding 3 hours onto almost every day (5 days on/2 off). This would be a major reduction in free time/rest. However the down side is that I am away from home and my wife for 3 to 4 nights a week. I tried B&Bs but the constant booking, check-in/check-out, pack/unpack, made it worse than driving all the way home".

"My drive to work takes 2 hours. Sometimes it is more practical to stay in overnight accommodation near to work".

"My permanent home is just too far to be driven on the work routine I now have. Permanent home to base is about 1 hr 20 min, plus the vagaries of the Staff Car Park bus service on top".[2]

"I use it because I'm commuting from Malaga, Southern Spain. This requires arrival in the UK the day before early reports. My Father lives close to LGW, and even though my base is LHR my commuting flights are often to LGW. I use car or coach to reach LHR".

---

2   Some pilots comment that while the drive to the airport can be made in a reasonable amount of time, navigating from their designated car park to the Crew Room can take a disproportionate amount of time. This situation arises at, for example, Gatwick Airport near London. Planners might wish to give more thought to crew access (because, effectively, it is a flight safety issue).

24.a. How long does it take you to commute to work?

Up to 30 minutes:	20.1%	87
31–60:	30.5%	132
61–90:	20.8%	90
91–120:	10.4%	45
121–150:	5.5%	24
151–180:	2.8%	12
181–210:	3.0%	13
211–240:	1.2%	5
241–270:	1.8%	8
271–300:	0.9%	4
301 or more:	3.0%	13

25.a. Have you ever driven/motorcycled home in a state of fatigue?

Yes:	92.1%	399
No:	7.9%	34

25.b. Did you have any doubts about doing so before setting off?

Yes:	78.2%	312
No:	21.8%	87

25.c. On arriving home, did you have any regrets about driving/motorcycling home in a state of fatigue?

Yes:	67.7%	270
No:	32.3%	129

Why did you feel regretful?

"Because I had several episodes of drifting across lanes or sudden head-jerking, indicating I had fallen asleep".

"Because I nearly fell asleep on the motorway at 04:00 hrs".[3]

---

3   The window of circadian low (WOCL) lasts from around 03:00–06:00 (although there are individual variations). During this period cognitive performance is impaired.

"I felt regretful because I know my reactions were not up to speed in the event of an incident. I'm aware that being fatigued is akin to having drunk alcohol".

"Because I nearly crashed! Hence my use of the train now. Also, I arrive at work better rested".

"Because it was dangerous. I had a number of near-misses and made mistakes during the drive. It's almost as if you are in a state of euphoria, or a trance".

"Driving home from work after a night flight is always done in a state of fatigue. It is by far the worst part of my job. In the work/life balance, it is a calculated risk which I take to be at home as soon as possible to be with my family. I wish there was an alternative. I feel grateful every time I get home unscathed, and regretful that I have driven in such a state".

"I felt regretful because I risked my life and the lives of others in my determination to get home to bed – so desperate was I to sleep well".

"Because it is only later when you're relaxing at home you realise how tired you are and how you can't recall certain parts of your journey. Then, of course, there is the moment in the car when you nod off".

"Because I nearly hit a double-decker bus".

"I felt regretful because I don't like putting my life and that of other road users at risk by driving in that condition. But practically speaking, there is not always an alternative. It can depend on how well your pre-flight and bunk rest go – if they go well then you might expect to be in a reasonable condition to drive, if not then you might not be. It's unavoidable that you will most likely be very tired after operating an overnight longhaul flight".

"I felt competent, dozed off momentarily, and hit the curb. I could have caused serious injury to another. Damaged the car".

"I felt regretful as it was a struggle to keep my eyes open. Often I pull in to the services area to rest for 30 mins. I have felt that sometimes I must not have been in a fit state to drive a car. Occasionally it's difficult to even remember the car journey, even immediately after finishing".

"Eyes closing spontaneously on the motorway. Micro-losses of wakefulness without even eyes shutting – like your brain just shuts down for a micro-second. Clearly dangerous and I normally pull over and stop to sleep whenever I notice this starting to happen. But there aren't many service areas on our motorway network (as opposed to, say, France, where rest areas, but not services, are extremely frequent) so you just have to keep going, as stopping to rest on the hard shoulder is illegal. Sometimes I have had to just carry on because I needed to get home for an appointment for my Mother, or similar".

"Almost falling asleep at the wheel. Stupid. Never done it since. If I'm ever that tired I pull off the road and take a nap. 20 minutes or so later I feel much better".[4]

"I felt regret because, although short, I couldn't remember the journey home".

"I did not realise I was fatigued when I set off. On the way home I came close to crashing on a corner. It was then that I realised how bad I was. The shock kept me alert for the next couple of miles. That got me home. The realisation I could have crashed and hurt someone else was the reason for regret".

"Having been woken by driving on the rumble-strip at the side of the Motorway, I count myself lucky. I have a young family, and it was irresponsible of me, but I was desperate to get home. Since, I have occasionally had a nap in the car prior to leaving for home. My wife isn't always understanding, as she often has a tough time at home with two young kids, also suffering from sleep-deprivation. She just wants me home as soon as possible. If I'm late, it means that I get more grief at home".[5]

25.d.i. Have you ever been involved in an accident while driving/motorcycling home in a state of fatigue?

Yes:	7.8%	31
No:	92.2%	368

---

4   One of the possible problems with napping is sleep inertia. It can take up to thirty-five minutes to become fully alert after a nap (Civil Aviation Authority, 2003).

5   Actions must be viewed in context. The back-story is relevant. Driving while fatigued is risky. But there are other factors in play, like the perceived need to support one's partner. The risk of having an accident may be traded off against the risks posed to a relationship by tardiness or absence.

25.d.ii. Do you think that fatigue played any part in the accident?

Yes:	96.8%	30
No:	3.2%	1

Please describe the accident.

"The following incident occurred when working for [a low-cost carrier] based at LGW: I was rostered a – not uncommon – five day block of work consisting of 18 sectors (4 x 4 + 1 x 2.). Each duty was planned to within an hour of discretion and each day ran late. The last day ran into a day off. After dropping off the paperwork and getting the bus back to the car I was on the road at about 1am. There was a torrential downpour. Despite this I decided to get home as quickly as possible. I lost control on standing water on the M25. I think I spun about six times hitting the central reservation at least five times. My fatigued state disabled me from making a rational assessment of the conditions and subsequently choosing a sensible speed to drive".[6]

"I rear-ended another car. Strangely having got in from a long-haul flight, slept for several hours, then driven".[7]

"In 1992 I was involved in a rear-end collision at 40 mph due to my inattention (my fault). I was driving home in the morning after an overnight long-haul operation. I was inattentive for 5 seconds due to being tired".

"I was driving along a dual carriageway, left the tarmac surface and ended up on the central reservation at high-speed. I had fallen asleep, but luckily I woke when the car started bouncing over the grass".

6   Fatigue degrades cognitive performance and judgment (Strauss, 2010).

7   Sleep inertia can last for up to 35 minutes after waking: "Sleep inertia is the main factor limiting the effectiveness of naps and it has been observed following naps as short as 10 minutes. It occurs on wakening and it may persist for between 5 and 35 minutes before performance returns to pre-nap levels" (Civil Aviation Authority, 2003). Sleep inertia affects cognitive performance: "Sleep inertia is a transient period of impaired performance and alertness which occurs during the period after awakening, and which may severely limit the pilot's effectiveness and judgment" (Civil Aviation Authority, 2007).

"I was involved in a back-end swipe. Hit by a youth late at night. He was driving too fast down a single track lane, misjudging where I was in relation to himself. He struck me as I was entering a passing place. Not fatigue-related, except that I misjudged his speed and perhaps slowed down too much whilst entering the passing place. Had I been fully awake, I would have known exactly what he was doing and anticipated the incident".

"My car (with wife and 2 children) was hit side-on while driving home from the airport. I felt afterwards that had I not been returning from a night-flight, then I may have been more aware of the other car at the junction".

"I was waiting to turn right across a main road. I obviously fell asleep. I woke up when the car crashed into the kerb on the opposite side, burst tyre, damaged wheel. Had drifted across opposite carriageway of main road. N.B. journey home from car park is less than 20 minutes".

"On completion of an 11+ hour overnight duty, I went into a hotel in GLA to get 4 hours sleep before taking a commercial flight back to SOU. After picking up my hire-car for the onward journey, I drove into a lamp post".

"Car accident. Driving along, aquaplaned off at slow-ish speeds due to very slow over-correction and unable to hold the car. I am dead certain this wouldn't have happened if I were rested".

"Long-haul sector, post-minimum rest. Basic crew. In-flight emergency (engine failure – mid-Atlantic), extended duty day. Tired and fatigued post-flight. I lost control of the car. Vehicle written off. I sustained minor injuries".

"On a wet drive home, after a long, stressful, fatiguing day, having had to fill in Air Safety Reports due to an incident, I drove too fast round a bend and spun my car. No-one else was involved. But my car was damaged. I wasn't concentrating!!"

"Last week (January 3, 2011) I hit a deer on the way home at night. I was tired and slow to react. Have also driven straight across junctions without slowing down/stopping. Fortunately, on each occasion it was late at night or in the countryside, so I didn't hit anyone".

"I briefly fell asleep at the wheel. When I woke I was driving across on the wrong side of a dual carriageway ... it was late at night and thankfully the road was very quiet – I skidded to a stop on the far verge".

"I was in standing traffic, which was start-stop-start-stop: I drifted off to sleep, and ran slowly into the back of the car in front".
"I fell asleep behind the wheel of a car. Crashed into woods off the M4 near Newbury".[8]
"I was driving late at night and in order to press on I drove much faster than the weather conditions merited. It was winter with a hard frost, and obviously slippery conditions. I was on a country road and frustrated by what seemed an excessively cautious driver in front. I eventually overtook this car but lost control at the next bend, crashing into a safety barrier. I now nearly always take the train to avoid this situation".

26.a. Does your airline provide sleeping accommodation for flight crew at/near your designated base?

Yes:	18.9%	82
No:	81.1%	351

26.b. What form does that accommodation take?

---

8   Sometimes losing control of one's vehicle is inconsequential, sometimes consequential: In December 2001 Gary Hart was convicted of causing the deaths of ten people by dangerous driving in the Selby train crash. After staying up all night Hart lost control of his Land Rover (which was trailering another vehicle). The vehicle left the M62 and crashed onto the East Coast Main Line, causing two trains to collide: "[E]xpert prosecution witnesses claimed he had too little sleep after a night on the telephone" (*The Independent*, 2001). Mr. Justice Mackay sentenced Hart to five years (Hart served half his sentence), commenting: "You either actually knew, or could be expected to have known from feelings of sleepiness that you were experiencing, that you were at risk of falling asleep and, notwithstanding that, you carried on" (Mackay cited in Oliver, 2002). Detective Superintendent Peter McKay, of North Yorkshire police, said Hart was a "mobile catastrophe waiting to happen" (McKay cited in Oliver, 2002). Hart, of course, had the option of going to bed the night before the crash. In choosing to stay awake (he was on the Internet/telephone to a potential girlfriend) he displayed willful irresponsibility. Professionals like London Underground track engineers, doctors or pilots have no choice: they must work their night shift. They must work through the WOCL with all the accompanying physiological and psychological decrements.

Apartment/Flat:	2
Land-side/air-side beds/bunks:	10
Crew Room recliners:	42
Other *(please specify)*:	35

Other:[9]

A 'Quiet Room,' but not particularly quiet or restful as other people continually coming/going
A hotel, but only if flying from a certain London base. Not from the other bases
A hotel can be provided in exceptional circumstances, but most crew never ask
A post-flight rest room. However it is noisy and too disturbed to get any quality rest
But they're not exactly very good, nor is the room quiet enough
They provide camp beds in a dark, quiet room
HOTAC[10] if duty > 16 hours
Hotel (but only on in-bound duties)
Hotel for LGW reports
Hotel room if operating from second base only (LGW)
Hotel room – but only provided under certain conditions
Hotel, but only if on rostered minimum rest!
Hotel, but only in very limited circumstances
In a dark room. Sometimes disrupted by noise
Only after long haul flights – not following 'short-haul'
Quiet room with large, comfy sofas
Quiet room, camp-bed type
They provide the most uncomfortable chairs they have. The back is absolutely vertical, making a relaxed sitting position difficult. Also one of the rooms is windowless and very small, which is hardly a relaxing environment
There is a 'quiet room' with mattresses. But it is often full
Uncomfortable 'Quiet Room' with soft furnishings (BUT NOT RECLINING)
Virgin does. The airline provides a quiet room with big chairs. EasyJet didn't. They said that if you were fatigued they would get you a hotel room. However, I don't know of anyone who ever achieved this

9   Duplicate entries have been removed. Although quotation marks are not reproduced
    in tabular entries, the words are those of the respondents.
10 HOTAC is a common abbreviation for hotel accommodation.

27. Will your airline pay towards (i.e. subsidise) local hotel accommodation for fatigued flight crew returning to home base?[11]

Yes:	16.9%	73
No:	83.1%	360

28.a. Do you overnight down-route?

Yes:	95.60%	414
No:	4.40%	19

28.c. In terms of quality, how would you describe your down-route accommodation?

Poor:	1.9%	8
Satisfactory:	20.8%	86
Good:	57.5%	238
Excellent:	19.8%	82

28.d.i. Are you able to get all the sleep you need in your down-route accommodation?

Yes:	36.2%	150
No:	63.8%	264

28.d.ii. Why not (Please specify the main reason)?

Minimum rest:	98
Noise disturbance:	171
Inability to regulate room temperature:	122
Lack of comfort:	54
Inadequate blackout:	78

11   The possibility exists that any charge levied on flight crew for HOTAC would discourage its use. Those on relatively low incomes (First Officers, for example) would be more inclined not to avail themselves of the facility. Charges discriminate against the low-paid (because they constitute a larger percentage of salary).

Interruptions from hotel staff (telephone calls, etc.):	93
Other *(please specify)*:	120

28.f. In your opinion does your airline understand the rest and recreational needs of its down-route pilots?

Yes:	76.1%	315
No:	23.9%	99

What does the airline not understand?

"The airline used to understand, and accommodation was first class – since merger HOTAC has deteriorated considerably for cost savings. Company are fully aware of pilots' requirements".

"Actually, I think they do understand and do their best. Unfortunately this is a commercial world, so they have to roster to make efficient use of pilots (with regard to FTLs and the other airlines), and hence be competitive".

"Financial pressure is pushing the standards of the down-route hotels downwards".

"My airline goes for the cheapest option. This may mean long rides from the airport to the accommodation and back. As long as there is a room with television and food available, that is it. Location and facilities do not come into it".

"My airline may understand, but does not always address the rest needs of pilots. However, my airline does provide good accommodation/ rest down-route on majority of occasions".

"Because they are image-focused and interested in appeasing 20 year old cabin crew we often stay in down-market hotels near popular night-life spots or beaches. All I and my colleagues want is a clean room, blackout curtains, air con that works, peace and quiet and a place where I can eat whenever I like".

"Being at an airport hotel for a week can be a lonely experience".

"Because CAP 371 says that minimum rest can be reduced by 1 hour when down-route. When you're down-route you don't have local passes so going through security takes longer. You then have to wait for the courtesy bus or a taxi to get to the hotel, then check in. This routine takes longer than the average drive back home, not to mention an unscheduled overnight due to a technical problem or weather when you rely on operations personnel several hundred miles away to sort out accommodation and transportation. On one occasion, recently, transfer from the airport to the hotel 15 miles away took nearly 6 hours".

"Things are generally OK, but there are a few hotels around the network which fail due to poor quality or not being able to get decent food 24 hr".

"It only grudgingly accepts these rest and recreational needs – they are slowly and constantly attempting to trim them back".

"In general I'd like to answer 'yes', but one thing prevents me from doing this: reducing a pilot's minimum rest by one hour because s/he is out of base. So you have done 11h 50mins of duty. They can now make you rest for 10h 50mins, instead of the welcomed 12 hours you'd get at home".

"Lip service is paid to fatigue and its management. Cost-reduction is number one on the list".

"The airline does not understand life away from home. You have to cram your life into your one or two days off at home. It's a long-haul lifestyle on a short-haul roster, except we don't get the rest – we just get min rest every night. They don't understand you can't keep healthy. You don't always have access to healthy food, or regular exercise. It's also very expensive. Most cabin crew can't afford to eat with the current Euro rate – then our stress levels are increased making sure the cabin crew are fed and rested and not about to pass out mid-duty".

"No. It doesn't give a hoot if the hotel is right next to an eight-lane Highway in the USA (BA crew, Houston). I mean RIGHT next to. All they do is count the cost and go for the cheapest option. Time and time again. We are often put in dodgy areas, with no facilities, no restaurants, etc".

"We are increasingly getting minimum rest in hotels farther away from the city centres, with little to do. Most hotels do not provide Internet access since it is not part of the contract, so we cannot do our [roster] bidding, check weather or keep in touch with the family".

"Noise is a massive issue. Hotels can be noisy, and that is no good".

"The airline does not understand that a top hotel does not necessarily provide a top night's sleep (ref poor room temperature regulation). They do not understand that few people can 'switch off' and sleep at 8pm for a 4am call, or go to bed at lunchtime to prepare adequately for a night duty, or sleep in an aircraft bunk at 4pm (body time). They set the rules according to what is theoretically achievable, rather than what occurs in practice. In short, they do not understand (choose to understand?) the concept of the body clock, jet lag, circadian rhythm".

"I believe the company regards me as simply a tool for its objectives, and not as a human being. I believe it regards my downtime down-route as an inefficient use of its resources".

28.g. Have you ever felt lonely or isolated when down-route?

| Yes: | 43.0% | 178 |
| No: | 57.0% | 236 |

Please describe why you felt lonely or isolated, and how you managed these emotions.

"I felt lonely because I had not seen my girlfriend for more than 3 days that month. Always in hotels. Managed it by cultivating anger towards work, and purposely no longer going 'the extra mile', so to speak".

"A lot of time is spent at work and at times when there are issues at home it is hard to keep communications up unless the Internet is free down-route. If I can talk to the family I feel I can stay involved in the situation and communications keep me calm".

"Cabin crew resent pilots".

"I have felt lonely because the cabin crew, especially, are much younger and do not understand our job either, and socialise in a different manner. That leaves one other pilot to socialise with. If they are doing their own thing, or have someone with them, then you are on your own".

"Break-up of a relationship, stuck in Australia. Felt very isolated".

"During periods of stress or emotional upset i.e. missing a family get-together (wedding, christening, etc.) personal feelings can be amplified and get on top of you. This, coupled with time-zone shifts/differences, can mean you find yourself unable to talk to people. I manage these emotions by trying to socialise with colleagues, watching T.V., going on the Internet. Generally by trying to get out of my room".

"Anti-social hours and jet lag often meant I would spend hours in a hotel room awake, waiting for the sun to rise. I managed by working, reading and maintaining contact with home".

"Cabin crew in 9 out of 10 cases despise pilots at this airline. In the past three months, and in over 40 nightstops, I have had social contact (dinner) with one crew. I get on with the job, read a book, go to the gym and simply no longer care. I simply state that I'll be in the lobby at a certain time to go for food and should anyone wish to join me they can (a sense of duty of care to my crew)".

"Missing my young family when away from home and not being able to deal with normal domestic issues from thousands of miles away. Managed by trying to talk at least once a day to my wife to keep in touch".

"In a destination where the cabin crew stayed in a different hotel and the other pilot(s) didn't want to socialise, I could feel quite alone and depressed as I am quite a social creature and haven't historically liked my own company very much. I dealt with this in the past by often going out drinking on my own and trying to meet other people (strangers) to interact with. Alternatively, I just had to 'man-up' and accept the situation and get over it! Lately, I have become more spiritual and find myself more at ease with my own company and less in need of social drinking... It really helps!"

"I missed home and felt cut off from loved ones. Met with the crew, had a beer and got it off my chest and/or I rang home (but this does not always work as it can make me feel more lonely)".

"I feel detached from family life. With proper rest periods at home this is easy to deal with. With increasingly busy rosters and shorter time off this is tricky. I manage these emotions by spending less time getting required rest at home after trips in order to spend this time with the family".

"It is lonely. It's obvious!"

"It feels lonely sometimes being down-route as people believe you lead some sort of amazing lifestyle, but being detached from reality, it frequently does not feel so amazing. I try to counter this by bringing my computer and staying in touch with friends".

"I miss my family. I get fed up socialising with crew I don't know. Cope by running and tourism!"

"Leaving domestic stresses behind when going to work makes me feel like a bad parent and the inability to deal with them whilst away compounds the feeling. Eventually, I just bottle it up and try to be sociable because we all have our problems to bear!"

"Middle of the night, too tired to read, complete any meaningful activity ... many, many occasions such as this. Learn to cope ... helped by the bidline which enables certain trips to be 'meaningful' i.e. do something enjoyable rather than exist".

"Generally it's due to being awake in the middle of the night due to jetlag and time-zone issues. Generally our hotels are in good locations and have good facilities, although this is gradually being eroded in some instances. I find the quality of the hotel and its location make a HUGE difference to the quality of my rest. In the poorer hotels the lack of e.g. reasonably priced in-room Internet access can lead to feelings of loneliness, plus a poor range of English T.V. channels, poor food (particularly overnight room service) etc. I have a Smartphone with unlimited worldwide data roaming and a good deal on SMS back to the UK, which helps me keep in touch. During the day it's fine. It's mainly being up during the (local) night which is the problem. In some cases the report for duty is early in the morning which can add to the unpleasantness of the situation if you can't sleep, as you know you will be very tired for the flight home".

"It can be a very lonely job if down-route for multiple days and no-one to talk to. Not always easy to manage, and there is no real reasoning for it. You just 'deal' with it".

"Isolated from home/family – with work colleagues who I have never met before (and may never meet again). Despite 13 years in the airline I am often flying with a crew where I may not know the other pilots and none of the cabin crew. Sometimes positively managed by being active, e-mailing family back home, etc. Other times less positively managed e.g. going to a bar and perhaps seeking an inappropriate friendship with a person of the opposite sex (maybe not for sex per se, just for some human contact)".

28.h. In your experience do hotel managers understand the needs of down-route pilots?

Yes:	53.1%	220
No:	46.9%	194

What don't they understand?

"Hotel managers don't understand because the airline doesn't pay the hotel enough to understand".

"Most do understand, but some don't understand the need for sleep at odd times compared to the local time of the hotel".

"My company and union agree certain stipulations to the hotel contract to ensure adequate rest (i.e. non-adjoining rooms, away from lifts, above a specified floor, etc.). These are often ignored or not known to check-in staff who put the hotel's commercial considerations on the day ahead of our agreements".

"Don't seem to understand that maintenance work disturbs rest (during day, for a night departure)".

"I believe they see us as difficult customers and often put us in rooms close to lift shafts, cleaners' store rooms, etc. Often when you speak to managers it is after the event and too late in the day for you as an individual. Thus they appear to simply pay you lip service, knowing with roster rotations it is unlikely you will be back the next day or night, so the problem will go away. Many times the same issues arise if you do happen to return to the same hotel within a short period".

"I don't think they are interested really. We are a cheap corporate contract".

"It's difficult to appreciate someone else's situation when it hasn't been experienced first-hand. And so understandably hotel managers don't fully appreciate each airline's 'down-route' pilot needs. 24-hour facilities, for example, are quite a rare thing".

"Despite company guidelines, rooms are sometimes allocated next to lifts and building works".

"They don't understand disturbances! Staff coming into rooms to service mini bar, housekeeping – it's an intrusion of privacy. As a woman I have had several male hotel staff let themselves in when I have been changing or in the bath. You feel violated (I have never followed this up at work). It's similar to the security search where some searchers are over-zealous (under the wire on bras) and open your bag in front of all your crew and put personal items on view. It's difficult to concentrate at work after such events. They also don't understand that we pay for our own food, unlike business travellers who can claim it back. We receive 1.90 an hour down-route – that is it! When a burger cost 23 Euros it's stressful – you would like to spend this money with your family".

"It depends on the quality of the hotel and the part of the world. Almost everywhere there are disturbances from cleaning staff during the day just when I'm sleeping before pick-up".

"It can be difficult for non-flying people to understand the effects of being away from home, time-zone changes and stress can have on someone. Also the need to sleep during odd times of the day can upset the 'efficient running!' of the hotel".

"Cleaning outside rooms with late pick-ups. Rooms near lifts, stairs or food dispensers, ice machines".

"I don't think they really think about it. I think it is difficult for anybody to fully understand unless they have done the job".

"It's a mixed bag. Sometimes they are excellent, and other times either very inconsiderate with noisy room allocations, or strange requests for new rooms because of noisy neighbours, etc. Sometimes they try to take advantage of the fact we don't have transport and charge over the top prices for shuttle buses, etc. Sometimes we just feel like the poor relations! Usually we are very fortunate in that the hotel staff are very accommodating. Obviously, some of our colleagues perhaps don't enhance our reputation by poor behaviour, which then reflects badly on all of us".

"Often Managers don't realize how long we've been awake when we check in. They don't realise how long we will have to be alert and fit when we leave their hotel. In other words, how valuable even the shortest nap can be for us".

"Some do, but many treat airline crew as a necessary evil – to keep their hotels financially secure during the lean years. They don't understand that their hotels are our homes – we spend twice as much time in a hotel as we do in our own homes. They need to understand that what we have access to in our homes we expect to have access to in the hotel – without paying extra for these things!"

"Managers don't understand the condition of a long-haul crew when they are checking in to a down-route hotel. We are all exhausted and the hotel staff often don't seem to have a clue about this (as evidenced by lengthy check-in procedures, room keys and rooms not ready). When I arrive at the hotel I just want the whole crew to immediately be given envelopes with room keys so we can go and sleep/relax. Often cleaning staff are noisy in the corridors too – we can't expect them to be quiet but often I don't think managers explain to staff how important it is to always assume that somebody could be trying to sleep in a hotel, regardless of the time of day".

28.i. In your experience, do hotel staff (desk clerks, cleaners, etc.) understand the needs of down-route pilots?

Yes:	29.2%	121
No:	70.8%	293

What don't they understand?

"That 'Do Not Disturb' means just that. It doesn't mean, 'OK to Hoover the corridor, slam doors, have loud conversations with your colleagues'".

"Cleaners are not to blame, I think. They're given a job to do, and they do it well. Rooms should be allocated according to check-in/out times. Keep everyone on earlies at one end of a corridor, and people on lates at the other end of a corridor, so the cleaners cleaning the rooms of the people that checked out early do not wake the people that came in late the night before".

"Hotel staff are generally very inexperienced, changed frequently and most of the time unaware of the agreed contractual arrangements for the provision of quality rest facilities".

"Some are quite good, others not so. US hotels are usually the worst offenders".

"British Hotels are the worst for treating pilots very badly, where European hotels are much more helpful (e.g. quiet rooms, crew room, access to Internet, etc.)".

"The majority of any problems, for me, occur in the USA or USA-dominated territories, in that the basic hotel staff do not seem to get much training and/or are not paid enough to make the job matter. Only in the US are DND notices completely ignored, and you wake up to find someone cleaning round your bed".

"Often rooms aren't ready (the last thing you need after 10 hours on duty is to sit in a hotel lobby for 45 minutes). Hotel staff often ignore the need for quiet rooms (given adjoining doors / opposite lifts / by ice machines). Staff often knock on door even though 'Do Not Disturb' sign is on. Cleaning staff and porters often talk loudly in corridors".

"Cleaners can be a bit hit and miss with their noise/timing but, with the best will in the world, a hotel on the west coast of the USA, for example, doesn't march to the beat of my circadian rhythm".

"Cleaners could close doors quietly but instead it takes 5–15 door slams to clean the next-door room. Vacuuming the corridor 2–3 hours after we have arrived to sleep is another favourite. I do not remember ever having any issues with hotel desk clerks".

"Cleaners don't understand that we are often trying to sleep when they are cleaning other rooms and they often shout between rooms and make a lot of noise. Some also try to enter your room even with the 'do not disturb' sign displayed".

"Lower-level hotel staff do not regard airline crews as proper customers and do afford the same level of service or consideration".

"They don't care. Probably a lack of organisation by the housekeeping department/Manager. I have never been asked until what approximate time would I like to have peace and quiet. I'm sure it could be done".

28.j.i. Have you ever asked to be moved to another hotel room?

Yes:	86.0%	356
No:	14.0%	58

28.l. Have you ever gone sick when down-route?

Yes:	35.7%	148
No:	64.3%	266

Why did you report sick, and how did your airline react?

"At 04:30 on both occasions. Once with a fever and another time with an injured back. I called Ops as soon as I was aware I could not operate, and told them I would be able to operate back to base. They then had me replaced at base. No issues with the airline at all".

"Bad tummy. They acted like I was doing it on purpose".

"'Kept show on the road' for 3 sectors during day ... progressively feeling worse with cold symptoms. During last sector descent, ears blocked ... drove infection to sinuses. Initial reaction from Operations was frustration at having to cover my trips, but longer term the Company was very accepting once they realised I was not faking!"

"Appendectomy. Good support from BA".

"At a hotel I felt dizzy and nauseous, so much so that I had to have the paramedics called. Company wanted to keep me out for a couple of days to see how I felt. I wanted, and argued for, and got repatriation. Company was VERY unsympathetic and generally thoughtless".

"Burst appendix, dengue fever, fully supported".

"Had an allergic reaction to something. The airline was amazingly supportive and put no pressure on me to report fit until I was".

"I had a blocked ear. Not much contact from them i.e. I had to do all the leg-work, phoning around arranging appointments, etc., but they did position me home".

"Chest infection, airline was fine about it".

"I'd rather not specify the event as it is remarkably specific but, although home base were grudgingly OK, the local station manager was inconsiderate, rude and unrealistic – he wanted a minor surgery to be carried out on me without a local anaesthesia so I could operate home that night. Needless to say, this did not happen".

"Food poisoning and a cold. Impatience and disbelief from my airline".

"Food poisoning ... the airline reacted well and in accordance with their pre-defined procedure".

"The answer to this question is 'no' but I wanted to put a comment here: There are many times – and this goes for the majority of crew – when you will not go sick so you can get home. I have flown home when I would not have reported for duty if I was at home".

"Food poisoning ... they forget you exist".

"Food poisoning from hotel food. Airline provided time off, but required explanation and proof of illness".

"I was run over in Naples one morning before pick-up. Airline's handling of the incident was awful. Detailed flight crew report submitted about the handling of the incident. No response received. I was emotionally

unable to chase up the report at the time and was later diagnosed with
moderate-to-severe PTSD [post-traumatic stress disorder]".

"Food poisoning. Upset tummy, etc. Part and parcel of night-stopping.
Airline normally asks how sick you are (!) and if you can operate later.
Answer 'no' means mild panic at Crewing".

"I could not clear my ears. The airline were fantastic. Doctor provided,
and passenger tickets back home when fit to dead-head".

"I was coming down with a very bad cold. I offered to bring the aircraft
back to London flying only 1 of the 3 sectors planned. The rostering officer
(clever sod) said if I was fit enough to fly one, I was fit enough to fly three
sectors (that'll teach me). On reflection I agreed with him, and told him
to figure out how to get the aircraft back from Barcelona".

"The answer is actually 'no'. But I wanted to expand: I would be
extremely reluctant to go sick down-route due to the possible reaction
from the company".

29.a.i. Do you have any issues with food when at work?

| Yes: | 74.4% | 322 |
| No: | 25.6% | 111 |

29.a.ii. What are those issues?

No/limited access to food:	107
Lack of variety:	204
Poor-quality food:	298
Cost of meals:	32

31.a. Do you run a business from home?

| Yes: | 3.2% | 14 |
| No: | 96.8% | 419 |

31.b. How many hours do you devote to it in a typical non-flying week?

| Less than 5: | 42.9% | 6 |
| 6–10: | 28.6% | 4 |

11–15:	0.0%	0
16–20:	28.6%	4
21 or more:	0.0%	0

33.a. Would you describe your home as a restful place?

Yes:	81.5%	353
No:	18.5%	80

33.c. Why is it not restful?

"Simply the business of family life with a husband who spends half his time out of the UK".

"There is always something needing to be done, either domestically (cleaning, cooking, shopping, laundry, etc.), organisationally (correspondence, financial, car, doctors, dentists, school, etc.), or socially (children's activities, sport, school, dog-walking, etc.). My wife works, and is unlikely to be accidentally mistaken for Nigella Lawson/Delia Smith or any other 'Domestic Goddess'. (As you may have deduced, she is at work at present and not liable to come and look over my shoulder ...). I do get frustrated that 'jobs' seem to be left for me to cope with on my 'days-off', with the result that if I've been away for several days, there is generally a list of things that need attention – frequently ones which are mundane, but time-consuming (food shopping, gardening, etc.)".

"With a two-and-a-half year old, even though my wife gets up in the night, I still have disturbed rest".

"Pressures of family life. Heavy concentration of home-related duties into available time at home, including marital attention, parenthood, finances, home maintenance, social engagements. My marriage is challenging at times – in no small part due to my being away 65% of the time".

"Young family. Pregnant wife".

"As a mother of two kids and a husband who works full time there are always household chores to be done. They build up when I'm away and never seem to reduce".

"I've got a dog that needs walking twice a day, admin to do, and I'm home just as my partner leaves, but I just crack on and stay awake like a zombie".

"Purely because young children do not understand that they need to be quiet during the day if you need to sleep".

"Children – a lot to do, and with my partner working in a 'more important' (in his opinion) job than mine, complicated arrangements to keep the show on the road. Having said that they do sleep well so are only awake 7am till 7pm".

"Residing with parents following relationship breakup. Lack of own space".

"Inability of young children to consider the needs of others. No matter how many times you tell them, it is like trying to sleep with a herd of elephants rampaging up and down the landing, although earplugs do help somewhat".

"There are two young children around and often awake in the night".

"Always 'stuff' to do, also my partner suffers from mental health difficulties".

"Generally it's O.K., but a small rented flat also has noise issues at times. Most of the other residents work 9 to 5 hours with social events at the weekends. This can make going to bed at 8pm for a 4am alarm call sometimes difficult. Formerly I lived in a detached house and this was never a problem".

34.a. Have you ever failed to get adequate rest at home before report?

Yes:	84.3%	365
No:	15.7%	68

34.b. Why did you fail to get adequate rest?

Family-related stress:	196
Work-related stress:	100
Medical issues:	30
Household noise:	89
Extraneous noise:	85
Visitors:	54
Telephone calls:	84
Household duties (e.g. shopping, collecting children, etc.):	158
Other (please specify):	112

Other:[12]

'Jet lag', that is, body-clock issues
Attempting to sleep when everyone else is up and about
Because report time is when I want to sleep, body-clock time
Body in the wrong time zone. Plus, after a series of longhaul flights with in-flight rest, my body gets used to taking sleep in snatches. Consequently, I can sleep for 3 hours and then wake-up, unable to get back to sleep
Children up in the night/up too early
Circadian rhythms
Clock-watching for early report
Difficult report times i.e. mid-day, hence difficult to get rest due to previous night's sleep
Difficulty sleeping when I know I have to be awake at 4am.
Dealing with ill children in the night
Early report – inability to get to sleep
Early report and not tired leading to a late night and not enough sleep
Early report requiring rest to begin at a very early hour means sleep is difficult
Early reports – I can't just go to sleep early if I'm not tired
Early reports … most flight crews find it difficult to sleep before earlies
Early start, sleep anxiety
Early starts shift body clock. It is impossible to sleep on demand if you are not tired!
First early after a few days off. Lie-in on last day meant difficult to sleep in the evening
General inability to sleep before commencing the 1st early duty
Having to sleep during the day at home in preparation for a night duty is impossible due to your body not used to the change, and noise
Heat
Home renovations
I'm just a poor sleeper
Insomnia caused by jet lag
Insomniac baby
Just life-problems, on occasion, like any normal person
Just too much to do at home to go to bed early before an early start. Mostly due to insufficient days off each month

12   Duplicate entries have been removed.

Just waking up too early before an early report
Light
Nanny not arriving on time
Neighbours
Over-active mind due to all that was going on preventing sleep
Pressure to get sleep, and then not getting it
Regularly having to get up at 2 am for a 6 am report
Report time means sleep is required at peak alertness time, that is, 4–6pm
Reporting for work in the evening, it's impossible to get good rest during day
Sharing household duties with wife, getting kids to bed etc., doesn't enable me to get to bed as early as I'd like prior to an early start
Sometimes just the inability to sleep, or worrying that I will miss the alarm for an early start
Sometimes sleep simply does not come!
Sometimes you cannot force yourself to sleep at strange times of the day
Sometimes you just can't sleep to order at odd times
Sometimes you just cannot force yourself to sleep the night before an early start, if you are not tired. I have had as little as 4 hours rest before, but still reported for duty
Text messages from work waking you up early
Transitions from earlies to lates disrupting body-clock
Trying to 'Nap' before a late report for a night flight
Very early report times. Inability to go to bed very early
With a 1 hr 30 mins journey to and from work, a minimum rest period does not give time for eight hours' sleep

37. Have relationships with work colleagues ever affected your home life?

Yes:	17.8%	77
No:	82.2%	356

In what ways?

"The stress of managing young 'Generation Y' first officers who lack self discipline and find it hard to accept constructive criticism".

"When you have to debrief a crew member for poor performance, it eats into your home life!"

"I was unable to switch off at home due to being summoned to explain myself at work because of a false allegation. Thought I was going to have a black mark against my name for nothing".

"My wife doesn't understand the nature of my relationships with work colleagues".

"Too numerous to mention. As a BALPA Rep, it was 24/7 with members' issues".

"It's a little convoluted as my wife works for the same operator, but recent industrial issues have caused problems with mutual friends of ours".

"I have divorced twice – a factor each time has been a relationship with a work colleague, or someone I have been meeting regularly in another city in another country".

"Stress at work over redundancies and industrial issues have brought stress back into the home".

"One of the captains is a bully (everyone else is great!) and flights with him are a nightmare, especially in the summer. The busier the roster, the moodier he gets".

"Paranoia about down-route affairs".

"I got a bit fed up for a while when I went through a period of continually flying with people who were not natural matches with me personality-wise. Seeing names on your roster that you know are going to be hard work for up to 5 days can play on your mind in the preceding month. Yeah, I know ... it's part of the job and we have to be able to work with everyone. It's still depressing compared to flying with someone who could be your best friend out of work, though".

"A difficult colleague may ruin your day and put you in a bad mood for when you return home".

"A company informal disciplinary action required me to tell my wife about (completely unfounded) sexual harassment allegations made against me".

"Small clashes play large on your mind".

"I believe that the stress incurred with having to deal with cabin crew's current attitude (plus usual home stresses) has caused a mild illness, for which I have seen a GP".

"I was assaulted by a Captain on the flight deck ... It was brushed under the carpet by [my airline] and has caused me a lot of disturbed sleep and stress since".

"Conflict or dissatisfaction with a colleague is a major cause of stress and affects the wind-down".

38. Have relationships with partners/offspring ever affected your work life?

Yes:	40.4%	175
No:	59.6%	258

In what ways?

"Arguments just before leaving the country to go on a long trip. Left to 'stew over it' in a remote hotel thousands of miles from home".

"Concern about how partner is coping, and details about my toddler. So he has phoned with an 'emergency' as soon as I've got to Lyon ... as if I can help. After a while this has improved, but the stress for a Mum leaving her 1 yr old, and for a Dad suddenly being left in charge, is significant. I'm more relaxed now: I just leave my phone on until push-back from LHR, in case they need me".

"A very nasty divorce petitioned on the basis of my unreasonable behaviour – 'unsociable work hours, missing family events, grumpy on the first day back from a trip', etc., were all cited in the divorce papers".

"Being away on a trip when your partner needs your support at home".

"New partners, needing to understand and experience a typical weekly roster of a pilot. They don't always understand why you want to sleep on the sofa at 14:00 while they expect jobs to be done/meals to be prepared, etc., etc., even though you were up at 03:00 and didn't get home till 12:00. They want to go out for meals/drinks at weekends: you go along but can't relax properly since you know you've got to be in bed for 22:00 if you have an early start".

"Being dumped just before a two-week type-rating simulator course in a foreign country!! I found this emotionally very hard. It was hard to keep focused on studying and performing to the required standard. I had to repeat various items of assessment".

"My girlfriend does not like me working days off. She feels we do not spend enough time together due to my job, as it is".

"Times of heightened stress have reduced my 'capacity bucket'".

"I have had a separation with the mother of my child which still causes me pain and stress after four years. I try to put this out of my mind at work and fortunately am able to concentrate and avoid the distraction at work".

"I have found myself distracted during important phases of the flight".

"We have a lot going on at home; I love my wife dearly, but issues with our youngest son throw up a lot of problems that we had never anticipated. I sometimes 'tune out' for a while in the cruise whilst contemplating various care issues for our boy".

"Of course. My wife has early menopause, meaning that we can't have our own child. We are exploring IVF. But that may not work, so that's very stressful".

"Stress over my marriage break-up. My children live with my ex-wife, and live many miles away with a helplessness resulting from their personal problems and an inability to be on-site to help".

"Obviously the answer is 'yes'. Almost divorced (one of the lucky ones so far), young child issues, etc".

"I was distracted when attending work. I knew the company would not take it as a valid excuse. They regularly state that you should call in sick because of all the usual suspects: stress, arguments at home, death in the family, etc. But they practice something different. One Captain recently had his daughter pass away. When he called the company they asked him 'would he be in work the next day?' And he was back in work within a week of the funeral. The company pressures pilots all the time, and everyone ignores it".

"Finding out when down-route that my daughter was being taken to hospital with breathing difficulties while I was in a hotel".

"It's very hard to be away from home for 180 days a year with a young family. My wife suffers from increased stress levels due to my absence, and often that results in arguments when I return home. This, in turn, makes it hard to leave again for my next duty, as I am usually settling in to the family routine by that stage. If I leave home for that next duty without resolving the issues with my family, it plays on my mind at work, and if all is well at home, I long to be there with my family. It's a Catch-22 situation".

"I'm probably quite close to breaking up with my wife".

39.a. Have you ever sought advice/help for a domestic relationship issue?

Yes:	19.9%	86
No:	80.1%	347

39.b. Who did you consult?

Family G.P.:	19
Aviation Medical Examiner:	5
Partner:	14
Offspring:	1
Trusted (non-work) friend:	37
Trusted colleague:	30
Chief Executive Officer:	0
Personnel Director:	0
Operations Director:	0
Chief Pilot:	1
Fleet Manager:	7
Rostering Manager:	1
Crewing Officer:	0
Other *(please specify)*:	43

Other:[13]

Base Manager
Best friend
Cognitive behaviour therapist
Company-sponsored support line
Father
Mother
One of the Help Direct-type numbers
Other family members
Psychologist
Psychotherapist
Relate books
Relate
Relationship/Stress counsellor
Relationship Counsellor
Sister, counsellor

13   Duplicate entries have been removed.

Sister, Crewcare
The Counselling Partnership (Tavistock Institute)
Therapist/Counselor

39.c. When did you seek advice (date), what was the nature of the relationship issue, and what was the outcome?

"2007. Stress of partner not wanting me to go away to work. We discovered it could have been to do with the fact that my wife's mother was cabin crew. She was a single mother and left her daughter for prolonged periods. We think this has caused the problem, as the pattern is repeating itself and she experiences feelings of abandonment. It has helped, but the feeling is still there".

"2007/2010. Ongoing depression in one child".

"Several times in 10 yrs. Last was in 2007 – when my infidelities led to a stressful divorce. I probably should see the counsellor again, longer term, as I regularly feel I live my life just to be a pilot – and I wish I could have a family/maybe children and a life outside of my lonely existence at work".

"A few years ago. Was cheated on. Broke up and got over it!"

"Arguments that were getting bad enough that I was being distorted all the time at work. I have worked hard to get the job I have, and didn't want it to continue. Things calmed down over time, but sometimes still surface".

"2006. Attempted suicide of partner".

"2003, when my Wife and I were having relationship problems after 3 difficult years with ill child who rarely slept – we undertook 'Relate' counselling together which eased problems a little. Moving abroad to Spain a year later seemed to help, as child's health improved".

"2009. The issue was infidelity on my part. We managed to pull through".

"Start of a divorce in 2009. Offered some time off work if required (didn't take it) and a temporary, part-time contract for a year to allow for regular contact with the children".

"Wife's adultery – she refused to attend counselling. Got a divorce".

"In summer 2007 (July) after a move of base to Madrid. Break from partner after 7 years. But got back together after 4 months apart. We are better than ever now".

"December 2008 to July 2009. We were advised to have a trial separation". "Several occasions over the last 15 years, both for marriage guidance and child behavioural issues. These consultations have generally been beneficial". "When I was taking care of my mother, who had Alzheimer's disease. I did this for 3 years".

40.a. Have you ever sought advice/help for a relationship issue with a work colleague?

Yes:	13.2%	57
No:	86.8%	376

40.b. Who did you consult?

Family G.P.:	0
Authorised Medical Examiner:	0
Partner:	17
Offspring:	0
Trusted (non-work) friend:	15
Trusted colleague:	42
Chief Executive Officer:	0
Personnel Director:	0
Operations Director:	0
Chief Pilot:	5
Fleet Manager:	12
Rostering Manager:	0
Crewing Officer:	0
Other *(please specify)*:	6

Other:[14]

BALPA ... the only reliable backing/advice I am likely to get
Base Manager
Friend
Training pilot

---

14   Duplicate entries have been removed.

40.c. When did you seek advice (date), what was the nature of the relationship issue, and what was the outcome?

"1996. A good friend and colleague was turning up for work having been drinking. I didn't know how to deal with this and sought guidance. I confronted my friend and told him what I had observed and therefore what others would notice. I said I was offering him the opportunity to do something himself before that option was taken away from him (by someone else reporting it)".

"2009 was the last occasion and it involved very poor CRM from a colleague. This is not the first, nor will it be the last occasion".

"2007. First Officer with a poor attitude and dreadful CRM skills caused clash of personality which affected professionalism, hence my reporting it. Several meetings with Fleet Captain/HR. First Officer left employment of his own decision during this period. Therefore, disciplinary status was never formally closed".

"2001. Personality clash-difficult colleague. Positive resolution".

"2004. Positioning as crew and denied correct handling by ground staff (who knew they could try it on). Stood my ground ... surprise, surprise, a complaint against me, but handled correctly by me and given excellent support by BALPA. Got the correct outcome ... begrudgingly by management. This has happened twice. Again in 2005".

"An awkward Training Captain and his approach to training. I resolved it through talking with the next Training Captain".

"About 2 months ago. The issue was another colleague being very hard to work with. I simply try and swap duties with people who don't mind flying with the person in question, as the company does not truly understand why people cannot get on sometimes. They never address the issues at the heart of the matter – as it costs money".

"Insubordination, bordering on violence by Cabin Crew member. Managers more concerned with relations with Cabin Crew managers than solving the issue. Total lack of support".

"It was about someone that I had a difficult personality clash with (along with many other people, I might add – this guy was *really* weird, and it wasn't just me that thought so). I asked a senior training captain and union rep whether I could flag up my problem and ask not to fly with the individual ever again. He asked management anonymously on my behalf and the answer was 'No chance'. If I were to raise the issue, then we'd both be hauled in to speak to the fleet manager/chief pilot and have our heads knocked together until we could resolve our differences. Not a good outcome for me since the individual I was concerned about was the sort of person who would wind you up deliberately. He would have said all the right stuff to the management, and then just kept doing the same stuff anyway (but probably worse, just to rub it in). But maybe not, I didn't find out as I decided to keep quiet thereafter and hope I didn't get rostered to fly with him again. We didn't fly together and I ended up on a different fleet soon afterwards, thank goodness. Not good support from management on that one!"

"2008. A particularly obnoxious Captain made accusations concerning my private life to my mother! I asked management to rectify the situation which occurred".

"2005. Flew with a First Officer, who at the end of the flight I was unsure if I'd operate home with! Decided to think about it over the 24 hour slip, and talked to a friend. On the flight home tackled the First Officer over the issues I had with him. The feedback was accepted and he responded".

"2009. Management threatened me with dismissal. I now keep a low profile. Avoid crew down-route. Try not to get involved".

"2007. An unnamed Captain I was about to operate with 'jokingly' hit me across the head with some documents, in front of other work colleagues. However, I was so insulted and angered by his actions I had to walk away to compose myself. I felt like I didn't want to fly with him, but duty-bound I got on with it. I discussed it with my wife at home, and afterwards was glad to have to not reacted at that moment. But I decided that one more transgression like that from that individual and I would confront him. But this never transpired again".

"Unsure of date (several occasions). Flying with a 'prat' in the other seat. Merely to offload and share the problem".

"Last July. Just chewed it over with a colleague, but nothing could be done about it, as said Captain is very popular with management".

41. Some trades unions (BALPA, for example) offer a confidential peer-support system. Have you used this type of service?

Yes:	2.1%	9
No:	97.9%	424

If yes, please describe when you did so (date), the circumstances and outcome(s).

"In 2002 for advice relating to company procedures".

"Was reported by an unhelpful TRM, so was asked mid-rest period whilst airborne to file a written report. Was so incensed the rest period was useless. Got no response from company".

"For spouse; helpful".

"After a sim check. It had gone badly, but although still passing felt I was in trouble. No support or feedback ever came from the company, so felt very lonely. Spoke to BALPA rep who lifted my spirits".

"I used BALPA in 2001 after an argument about a work-related issue which was very upsetting".

"I had an issue with a training captain who was suspected of drinking before work ... He was to operate with me on a 2 sector short-haul trip. A senior manager replaced him at short notice, then spent my 'training' sectors quizzing me over the previous captain! I phoned a BALPA advisor to talk it all through. Very useful indeed, if for nothing other than to clarify your own thoughts on the matter".

"Their advice is regimented and only concerns the legal side of one's options".

"2003: made contact with counsellor at BALPA but continued with Relate".

42. In what ways might peer-support be developed/improved?

"Perhaps it could be better advertised – I had no idea that BALPA's existed!"

"Make it known that it happens more than we think, and that many of our colleagues have used it, and it is not a sign of failure, but a positive way of resolving an issue".

"I have not used it so it is difficult to answer. Having reminders of its availability would be good. I would certainly use BALPA's support rather than company support, which I would not trust".

"More low-key active supporters rather than a small list of the same old names. Discretely identifiable, trained for and trusted by the aviating community".

"Make it more obvious. Make an example of some outcomes (anonymous). I am always reticent to use these systems as I am worried I will be discovered, or that the system is not as confidential as it should be".

"Pilots do not appear to have the same level of peer support as cabin crew, who have a 24hr free helpline number on the station briefing sheet at every night-stop destination. Pilots do not have access to this number, and no alternative is offered by BA for pilots. If a pilot is a BALPA member, s/he might be able to contact BALPA for support, but it is not clear who to contact first, and so the facility is unlikely to be used".

"I am personally not interested. I sort problems out by thinking them through myself and by talking with my wife/family".

"My top-level management need to understand that we are all individuals and have different coping mechanisms with the day-to-day pressures of our job. My employer does provide support, but that only tends to be support once an individual reaches the lowest ebb or highest stress. Counselling on a regular, individual basis might trap any problems".

"Needs to be publicised and accepted more".

"Not really sure as I haven't used one. But I would imagine that a patient listener/empathetic ear is required. I would like to think that anonymous feedback is passed to the company concerned regarding the numbers of people using the service, and common complaints".

"I would rather use people unknown to me".

"The pilots advisory group (PAG) gets very little mention in newsletters, apart from contact details. Need to publicise the facility more, and explain the group's function".

"Online accessibility and text chat, perhaps?"

"I would not wish to raise any personal issue at work, and even work-related issues I would think long and hard about raising. There is too much a feeling of opening a can of worms and making your life more difficult".

"I have no experience of them, but I guess there is a risk of being stig-matised in what is still a reasonably masculine environment".

"I doubt it can be improved. The BALPA PAG is well advertised, and most pilots are always ready to lend a sympathetic ear".

45. Has the profession met your expectations?

Yes:	65.1%	282
No:	34.9%	151

If no, why and in what ways?

"It has mostly met my expectations, but it seems that over the last ten years the terms and conditions and general lifestyle has gone down, and is still on its way down. The new FTL scheme being proposed is one example. Airlines' lobbying to have a more relaxed FTL so they can squeeze even more out of pilots, and their disregard of scientific research by the EU is criminal, and will lead to accidents".

"Largely it has ... up until recently. Every year now the job becomes more arduous and intrusive, and the rewards reduce. I have been forced to request part-time working which I can ill-afford in an attempt to have some semblance of a normal life".

"Because my employer, and every other, seems to be hell-bent on demeaning the status of a Professional Pilot. As our HR department keeps reminding us, we're all equal. They wish to remove parts of our Salary and Benefits package by insisting they are not 'contractual'".

"After many years of military flying, airline flying is very routine, with an almost slavish insistence on using aircraft automatics. 'Safety' is used as the excuse for that. It's not really flying anymore, it's just monitoring".

"Airline senior management look to be more interested in their bonuses than in maintaining a high level of morale and welfare amongst the crew (flight deck and cabin). That, and achieve what is laid down in the business plan. Crews seem to be a necessary evil to modern airlines".

"Having left the RAF, in search of a change, after 19 very happy years, I had high expectations. My desire for greater family stability has been met, but sadly my professional expectations have not. Intense competition and difficult economic conditions have resulted in a huge drive to cut costs. To do this effectively it has been necessary to attack our terms and conditions and devalue our worth. Whereas in my previous job I was proud to serve my country and was well supported, I feel that this job is based on a requirement to buy a resource as cheaply as possible. That does not imply poor management, we have one or two excellent Flight Ops managers, but the reality of commercialism means they will always try to get more from us, for less. This 'race to the bottom' will eventually devalue this profession and all who work within it. My hopes for learning so much from working for a successful company have yet to be realised; it seems that some, but certainly not all, of our manager-colleagues are rewarded for trying to destroy the profession they are supposed to represent".

"I am a very fit and healthy person. I feel that even at this stage in my career I find it hard to maintain the pace of work demanded of me. I exercise down-route and sleep as much as I can. I still feel very tired after a normally long 3/4 sector day".

"1) The attitude of management to pilots is very poor. We are treated as a commodity and afforded no respect whatsoever in my company. 2) There is too much emphasis on the profit motive, to the detriment of safety. 3) Attitude of public to pilots: They see us as pushing buttons. How can they respect pilots when they see fares advertised for £5.99?"

"Generally it is what I expected, except for the relentless focus on cost. Crew are treated as costs and not assets, therefore are not fully appreciated".

"I am just a number. I am not allowed to make a single decision. If I do make a decision, then I am open to concentrated micromanagement-inquiry which is intrusive and demeaning. The company are prescriptive in everything to the extent that knowledge of the small print is of supreme importance, taking priority over flying ability. Experience has been subverted by the requirement to be able to recite lists from manuals. There is not enough interaction with other human beings following the closed-door policy. You are stuck with one person all day long".

"I expected more camaraderie (I feel I have no friends at work and very, very few friends not at work due to the limited and random time-off). I expected to feel more valued by my employer – we work hard to get into this profession, but we are so poorly managed (I have never met a manager since the day I joined) that we do not get any sense of appreciation from the company, or any feeling that we are valued for the wealth of our talents – i.e., we fly the planes when they say – that is a given. They do not realise we can do more, and often do do more – e.g., sorting out cabin crew problems (work or personal), interacting personally with passengers, using a professional yet friendly manner to keep ground staff 'on side' to get the job done at times".

"Given less respect and trust than I was expecting, and continually fighting the company to keep the authority and respect to affect the operation. It is also a constant battle to maintain the lifestyle that has traditionally accompanied the career of an airline pilot".

"I haven't moved on the 777 list for five years now. I have had three weekends off this year (not including leave) and am unlikely to move up the list for at least two or three years. Eight years of working every weekend, and having very little choice in rostering, is not an acceptable way to live".

"Financially ... always jam tomorrow, and now severe pressure on terms and conditions will mean that it is obvious I will never achieve the lifestyle I had hoped for. Satisfaction: there have been many good aspects and great people I have had the pleasure of working with ... But far too much dross with too big an influence on my job status, much of it driven by envy. I have really worked hard at my career and have gained satisfaction in some ways, but overall I feel unfulfilled".

"I love my job, but it is a very archaic industry".

"Hmm. This will be a rant. It's intellectually unstimulating, remarkably boring. It's not peopled, in the main, by the sorts of people I thought would be doing this for a living. On a general level it uses alcohol as a crutch for fatigue/dysfunction. There's a general lack of enlightenment on the part of operators regarding fatigue, work environment, etc. Compared to, say an HGV driver, we seem to be charging headlong into a push for limitless duty durations. We're expected to sit on aeroplanes in summer with no air conditioning as the cockpit temperature screams into the high 30s degree C, and beyond. Any attempt to mitigate/ameliorate is met with veiled hints of disciplinary action from some of the more career-ambitious managers. A shambles of an industry in many ways I feel. I would not, knowing what I know now, go into this career. It's just odd".

"It is not what I thought. I never expected it to be 'about the flying', but I have been surprised at how 'behind the times' the pilot community as a whole is. There is still a huge amount of 'old school-ness' stemming, in my opinion, from the ex-forces pilots. Those that were trained for civilian aviation from the start have a much more open and appropriate view-set. For them it is not about being respected by default, but about being professional and generating respect for their behaviour. The ex-forces pilots seem to think they are entitled to it because of the stripes sitting on their shoulders, again, stemming from their past-times".

"It isn't the pay – generally happy with that (although losing 10% of the full salary for a year for moving base or getting promoted seems unfair and unnecessary to me). It isn't even the overall workload per say – would be happy to work more hours in a year. I think I'm disenchanted with it because of the workload on a daily/weekly basis – earlies take a lot out of you and there doesn't seem to be much thought given to the structuring of the roster pattern to take this into account. I'd be happier to work longer hours on lates and shorter ones on earlies, for instance. Management don't take human factors at all seriously (other than knowing we're a weak link and designing us out of the equation by ensuring automation as much as possible). Therefore my role as a 'pilot'– someone who flies planes – is diminished to the role of systems monitor. By automating the process it is assumed we have an easy role – and due to automation we have fewer accidents – therefore it must be possible to work us harder! What they don't see is us getting a nap during the cruise because we're too tired to stay awake, or us missing calls or getting muddled on procedures where nothing goes wrong or the other guy was there to cover our mistakes. Management do not factor the cost of losing the good-will of the workforce. Before they became so top-down pilots would go out of their way to help them out. Now they do so only because they feel pressured into doing so – the company doesn't care if they lose those pilots in the long-run because they'll get someone else in who is cheaper/more profitable (through the training dept). Not enough consideration is given to training for multiple/concurrent problems (as often happens in real emergencies). Therefore I often think I am ill-prepared to face such problems (although we are prepared very well for linear, singular problems). I feel there is a lack of communication between the pilot and management bodies. Management is top-down and dictates.

We do not have union recognition, and our Employment Representative Committees (ERCs) are seen as mouthpieces for management (some bases do not even seem to have one and a lot of pilots do not know who their representatives are). Due to the imbalance of power, crews (pilot and cabin) have to pretty much take whatever we're given. There is a feeling of 'make the most of it while you can', and 'if you don't like it, leave'. New SOPs are introduced at short notice and are often re-hashed or not relevant to pilots (they are generally issued every Friday before the rosters come out – they are required reading before accessing the roster, therefore a lot of them get discarded as 'noise' just so you can get to the roster)".

46. Would you recommend a career in commercial aviation to your offspring?

Yes:	19.2%	83
Maybe:	38.1%	165
No:	42.7%	185

If No, please explain.

"All the financial liability is now placed firmly with the individual. The total sums involved of approx £100,000 make it a very high risk venture with a variable success and return rate. The job of pilot varies dramatically between employers, as does the remuneration and lifestyle. Unfortunately, there are less and less good employers out there, which means there's a greater risk of ending up having to work for a bad employer to service a stupid amount of debt!"

"It is a rapidly changing job, constant pressure to work harder for longer, with less appealing working conditions".

"Falling income and lifestyle, work-life balance and the lack of a any place (other than a flight-deck) of feeling like you belong after a few years".

"1) Cost of entry to the profession. Around £100-£120k + £30k for university = up to £150k. 2) No guarantee of a job. 3) Pay as you fly. 4) Poor attitude to pilots by management and public".

"Health issues. Shift work and lack of regular sleep, poor diet, dry atmosphere, pressurisation, toxic fume events, cosmic rays, social/marital problems due to shift work. Heavy burden of debt to acquire a licence, salary not reflecting investment, poor lifestyle, responsibility, stress, health issues, risk of incident and loss of social life".

"I think it is an awful industry for young people to try to get into. The costs of training are unbelievable, and the available jobs, when they arise, have utterly dreadful terms, conditions and prospects".

"Absolutely no; VERY long, unsociable, hours, continuous assessment (sometimes not entirely objective), lack of respect from management and a constant bearing down on pay, terms and conditions, whilst the progressive pressure for more and more flying, with less and less rest, is not something I'd recommend to my child (or anyone else). This is a 'mature' industry, run, in the main, by poor managers, producing little profit and with a far from 'secure' career path. I'd recommend becoming an investment manager or a banker(!)".

"It is in a gradual state of decline and managed by short-term bonus-grabbing people".

"There is a downward trend in terms and conditions. Who is going to borrow £120,000 to become a pilot when they can only expect £15,000 per year on a temporary contract? Directors are bonus-driven, and don't care if the airline exists in 5 years time. The contempt shown to the profession by managers says it all".

"I would suggest they earn money elsewhere and fly for fun".

"In the 11 years I've been doing this job, I've seen a large change in the industry. There is a relentless downward pressure on ticket prices which leads to downward pressure on terms and conditions. When I joined I paid for my own licence, but no further. Nowadays it seems to be the norm that people pay for type-ratings and line training as well. I would actively advise anyone not to pursue this as a career, when one would have to spend upwards of £100k to then look forward to a career where you spend 1/2 your time away from home, working shifts in an unhealthy environment (dry air, cosmic radiation). Added to this is pressure from policymakers where we have to contend on a daily basis with the ludicrous and illogical position where the pilot is supposed to be trusted to fly the aeroplane, but is not trusted to come airside without being subjected to the same security regime as passengers. They are now even proposing we be screened by back scatter scanners for no gain whatsoever, apart from enhancing the illusion of security, and at the expense of an increased ionising radiation dose".

"I'm never home; Difficult to have a social life at home. Airlines are becoming bigger and more powerful. Some take advantage of people and if they're worn out / burned out / are too demanding, you get replaced, or get a negative assessment. There's the permanent stress of being at risk of losing your job. Being almost unable to do anything else but fly puts you in difficult position".

"I have two boys and both have no interest in flying. They both have remarked on several occasions that dad's temperament changes after a long flight until he is fully rested. This of course is disturbing for me".

50.a. Please describe your financial circumstances (training costs, debts incurred, etc.) in as much detail as possible.

"Good. Was a BA-sponsored cadet, hence no training debt".

"Total training costs £118,000 (ab initio and two conversion courses). One conversion course of £23,000 paid back by airline over 5 years. Current debt left after repaying for just under 10 years = £62,000. Monthly payments to the bank of £1,050. About 5 years to go".

"Training costs were about £100,000 if you include living costs. This doesn't include the opportunity cost of not working. To be honest, my previous career paid for the training, as well as the house my family lives in. So, compared to most newish pilots, I can't grumble. I arrived with a lot of cash in the bank. To give you some idea, I live in a half-million-pound house, and was earning £22,000 when I bought it!"

"Having come into commercial flying later on, my financial slate was wiped in my 30's due to training costs. Therefore I have a large mortgage! Whilst I maintain a positive balance and a small amount of contingency savings, I have no other wealth. The future is a worry, as we have chosen to put our son into private education, so increased pension costs, lack of pay increase vs. inflation, and the prospect of increased interest rates cause me considerable concern!"

"£10,000 pounds personally, father helped with £40,000 towards ATPL".

"I am fortunate that my parents paid for my flying training. However, I am repaying them (just without the interest that would have occurred if I was financed through a bank). I also have a student loan from university. In total, flying training and university loans totalled £75,000. I have a

£180,000 mortgage, buying a house near to my workplace in the south-east of England is incredibly expensive. In all I pay over £2,000 each month towards flying loans, mortgage and student loan repayments. My wife is American. Her Indefinite Leave to Remain visa application cost £1,095. Needless to say, I rarely have any money left at the end of each month, and I rarely ever get any luxury items. I can barely afford to heat my home".

"I entered via the cadet scheme 10 years ago, so no training costs and little debt. Lucky!"

"Comfortable, but by no means flamboyant. I do not have to worry about any of the basics in life (mortgage/food/heating, etc.) but I drive a 13 year old car, we do not have holidays, and I certainly don't have a boat! I still have a mortgage (taken out for the second, crew-address house) which costs about £1800/month, but that will be paid off in 8 years".

"Ex military helicopter pilot, so it cost me about £18,000 to convert to a civilian fixed-wing licence. I also paid £6,000 to leave a former employer".

"I currently owe around £65,000 for my training. My loan is in Euros, so the 2008 interest rate cut added £500 a month to my payments. As my employer pays me a fairly low wage I have run up around £12,000 in credit card debts since I starting flying. In mid-2010 I renegotiated my training loan, increasing the term from 6 years to 10 years. This has finally enabled me to reach a point where my year 3 FO's salary gives me enough to break even every month".

"DIRE!!!! 4th airline. Been at it for 30 years now so ... pay freeze, pay cut, increased taxes, costs, etc., but we have made it through, my family and I, and we will fight another day!!"

"I finished university with £15,000 debt. Took out a professional studies loan to fund training cost of £30,000. Finished paying them off after 7 years".

"Currently a large mortgage and children at private school. Combine this with a pay cut and loss of personal tax allowance and my disposable income is the lowest it has been in the last 20 years. Presently struggling to pay all the bills".

"I have a mortgage and 2 children in private school. My outgoings are massive and we have no extra funds for luxury items. Our house is rather less substantial than many other professionals of similar standing, but it is comfortable, and in the wider scheme of things we are fortunate. I live in constant fear of a cut in pay because it could end my children's' education at a critical time. I am also frustrated by the constant negative changes to my pension. My benefits are a fraction of those that I expected when I joined, meaning that I will have to work longer for less money in retirement (like many others). I see little opportunity to generate significant wealth but I am hopeful that I will end my career with the prospect of being able to live in some comfort. My situation is a far cry from those of previous captains, but it is also rather better than many of those who will follow me. It seems the 'race to the bottom' is running at full pace".

"I currently owe around £75,000 to the bank for training costs, due to interest and a period of unemployment (causing me to not be able to repay the loan). Salary with sector around £45,000, so comfortably paying back my loan".

"Captain, aged 60, family grown, separated. I am financially sound, though not wealthy after two divorces. My future is secured with a BA pension".

"I trained at Oxford ... I had no money of my own, and they were the only organisation to have a deal with a bank that did not require your parents to put up their house as security. It cost 130,000 Euros by the end of my training ... That includes the cost of a partial on my IR. I found employment in the UK, where I now live and work, although my loan is still in Euros. Because of the exchange rate I still owe more to the bank (in pounds) than I did when I started paying back the loan 5 years ago (at 1,200 Euros a month). I still owe 96,000 Euros, and have 15 of the 20 years left on the loan. I also have a mortgage that is currently £1,100 a month, and some 30,000 Euros debt to my fiancée's parents, which we needed for a deposit. A bleak situation really, considering I am working for one of the poorest paying jet operators in the UK. It causes me a lot of stress, and is certainly not what I expected from the industry".

"Eight years into airline flying, I still have £15,000 of debt. It was very stressful to start with, but manageable now. I spent £70,000 on training, £8,000 on a bond and £5,000 on credit cards for living costs".

51. Do you feel you have enough time and resources to adequately prepare for your duty?

Yes:	71.8%	311
No:	28.2%	122

Please describe the problems you encounter.

"Inadequate I.T. provision at easyJet means that OFPs can take a long time to print out. Added to this is terrible security at my base (LPL) which means that there is even less time to prepare if we are to get to the aircraft at the company's stated time of Off-Blocks minus 35 minutes. The report should be 1:15 before the flight, and not 1:00".

"Officially we have a report time of one hour prior to 'off-blocks'. One hour is not long enough to thoroughly study the paperwork, current weather, the forecasts, the NOTAMs and to brief the cabin crew and each other. I reckon 40 minutes is required for this as a minimum. Then, you need to get to the aircraft from the Crew Room (for me, approx 5 mins). Then you need to get into the aircraft and get set-up – 30 mins max. 75–90 mins should be the legal minimum in my opinion. As an FO, living fairly close to the airport, I'm ALWAYS AT LEAST 15 mins early for my report time. If I arrived on-time, I guarantee we would either depart late OR we would depart on time, but I probably could not tell you what the weather was doing at our destination or alternate".

"A 45-minute report before pushback is not enough, especially for 4 sectors, as there is too much paperwork to wade through. I have frequently missed important notam information. 25-minute turnaround with refuelling supervisor duties is not achievable safely, as it leads to rushed briefing and rushed pre-flight and rushed checklists".

"Our report time is designated as 90 minutes. We are expected to be at the aircraft at ETA-55, or we are questioned as to why we are late. In the 35 minutes we have to walk into the passenger check-in to check in our suitcases. At Gatwick it is then a 10 minute walk to our Crew Room where we have to print out our own paperwork, which takes a good 5 minutes, then brief, leave the Crew Room to pass through the security check-point and then pick up a bus (first come, first served) to the aircraft. Basically, unless you turn up 2 hours before, this is impossible. At Heathrow the system is to check in one's bag, pass security to airside, and walk to the Crew Room (normally about 25 minutes in total). In the Crew Room the flight paperwork is prepared for you, and the aircraft is parked very close, so you do tend to arrive on time, but under-briefed".

"As a new Captain I still spend time at home before a trip preparing for the flight, familiarising myself with the airfields, aircraft defects, etc".

"1-hour report time, 15 mins allocated to flight planning. This is impossible to achieve without reporting early, especially with adverse weather. Most come in early so they don't have to rush planning".

"The down-route briefing times are often too low, especially when the time required to get through airport security and immigration is high. It leads to rushed preparations on tricky departures. But the company (and union?) is reluctant to increase briefing times before a duty".

"Our standard one-hour report becomes eroded by extensive queues for security and difficulties getting to the aircraft. Crew are blamed for delays if they arrive late at the aircraft with no reference to how busy/ tricky/important the briefing stage is".

"Our Crew Room does not have enough briefing space at shift-change times. Printers are regularly not working. We have to get all our briefing materials separately, and this takes time. If we were presented with a one-click pack, then this would give more time for briefing and aircraft preparation".

"I tend to report between half an hour and an hour before official report time, to allow me to 'soak up the atmosphere' (as I call it). Printing off notices, doing the admin that can't be done accessing Crewlink from home. Picking up new manuals, etc., and most importantly, pulling off the paperwork to go through by myself, before the Captain arrives. I feel far better-briefed doing it like this than just once with the Captain rattling through it".

"If I arrived at the on-duty time, the flight would depart late. There are too many associated activities which need to be carried out prior to report".

"Increasingly down-route departures are too rushed/pressurised. Poor briefing facilities (none usually), poor briefing material. Delays due to security and unhelpful station staff. As usual the flight crew usually cope, but we should not be put under such pressure, and again our ability to control and influence is much diminished".

"We report 30 mins after the cabin crew and have to check in our bags first. We often don't meet the crew until we get on board the aircraft".

"Time-pressure with On Time Performance. It can take up to 15 minutes longer to reach your a/c if you are on a remote stand, but all this is not calculated. Every late arrival of crew is recorded and queried. This creates stress because the reason is obvious: not enough reporting time. Increasing this of course increases duty periods and diminishes production. Also: difficulties with checking in/printing paper/very stressful security search! What do you think about crew/captain having to 'undress' before all his passengers? What authority do you have after that? It is all a joke – a company/government game to have control".

"You always get to work early and/or prepare online from home to foresee problems".

52. Are current security measures for flight crew:

Too lax:	0.0%	0
Just right:	4.4%	19
Excessive:	95.6%	414

53. In your opinion has passing through security ever compromised flight safety?

Yes:	76.0%	329
No:	24.0%	104

How?

"Being picked on by security. Taking too long to repack a bag, irritating security man who speaks to the scanner lady who then sees something, then a complete search is required. They are unable to answer my question as to what the issue was ('You have an electric toothbrush'; 'No I don't'), etc. Basically making me angry. Ranting on about it to the Captain makes me a little calmer, but it's not an ideal start to a sector. Also being frankly groped in Copenhagen where the men there were only checking the women (whether or not the gate went off). 'It didn't beep'; 'Well, it's up to our discretion' ... with a smirk".

"Being patronised and humiliated doesn't set you up in the right frame of mind for the day! Being deliberately pissed off 10 minutes before you arrive at the aircraft is not the way to treat people you want to look after the reputation of the airline. Note, it's especially farcical and idiotic at home base – LHR".

"All the time. Worse now than ever. Non-standardised procedures, heavy-handed searches, inability to challenge security staff for fear of being accused of whatever they can dream up. Things are occasionally so bad that I have a pre-rehearsed line which if needed I will state to security staff just before off-loading myself from the flight. That usually gets the attention of their manager and mine, and a resolution is forthcoming. They seem to lack the understanding that I or the contents of my bag are not the threat – any day of the week I could take control of the flight deck and fly the aircraft into any structure of my choice in central London. Instead they obsess about my laptop coming out of its neoprene protective sleeve. Priceless".

"Aggressive behaviour from security staff toward me personally makes it difficult to keep your own blood pressure down. You are then supposed to climb into an aircraft and concentrate on that!"

"At any point onwards from first boarding the aircraft 'with the intention of flight', an emergency situation may arise. If you are still fresh from a run-in with security over toothpaste/contact lens cleaner/whatever, it will adversely affect your performance in what might turn out to be a critical fashion. It is possible that lives might be lost unnecessarily".

"Abusive/confrontational security staff. Searches more akin to a sexual assault. Most of all the total pointless actions required by the security NASP".

"Being told I cannot take my nail clippers onto the aircraft while being allowed an AXE on the flight deck is ludicrous. Being searched EVERY day by a low-skilled and generally poorly-educated individual is a complete farce and can and does wind up even the most relaxed crew!"

"Extremely antagonistic security staff not only to me but to my crew. They tried to take items from me that belonged to my mother who has recently passed away (liquids for testing and one item of 110ml that I had not spotted). They took my contact lens solution because it was 200ml.

I showed them my roster and licence that showed I was away from home from 3 weeks and needed the large bottle. It was very stressful. It's too much to think about the exact contents of your bag all day every day. Sometimes you need things that are bigger than 100ml and you cannot check your bag in because it has fragile things in it. Three times I've been groped whilst being checked. One even asked if she could do a bra search. I said no. She let me through with no further questions. Previous to this a security agent felt under the underwire on my bra. I felt violated and had to take a few minutes to myself under the pretence of going to the bathroom. It still makes me very cross thinking about it".

"Being treated with suspicion and rudely by security staff is never going to help your state of mind when you go to the aircraft! At the end of the day, pilots have to be trusted by the nature of our job. Publicly and proudly taking a bottle of mineral water off us is not going to enhance safety and security one bit. The U.S. now let's us take water through, as in the words of a TSA agent to me last year 'we've gotta trust you guys!'"

"Security caused a big delay. A lot of stress. Crew arrived at a/c late and stressed. Everything was rushed, to try and get out before a monsoon hit".

"By distracting us and making us angry with some of the pettiness that we are subjected to, and then taking so long that we rush our checks and potentially miss something. The UK is the worst in the world for its screening of flight crew. I accept thorough screening, but there are ways and means of doing it. Dare I say that, in general, our American friends make it a less arduous experience and have largely stopped treating us all as the greatest threat to aviation, which is how I often feel in the UK. (More so in the passenger channels)".

"By the intrusive and unnecessary inappropriate touching by a security operative. It was verging on sexual assault".

"Cabin crew questioned whether her solid underarm deodorant counted as a solid (exempt) or a gel (declarable) and was subjected to a humiliating 15-minute check of all her belongings which were tipped out on the counter in a display of petulance by the security officer at Gatwick. She was angry and distracted from her duties for the rest of the day. Another crew were forced to walk all the way back down the other side of an empty room having arrived at the sole search arch there because they had moved the wrong way round a temporary barrier. iPads, phones, belts and shoes are removed and you can be treated like scum at some of the major airports. Manchester won't let you leave to go 'land-side' after a duty unless you are escorted by someone from your own company through security. Difficult at 23:00 when you are the last flight in, and everyone else has gone home and you're on a night-stop. Leaves you feeling frustrated, distracted and occasionally angry".

"Captain not allowed to take mosquito repellent through, even though allowable. She got very stressed and took this anger to the flight deck. We were going to malarial Africa".

"Constant daily unnecessary stress and hassle over minor 'toothpaste' or 'shaving foam' issues, i.e. the ridiculous ban on liquids for flight crew, actually hindering the security effort. Most of us loathe 'security' in all its aspects. Pre-flight distractions are always a problem. I was a Flight Safety Officer (and, ironically, a Security Officer) in the RAF, and studied many well-documented cases of distractions contributing to accidents/incidents. However, UK Security PLC seems totally ignorant of, and uninterested in, these issues. The government is useless. The company does not care, and we are left with a shambles. BALPA seems powerless to achieve any improvement. I would say security is the number one avoidable and unnecessary stressor at work".

"Excessively intimate screening meant I arrived at the aircraft late, and very annoyed. Although the issue was resolved by push-back, it had compromised the set-up of the aircraft".

"Doing it sometimes several times per day on short-haul has a cumulative effect of winding you up with the nonsense of it all, bearing in mind that is doesn't really add anything to the safety and security of the operation. Once a pilot is through security and in control of a guided missile weighing up to 380 Tonnes with up to 120 Tonnes of fuel on board – how would even a radio full of Semtex make me any more dangerous at that point? It can become quite depressing. Finding yourself faced with a particularly rude/stupid security person, when you don't believe in the system anyway, can make you angry to the point of distraction in the cockpit, when your body is trying to purge all the adrenaline released by the fight-or-flight syndrome from when you had been angry 20 minutes earlier".

"I had a very stressful shakedown by security at Manchester which involved abusive, aggressive behaviour, which I ASRd[15] at the time".

"I end up getting stressed, and late into the cockpit, causing things to be missed, and a rushed atmosphere, however hard I try to prevent it from pervading the cockpit. BALPA REALLY need to address this issue, and stop faffing around with letters. Got to do something – PLEASE".

54. Is there anything else you feel strongly about?

"An increase of annual duty hours WILL lead to an accident in the near future".

"900 flying hours per year is a limit, not a target. The law says this. The law is not enforced".

"There is a lack of appropriate status and respect from within the company as a whole. We are reportedly the 2nd most trusted profession in the UK, but we are not treated as such within the company. We go through 2 yrs of training and numerous checks and assessments, versus cabin crew's 2 weeks and yearly SEP. Yet we are repeatedly compared with, and aligned to them".

"Brussels bureaucrats coming up with a FTL scheme heavily influenced by airline management with an eye solely on cost and scant regard to safety, while ignoring previously-used, scientifically researched FTL schemes".

"Crew food is terrible. Our bottled water is so cheap it smells, and the company will not take notice of anything. Our food bags with sandwich and salad costs the company £4.75 per person. Go and try to buy a sandwich, salad, chocolate bar, cheese portion and crisps for £4.75. Now you might realise how poor the quality is".

"Automation levels. Over-reliance on automation and the dumbing-down of manuals and modern check lists".

"BALPA – take a proper, firm and resolute line on security. BALPA – take a proper, firm line on Pay to Fly schemes. BALPA – take a proper,

15   Filed an Air Safety Report.

firm line on EU FTLs. BALPA – please grow some cojones [testicles] about the more distasteful issues in the industry! PLEASE".

"Fundamentally, aviation is a dangerous business that is only made safe by the professionalism of those who really care. Whereas a control of costs is necessary for success, the pendulum has swung way too far in favour of reducing costs and away from maintaining safety. Huge debts for training, and increasing duty hours, are just two examples of the damage of excessive cost-cutting".

"The attitude of passengers to the whole process. Drinking their own alcohol on board and flying when obviously medically unfit to do so. Aggression (bullying) shown to staff who are doing their job to the best of their ability. I often allow the cabin crew to sit in the flight deck and offload frustrations and chill before facing the passengers again. There ought to be some sort of education program for the general public. *Airline*, etc., merely shows conflict because it is good television. It is not. I believe it can cause problems in the air if the general public believe that what is shown is the right way to act on board. Security overseas is a joke. All the agents want to do is to get the passengers on the aircraft so that they become our problem".

"The bottom line is if the airline could fly us twice as much, for half the pay, they would. That's why union solidarity is so important".

"The fatigue issue is the 'elephant in the room' for the public. Nobody wants to think about it and admit the drawbacks of pilots up all night trying to land aeroplanes. They come close with studies showing performance degradation with disrupted sleep. Even a T.V. show talking about the effect on cabin crew(!) of being awake all night! Perhaps they don't think we're also human? Complacency will lead to longer hours. Accidents will occur due to fatigue. But the focus will be on the error made, not the context. Degraded performance is caused in part by fatigue".

"The excessively hostile attitude of the British Government towards aviation. The UK aviation industry is being sacrificed to placate the Green movement, while our European competitors steal our business, causing increased carbon emissions to boot".

"Body scanners!!! Please do something about this. I am not happy with BALPA's response that they are not a health risk, because many countries, other unions and medical professionals say they are ... or could be. I do not want to die of cancer, or just get cancer because of some useless scanner. Why do we do security clearances if they still insist on treating us like criminals?"

"European FTLs. Some operators will bully crews to go to the limits. To remain competitive other carriers will follow suit. We have strict alcohol limits which are fair. I've never made a mistake due to being impaired through alcohol consumption. But I've made many mistakes due to tiredness. Ironically it's when you are tired that it's so difficult to recognise the symptoms".

"Fatigue is not a phenomenon that is well understood by the majority of people. Indeed, it is only since starting my job as an airline pilot that I have learnt to recognise fatigue and its effects. Politicians and voters will share this (completely understandable) ignorance, which is why I am pessimistic about fatigue being taken seriously whilst reassessing flight time limitations in Europe".

"European FTL proposals are disgraceful as they are not based on biological studies or facts and are a blatant example of commercial lobbying. I don't think the travelling public have realised yet that they might be a passenger on a flight where the most fatigued person on the aircraft is the Captain. A sobering thought!"

"Fatigue over time is a real problem particularly in Long Haul when rosters can have you flying across many time zones, with only a 'scientific' view of sleep patterns. It is not possible for all pilots to sleep the same. Some will have more difficulty with particular patterns than others. This builds up over time leaving the individual exhausted mentally, but not physically. I often live in what feels like a 'fuzzy bubble'. Flight Deck security needs reviewing – there is no justification for banning my family from the flight deck during flight. I have been scrutinized enough not to be stupid enough to let a terrorist in there. I know my family members well enough not to doubt them. The government should not insult us, or them, by thinking we are that stupid".

"The authority of the commander in British Airways is constantly being eroded. However, the responsibility and accountability is remaining. All three must be kept in balance".

"Flight time limitations in their present form were implemented in a different commercial operating environment. Multi-sector shorthaul operations to maximum hours are now the target, and the norm. This is very tiring and fatiguing. It seems that when FTLs were introduced, shorthaul flightcrew would be unlikely to get to 900 hours on a regular basis. Unfortunately, for many pilots this happens year in, year out, leading many to just about operate within safe boundaries. No increase to the present scheme must be accepted. To do so would risk the lives of pilots, crew and passengers alike".

"Industry mortality rates will go up if companies seek to explore the limits of the amount of flying a pilot can do. I feel the company knows the cost of everything, but the value of 'not a lot'".

"There appears to be an erosion of professionalism within the industry, mainly from Captains concerned about commercial issues. Rushing around to meet OTP targets, and taking no fuel to save a little here and there. The Captain needs to be the restraining bastion of safety. Maybe it is because they fear underhand disciplinary action, demotion, criticism or simply that they are not 'compliant' individuals. I flew with one Captain who commented: 'Ours is not to reason why, ours is to do or die'. As a Public Transport Licence holder and so-called professional, he couldn't have been more wrong. It is entirely his position to reason why! Especially with ill thought-out commercial targets. I feel this attitude reflects the current state of the industry".

"The European political-messing in the science of fatigue!!! What happened to the European Working Time Directive? Bring on the crashes! The Buffalo air crash in America is an important lesson for us all. Wake up public, this is your life at stake. If you want to fly for a £20 fare, somebody pays for it!!"[16]

---

16 The retired CEO of American Airlines, Bob Crandall, has argued for the partial re-regulation of the industry (Crandall, 2008). Crandall's interventionist view is challenged by free-marketeers like Professor Steven Morrison: "[A]irline competition is working in the sense that those carriers that enhance traveller welfare are rewarded with higher profits. This is an important finding because it indicates that policymakers should not intervene in the competitive process" (Morrison and Winston, 2005).

Interview Responses

Notes

While the intention was to conduct up to 100 face-to-face semi-structured interviews, fewer than a dozen were conducted due to the volume of data generated by the web-based questionnaire and the SLOGs. The shortest interview lasted 90 minutes and the longest 150 minutes. Responses were recorded on a digital recorder (by the author). The answers were transcribed verbatim (by the author). The interviews were conducted at the University of Leicester, as this was felt to provide a more relaxed and controllable setting (the author's experience of conducting interviews in the field is mixed – interviews can be interrupted, the recording can be contaminated by extraneous noise, the interviewee may feel s/he is being 'watched' by colleagues/superiors, etc.). A representative sample of responses is reproduced below.

1 Motivation

1.1 Why did you become a pilot?

"I was born and brought up on the east coast of Lincolnshire. We had military aircraft flying over our garden, in those days. I could see all the Bloodhound SAM sites. So every time I opened my curtains in the morning I'd see the military. I didn't think my psyche was suited to a regimented lifestyle, however. I first sat in an aircraft when I was about five years old. My parents bought me a trial lesson for my sixteenth birthday. From that point the fascination just grew" (Captain, medium/long-haul charter).

"I remember at age nine reading about and drawing aircraft all the time. I didn't think I'd ever become a pilot. I didn't know what I wanted to do, but I was interested in aircraft. I joined the ATC at thirteen. I decided that I wanted to become a pilot. I tried to pursue a scholarship through the RAF but was knocked back on eyesight grounds. They predicted exactly what my eyesight would become by age 21. They suggested I try the civilian route, which I had not thought about. I dropped out of A-levels, got a job and paid for flying lessons." How did your parents react to your dropping out of A-levels? "It wasn't unexpected because my O-levels were all geared towards joining the RAF. I worked hard to achieve the necessary grades to get the best possible chance of getting a scholarship. My parents have been very supportive throughout" (Turboprop Training Captain, regional carrier).

"I wasn't particularly academic. I was more interested in doing what I wanted to do. I left school and did an apprenticeship in development engineering with Honda U.K. My primary interest was engineering. I'd always been interested in how and why aeroplanes flew. Things like how the landing gear worked interested me. I was brought up on a farm working with agricultural machinery, so engineering seemed the obvious direction. Working for Honda paid for my PPL. I don't get on with things that are boring. The flying bug bit me when I was doing my PPL. It's always different. I like the fact that I get to see the sun. Even though I'm at work at three in the morning, I like the fact that my days off are predominantly in the week, so I can avoid the crowds at the weekend. I like being different. I don't like following the crowds. I fly little aeroplanes outside of work, gliders. I have a love of flying" (A319 Senior First Officer, low-cost carrier).

1.2 What is the best thing about being a commercial pilot?

"The best thing is the flying. It is still quite fun. There is a certain amount of variety. Although we go to the same airfields time and time again, the weather is always different and there are always different problems. At the end of the day you leave work and you don't take too many problems home with you" (A319 Captain, low-cost carrier).

"I like the machines. I find them technically very interesting. The theory of flight fascinates me. It is still nice to get up in the morning to go and operate one of those machines. I've never lost that interest. Even if I am having a bad time I can re-sight myself and think, 'actually, this is good'" (Turboprop Training Captain, regional carrier).

"Someone paying you to fly. The satisfaction from completing the job" (Helicopter Captain, business charter).

1.3 What is the worst thing about being a commercial pilot?

"It has changed over the years. I can't use the word 'fatigue' because I am told by the company I can't. It is just a tiring job. It does grind you down." Can you discuss some of the symptoms of being ground-down? "What did it for me was the fact that I had to commute for quite a long time. At one stage I was driving two hundred miles a day, for probably two years. That, together with flying a full-time roster, doing line-training, was really shattering. I used to be pretty fit. But I seemed to hit this level where I was absolutely exhausted. Recovering from that has been extremely difficult, to the point where I ask 'Have I actually recovered from it?' There's a kind of underlying base tiredness. If I have time away, yes I recover. But what does it take to get me back to that base-level of tiredness again? Not that much. A full roster, and I'm there. I'm tired all the time. Which I don't enjoy. I also feel that I'm slightly trapped in the lifestyle. How do I get out of this? Exercise. If I try to exercise outside of work then the family gets in the way a little bit. I'm duty-bound there. The older I get the more difficult it is to sleep." Did you ever take temporary accommodation near your base? "Yes. I was a lodger for over six months, because I was so tired. When I was driving along I was thinking 'surely, statistically, I am going to have an accident. I am putting so many miles in and I am tired. But then I was away from home. I thought, you know, 'for the sake of a 100-minute journey I could be at home doing the jobs that I need to be doing, in my own house'. I ended up only using the lodging for early starts, really, not having to get up at 02:30 to drive down for an early start" (Turboprop Training Captain, regional carrier).

"The management attitude. They treat us as hired hands, to be paid as little as possible. A lack of respect from management. I find some the management culture is very harsh. In my previous airline [a charter airline] there was an expectation that one would go into discretion, and if you did not go into discretion there would be an interview. My present airline [a low-cost carrier] is much better. I find the public's perception a little irritating. They think we have an easy time. That we just press buttons. They don't realise how difficult and stressful the job can be. They don't understand. I doubt they ever will understand. The travelling public don't really care about the flying or the safety, so long as they get a cheap flight. As long as they get their cheap flight they don't mind what goes on on the flight deck, whether we get holidays with our family, or not." Why do you think the public so misunderstands aviation? "People like O'Leary, saying we only work eighteen hours per week flying duty, or whatever it works out as, does not help. The public still has this perception of pilots from the 1960s, 1970s, the Golden Era of aviation, when pilots were paid extremely well, they are still paid fairly well, but in comparison to other professions not as well as they used to be. There were times when pilots probably worked half as hard as they do now. I think that perception persists. I think the public would be surprised at how much pilots have to pay for their training. We need to let the public know" (A319 Captain, low-cost carrier).

1.4 What would you change about your current job?

"It's not a bad job. It could be the best job in the world, you know. We have a fixed roster. Our pay is fairly good. But it is little things, like them trying to get rid of the tea and coffee, despite the fact that they make a decent profit." (A319 Captain, low-cost carrier).

"I would change the constant shift between day and night patterns ... It's a commercially-driven change to maximise crew duty hours. I would stabilise the patterns of hours" (Captain, medium/long-haul charter).

"The big issue for me at the moment is finishing on a late duty, and starting on an early. It is very difficult in a family home to get appropriate rest prior to earlies ... because the rest of the house is up until 23:00, or 24:00. And so am I, if I'm honest, because I have things to do. Then the alarm goes off at 04:30, and away you go. If you do that four times in the week, you are shattered by the end of the week. You never actually fully recover. There are five of us in the house. Different age groups wanting different things" (Turboprop Training Captain, regional carrier).

"I'd like to fly more ... Two days ago [February 8] I flew for the first time since early December. You lose some of your skills, I feel. In the Police I used to fly between 250–300 hours per year. That's a good number" (Helicopter Captain, business charter).

1.5 What would you change about the industry?

"The industry is very safe at the moment. But the pressures are there. Safety could be secondary to commercial priorities. I think the commercial priorities are too strong in the industry. There have been a few near-misses, certainly in my airline" (A319 Captain, low-cost carrier).

"The ability to achieve proper rest when you need it" (Captain, medium/long-haul charter).

"I'd like the guy at the top to listen a bit more to the people at the bottom. Things seem to get stuck in the middle. Having done a little bit of middle management it's not the easiest place to be because you get squashed from both sides. I'd like a bit more common sense. A lot of the business decisions made at the top don't seem to be sensibly implemented at the bottom. We need more forethought. We need to plan ahead. As an industry we seem to spend our time firefighting ... By listening to people at the bottom they might short-circuit problems ... The pilot psyche is that of a problem-solver. That's why we get frustrated when we don't see problems getting solved. We get frustrated when people don't listen to us" (Helicopter Captain, business charter).

2 Work experiences

2.1 What is the best thing that has happened to you at work?

"The confidence from being told that I am now fit to be the commander of a heavy transport aeroplane. To get the four bars was something that stood out. The day that you are entrusted to do that job is the most important thing" (Captain, medium/long-haul charter).

"Flying fighters was probably the best thing. Intercepting Russian aircraft was probably the best thing" (A319 Captain, low-cost carrier).

"Probably flying for the Police and getting a good result. If you do a pursuit, you are working hard, you are using all your flying skills, and also there is a tangible result if somebody gets caught. And working with good colleagues makes a difference" (Helicopter Captain, business charter).

2.2 What is the worst thing that has happened to you at work?

"Potentially being made redundant because of a medical restriction" (Helicopter Captain, business charter).

"When you come face-to-face with the management attitude I described earlier. You give a lot then you are met with a 'take it or leave it' attitude" (Turboprop Training Captain, regional carrier).

"When I told my company I was not going to fly because I felt stressed. I know I am not alone. I understand from an authorised medical examiner at Gatwick that thirty pilots [at a U.K.-registered low-cost carrier] have been taken off flying because of stress this Summer alone. I think it is a very poor state of affairs when so many pilots are getting fatigued and stressed. It is not conducive to flight safety. Stress is something people may not wish to talk about for fear of jeopardising their career. I think the incidence of stress is possibly under-reported. There are a lot of very stressed pilots out there, some of whom get to breaking point, some of whom are at breaking point and don't say anything. I think that is quite prevalent in the industry" (A319 Captain, low-cost carrier).

2.3 How just is your airline's culture?

"Very good, certainly on the safety side. The head of safety takes a very good approach. He appears at every annual refresher training course and has a little chat. He goes through the recent incidents. He tries to reassure people that he's there for safety assurance. It's not about policing SOPs. He has an unemotional approach, which is the right slant. There is quite a good reporting culture. We do put our hands up. There is very little cover-up. With Crewing and Rostering it's hard-nosed business. There's a certain amount of 'If they can, they will'. So the FTL limits become a target when times are tough, so that gets a bit frustrating" (Turboprop First Officer, regional carrier).

"We have two cultures in our airline. The airline management understands flight safety. They do their best to look after the crew. However, I feel their best efforts are at times undermined by the wider Group culture ... Group don't feel that pilots should be a separate group. They stick us in the same boat as cabin crew, which is a transient workforce, with travel agents, with holiday reps. We are in it for the long-term. We are a career-based profession. I have been flying for twenty-odd years and I have no intention of leaving until retirement age, or until I can afford to retire" (Captain, medium/long-haul charter).

"They are quite just. They have this 'just-but-fair' policy. If you do a reasonable job at work and you are open and honest and you report correctly then the just culture will stand up for you, but if you decide to be non-standard consistently then you are leaving yourself open" (Turboprop Training Captain, regional carrier).

2.4 Have you ever not reported sick or fatigued for fear of victimisation?

"Yes. In my previous airline, a charter airline. You would not want to be seen going sick too often because it would affect your career. I probably went to work sick more often then than I do now. My current airline is actually quite good. I have never had any comeback, despite having been sick quite a lot recently" (A319 Captain, low-cost carrier).

"Yes, pretty frequently. On these runs of five earlies, particularly on days four and five you are absolutely buggered. But because it happens all the time you get used to the fact that that is how you feel. So you turn up anyway. If you don't you get snotty e-mails. You get pulled into the office. People get disciplined for being off sick. They have even started saying that people use 'fatigue' far too often. So one of the few things we can say without being questioned is now being question because they think we say it too often. In the last three or four years I have only been off for two days" (A319 Senior First Officer, low-cost carrier).

"I have gone to work knowing I should not have done. Anyone who states something different is probably lying. I have never used the word 'fatigued' when I have reported in. However, I am pretty sure that fatigue has caused other illnesses. When you are so tired at work, so run down you get common colds that last for a month. I have never felt pressure from the company to have to go to work fatigued or sick. However, we do face peer-pressure. I know that if I don't turn up for work it is going to screw someone else's day up. We are probably our own worse enemies in that regard. We look after our own, without looking after ourselves. I'd find it difficult to believe that a manager would say to me 'You have got to come in to work today. I know you are unfit, but you have to turn up, otherwise you are on a disciplinary'. I don't think that would happen. I am in a fortunate position being a union representative. I know where I stand. There are, however, some who won't stand up for themselves. New first officers looking for a contract. Temping pilots looking for a contract. They are only working over the Summer and have no job for the Winter. They are more likely to accept anything the company says. They will turn up for work when they are clearly unfit to do so. I have turned crew away before when they are clearly unfit to work" (Captain, medium/long-haul charter).

2.5 How would you describe the management style at your airline?

"All the pilot managers have never been managers themselves. They have all come from the line. It comes down to their individual quirks. Generally they are open. They are quite accommodating to reasons and suggestions. Other than this attitude 'This is the company line – take it or leave', they are quite open guys" (Turboprop Training Captain, regional carrier).

"I don't think there's a great deal of animosity between the pilots and their immediate managers. But I think the airline is undermined by the wider group strategy. There is a massive disconnect between the pilot workforce and the group management. They offer the carrot. While you are looking at the carrot they whack you on the back of the head with a very big stick. Concessionary travel has just been removed pretty much for all of one part of the company. That is very divisive amongst the workforce. The airline management's hands are tied. They don't have the authority within the group to be able to change things" (Captain, medium/long-haul charter).

2.6 How would you describe the current FTL (CAP371)?

"In comparison to some of those in Europe it is very good. The problems come when airlines use CAP371 as a target. You can work to the rules and still be very, very fatigued. Airlines are now working you right up to the very limit of the rules. My airline is quite good. If I say I am fatigued, they won't question it. Not all airlines are like that. They say if it's legal, you have to come to work, despite being fatigued. There was no system for reporting fatigue at my previous airline. It was either report sick, or go to work" (A319 Captain, low-cost carrier).

"I think it's good. You feel the fatigue when you get near the limits. On the North Sea I was flying 800 hours per year. You certainly know when that's been going on for a reasonable period of time. You feel the fatigue. If the rolling total is at 800 hours then you know you are going to make mistakes. CAP371 is a fairly decent bit of legislation" (Helicopter Captain, business charter).

"After doing five days of earlies at my low-cost airline you don't know your own name. Currently I do about 700 hours each year. Because I have no control, I tend to get buggered about a bit, which is why my body clock is all over the place" (Senior First Officer, full-service long-haul carrier).

3 Commuting

3.1 How do you commute to your base?

"I live 130 miles away from my main place of work, so I go down there [Surrey] for five days at a time. I drive down. I drive the six miles to/from base. I stay at my mother's house" (A319 Captain, low-cost carrier).

"I drive. It's about 90 minutes to LGW and about 75 minutes to LHR. I could not fly short-haul for the company because I'd have to drive there and back each day" (Senior First Officer, full-service long-haul carrier).

"I have no option but to drive. I commute from Derbyshire over the Peak District. A and B roads, snow, fog, thick and thin. Public transport is not an option. I can't do it given when we start and end duties. The cost is not insignificant. Because of the weather conditions in the Winter I have to drive a 4x4. There is no other safe option of getting to and from work. My commute time is one hour ten or one hour fifteen. The traffic is heavy because of the quarries. A lot of slow-moving lorries" (Captain, medium/long-haul charter).

3.2 How long does the journey take?

"It takes between 60 and 90 minutes" (Helicopter Captain, business charter).

"It takes 30–35 minutes, but I allow one hour" (Turboprop Training Captain, regional carrier).

3.3 Has traffic ever caused you to be late for Report?

"Yes. Between 10 and 30 minutes. Fortunately because at the moment I am flying two-crew, one of us will be there on time" (Helicopter Captain, business charter).

"A few times. But I have a good feel for the traffic conditions, and I have an alternative back-road route" (Turboprop Training Captain, regional carrier).

"Yes. But this was when I was called out. I allow a lot more time than I need" (Senior First Officer, full-service long-haul carrier).

3.4 Do you drive or motorcycle when fatigued?

"I have driven when I am fatigued. I had concerns, but you are so tired you don't care. That's the problem with fatigue. You get so tired you don't think straight. That is true when you are flying the aircraft as well. I know people who have written their cars off. With my recent posting if they ask me to go into discretion on my last day I refuse to do it, because I don't want to wipe myself out. I have become more careful. My life is more important than my job" (A319 Captain, low-cost carrier).

"Yes." Have you ever regretted doing that? "I've never had an incident to make me regret it. Afterwards, in hindsight, you probably think 'That wasn't the wisest thing I could have done'. You weren't the sharpest you could have been" (Helicopter Captain, business charter).

"I used to do. I once pulled into a service station and before I had turned the engine off I had fallen asleep. That was the worst experience I have had recently. I woke up with the radio blaring and the engine still running. I had had two days away from flying. I'd been on recurrent training. Normal office hours, but if anything it makes you more tired. It's 180 miles from my home to the training base" (Turboprop Training Captain, regional carrier).

"All the time. There is no way to avoid driving whilst fatigued. I don't think there is any pilot out there who could say they are alert when they are driving home from a long duty. I don't think you really recover from fatigue in the short term. It takes a significant period away from work to be able to recover from it. We are tired every day. We work. We are driving home tired. Even flying a couple of sectors during an eight or nine-hour duty you are still away from home 13–14 hours. I challenge anybody to say they are not driving home while feeling tired ... I have had plenty of near-misses. Driving down rumble-strips. Thinking 'I can't remember getting on to this motorway' ... You will drive home and think 'I can't remember the last twenty minutes of my journey'." Does that ever concern you? "Yes, a lot." Why? "Because I feel pressured into getting home. I'd rather be at home in my own bed than in a noisy airport hotel ... my wife works in the airline industry ... ships that pass in the night ... you feel pressured to spend as much time at home as you can" (Captain, medium/long-haul charter).

4 Support

4.1 Does your partner understand your work?

"She does because she is aircrew herself. She works part-time for a different airline. She does understand" (Turboprop Training Captain, regional carrier).
　　"I think so" (A319 Captain, low-cost carrier).
　　"Yes. It frustrates her, but she understands it" (Helicopter Captain, business charter).

4.2 Does your partner support your career choice?

"It is something I have to do to earn the money. I can't go anywhere else" (A319 Captain, low-cost carrier).
　　"Yes" (Helicopter Captain, business charter).

4.3 Do your offspring understand your work?

"I think they do, which is probably why none of them want to go into aviation. They saw what my previous airline was like. They saw the e-mails I was writing. They could hear the conversations that went on with other pilots. I don't think there was any need to discuss career choice with them. They realised that aviation can be quite a harsh world" (A319 Captain, low-cost carrier).

"No." Are they interested? "They are not interested. Part of it is to do with me saying 'Can you be quiet because I need to get some sleep'. They react to that. I think it's down to the pilot's job being misunderstood. Sitting around all day, and having people look after you ... how can that possibly be tiring?" (Turboprop Training Captain, regional carrier).

4.4 Do your offspring support your career choice?

"My conditions are better than in my previous job. I was doing a lot of night-flying. Going away" (A319 Captain, low-cost carrier).

4.5 How well supported are you by your Fleet Manager/Chief Pilot?

"My Base Captain is quite good, but he has his hands tied. There is only so much he can do. They don't really care very much. They know they have to obey the law. They don't really care if they close a base and move your family around. They don't necessarily support you if they have to move you around. They don't necessarily give you the full costs of relocation. One good thing about them is if you say you are not fit to fly they say 'don't fly'. That is one good thing about them." When you moved base what support did you receive? "I received limited financial support. I would have ended up considerably out of pocket if I had moved house. It wasn't the financial problem, it was the fact that I have a family, I have friends. I have a son who has just done his GCSEs, so moving was not an option. So now I am faced with the stress of commuting, of being away from my family. Whatever they gave me in terms of money would not compensate me for being away from my family. It seems that airlines are quite keen to close bases at the end of one season and open a base at the start of the next season, and just keep moving the pilots around. That is the model that they would like to adopt. They forget, actually, that there are human beings there with families and friends. They don't understand that we can't just move at the drop of a hat. But that is what they would like to do at minimum cost. I end up out of pocket, which does seem unfair." Do you think that working away from home has affected you in any way? "It has affected me. It has affected my family. I don't like finding out what my son's subject choices are when it's too late, because I have not had any chance to discuss his career. Being away from home is definitely stressful. I am away more than I am at home. When I do come home there are jobs to do. By the time I've done those jobs it's time to return to work. So there is no time to relax. I know I am not unique. Having spoken to pilots in my situation they feel the same. They feel there is no time off ... no time to relax. It's busy, busy, busy all the time. There is a feeling that you are wasting your life being away from home. It is a stress on the family, but more so on the pilot. I think there is a great deal of stress on the pilot who commutes. I have spoken to quite a few who have taken time off due to stress. My last flight was with someone who has a wife in Canada, so he is trying to commute to Canada" (A319 Captain, low-cost carrier).

"Our flight crew managers are non-pilots. Our immediate management are pretty much message-men. They receive our comments, complaints, recommendations. They deal with queries pretty well, really. Anything more complicated they will pass up the line" (Captain, medium/long-haul charter).

4.6 Do you feel able to confide in your partner?

"Yes" (Helicopter Captain, business charter).

4.7 Do you feel able to confide in your flight-deck colleagues?

"Some of them, yes. The more you confide the more you find out how difficult their lives are. It's something we keep a little bit quiet about. But if you mention it to somebody the dam gates burst open" (A319 Captain, low-cost carrier).

"Yes. A lot of people confide in me. I feel able to confide in them. It's quite a special relationship, really, because you work so closely together" (Turboprop Training Captain, regional carrier).

4.8 Do you feel able to confide in your managers?

"I'd be a bit more wary about that. They can help to a certain extent, but their hands are tied because they only have so many pilots, and there aren't enough of them" (A319 Captain, low-cost carrier).

"I don't, no, because of the line they take. When they've got their pilot's hats on, the guys are fine, but when they've got their manager's hats on, no" (Turboprop Training Captain, regional carrier).

4.9 Do you feel able to confide in your Aviation Medical Examiner?

"I'd be a little wary because he has the capacity to take my flying licence away. So when I reported sick for stress I actually went to my G.P." (A319 Captain, low-cost carrier).

"My present one, I guess so. I'm a little scarred by the aviation medical side at the moment. Because our livelihood depends so much on our medical, you are very loathe to bring anything up that isn't really necessary. If I were to have a minor health issue I was unsure about, I would much rather go and confide in my G.P. first, to see what happens, then take it to my AME, rather than the other way around … because the AME has a duty of care to do things immediately if they hear something" (Helicopter Captain, business charter).

4.10 Do you feel able to confide in your General Practitioner?

"Yes" (Helicopter Captain, business charter).

"I probably could, but I have never done it" (Turboprop Training Captain, regional carrier).

5 Training

5.1 How could the current simulator check be improved?

"At my airline we are doing quite realistic scenarios. We get an easy problem, a medium problem and a difficult problem. You might simulate a flight from LGW to AMS, something quite short" (A319 Captain, low-cost carrier).

"I think we are going down the right road. We are covering the basics. We do some in a LOFT environment, which is great. We have taken on board the latest behavioural markers, which is good" (Turboprop Training Captain, regional carrier).

5.2 How could the quality of cadet pilots be improved?

"The quality is very good. They are very bright. The majority are easy to get on with. Trouble is, they have absolutely no experience. They've done very little light aircraft flying. Their experience in anything other than fairly benign conditions is negligible. I have had them struggling with cross-winds of two or three knots. Which is a bit shocking. If you get a horrible, dirty day there is no way they could cope safely. Everything else is generally very good. They know their procedures. They can fly an ILS, a VOR non-precision approach in text-book fashion ... but when it comes to the handling of the aircraft they actually know very little. You have to be on your toes all the time. I think we could improve the situation by employing cadets who go from training to flying a turboprop. They should get 2,000 hours on a turboprop where they can learn handling skills in a slower, lighter aircraft" (A319 Captain, low-cost carrier).

"I think the cadets we take are of a very high calibre. I am still reserved as to whether they have enough underlying experience should things happen" (Turboprop Training Captain, regional carrier).

6 Future of the profession and industry

6.1 Would you encourage your offspring to become a commercial pilot?

"I wouldn't encourage them, but I'd let them make their own decision" (A319 Captain, low-cost carrier).

"Definitely not. It's all down to the lifestyle, which has been taken away. I would not want them to feel they are existing, in the same way that I am existing. I don't feel it's much of a life at the moment outside of work. There is no time for a social life. There is no time for proper rest. If you are a single guy, and you have your own place, and you can sleep when you want to sleep, do what you want to do, then maybe it is still a reasonable job, lifestyle-wise, but I think for anyone else, no. I would definitely tell my children not to do it, unless it was all they ever wanted to do." Do you ever see a time when you will choose to move to another career? "Yes, I am looking at it now, actually. I'm not sure what I would do. Maybe property renovation, property development. I'm in flying because it's all I know at the moment. I don't want to come out of flying particularly. But I wake up some days and I ask 'For how much longer can I do this when I feel this tired?'" Does the possibility of failing a medical worry you? "Being a sim instructor I feel more relaxed about it now. There's a ticket there to continue working with the company, and I do think they would support me" (Turboprop Training Captain, regional carrier).

6.2 Are you more a systems manager than a pilot?

"My role has changed. The aircraft I flew early on were much older. DC-3s, Electras, various light twin-engined surveillance aircraft, there was very rarely anything called an autopilot on board. They were equally long days, to the same CAP371 limits, but with no automation. You are sitting there constantly flying the aeroplane, and having to monitor, and having to monitor the other crewmembers as well, and co-ordinate all the participants, like ATC, ground agents, etc. Once you got into the aeroplane you were more focused on flying the aeroplane from A to B. Your handling pilot skills were much better. Now, we pretty much won't get in one unless it has got an autopilot. Humans are very poor at monitoring, We are very good at decision-making, but we are poor at monitoring. The longer the flight, the longer the day, the less effective we become at monitoring. My role has changed. Before I would hand-fly for the majority while being watched like a hawk by my colleagues. Nowadays I could count on the fingers of one hand the number of times I have hand-flown the aircraft above 2,000 ft. in the past year. I won't do it because the airspace is so busy, the workload is so high.[17] The only way to do it is to let the aircraft manage itself and you manage the systems on the aircraft. Basically my flying skills have deteriorated. My company at the moment is emphasising the pilot's monitoring role, because we've seen a degradation in the monitoring role." Why is your company focusing on monitoring? "Because we are relying

---

17   Sleep researchers Dorrian, Baulk and Dawson (2011) say: "[R]esults indicate that, in addition to sleep length, wakefulness and work hours, workload significantly influences fatigue".

on the automation without checking the automation is working correctly – purely because we are at work so often these days the challenge of flying an aeroplane is being replaced by the chore of having to go to work. Using the automation gives you spare capacity. At the moment we need that spare capacity. We need to channel our resources" (Captain, medium/long-haul charter).

"We are both. You still need your piloting skills. Less now, because they go wrong less often. But that is all the more reason to promote those piloting skills. I think the industry has realised this. I think Airbus when they are producing their new aircraft are going to encourage people to fly. I think they are trying to get flying skills back into the equation. I think they have been forgotten. Autopilots are very reliable. When they do go wrong, you don't actually believe they are going wrong. There is a tendency to leave it until it is too late before you take over, because autopilots are so good. Then if you are not practiced you are in big trouble. I am one of the pilots who hand-fly. But 40–50% of other pilots do not like colleagues practicing their flying skills. And to be fair there are arguments for and against it. If you hand-flew all the time there is a danger you would make a mistake. But if you hand-fly the aircraft at an appropriate time when it's not too busy, when the weather is good, I think there's a lot of benefit to be gained. I think those pilots who do not practice their flying skills are asking for an accident. Because when they are required to use those skills, they won't have them. However reliable the aircraft, there will always be those instances" (A319 Captain, low-cost carrier).

6.3 Do you think your government understands commercial aviation?

"I think you have to be in it to understand it. As they say, if you want to be in government, that's a good reason not to be in government" (Senior First Officer, full-service long-haul carrier).

"No. They still think pilots earn vast fortunes and sit there pressing buttons. I don't think they have any idea how much it costs to get a licence, how hard we work, how many pilots are probably getting fatigued, and having stress issues." Why do you think there is that lack of understanding? "I think that while we fly safely there is the assumption 'It must be O.K.' Just because it's O.K. at the moment does not mean there are no underlying problems." How can we improve their understanding? "BALPA should start promoting what we do. I think we should stand up for ourselves more. There are a number of pilots who are frightened to say 'I am fatigued'. We have got to start saying to airlines that we aren't prepared to fly when we think it is unsafe. All pilots should state that safety is their first priority, and everything else is secondary. I am not sure that all pilots are able to do that because of the culture of their airlines. They are making compromises. They are going to work when they are sick. We have a number of cadets who only get paid when they fly. If they have too many days off sick, they won't get taken on the following year. Not only that, if they go sick they won't get paid. Some of them are very short of money, so they go to work when they have streaming colds, which puts me in an invidious position. If I, as Captain, tell them that can't work they get into trouble. So I fly the aircraft at a slightly lower altitude. One consolation is if they do burst their ear drums, I am pretty sure I can land the aircraft safely. I don't think the public know how much of a threat to flight safety it is" (A319 Captain, low-cost carrier).

6.4 Where do you see the industry in five years time?

"The industry might suddenly grind to a halt with retirements and people saying 'No, this is not acceptable. I'm not willing to pay this sort of money to get this job'. If EASA's FTL comes in there may be a potential for more accidents." Do you think the travelling public would be willing to pay a few pounds more for a significantly safer operation? Or don't they see it that way? "I don't think they see it that way. If they were made aware of the difference that a few extra pounds would make then yes, they would. If they were not educated about safety, then probably not" (Helicopter Captain, business charter).

"Businesspeople will always want to meet face-to-face, but they won't be willing to pay what they once paid. I can see taxes on air passengers making other forms of transport more viable. If I wanted to get from Manchester to London I probably would not fly. I'd probably take the train. Security is a massive issue with airports now" (Captain, medium/ long-haul charter).

6.5 Where do you see yourself in five years time?

"Working part-time, I think. The low-cost model is unsustainable. It is not conducive to a social life. Many people I have spoken to want to work part-time. Which is very sad, really, because you should be able to do a job full-time without feeling that to have some sort of life I have to work part-time. I don't think it says very much about the industry" (A319 Captain, low-cost carrier).

"Realistically, doing the same job at the same base, maybe on different equipment. Financially I would not be ready to give up flying in five years time." If the opportunity arose to become a management pilot, would you take it? "Definitely not. I don't like the company ethos of 'If you don't like the job, leave'. That has really done it for me." But if you became a manager, you might be able to change that. "No. Not in these companies. I'd much rather work on the training side. These guys are told what to do by the bean-counters" (Turboprop Training Captain, regional carrier).

6.6 If you had your time again, would you change anything?

"Probably not. It's been a little frustrating that it's taken longer to get to where I wanted to be ... flying. The two years experience that I got as an engineer working for British Aerospace was great. Working as a Flight Test Engineer allowed me to see different sides of the business. The time I spent on the North Sea, although a little bit frustrating because it is a little bit of a bus driver's job with some very long transits, gave me lots of experience. It's a great place to get nurtured. It's a fairly safe learning environment. You are working with some very competent and experienced people. It gives you a very good grounding." Do you think it's desirable for people to have something to fall back on? "Yes. I wanted to go to university, and was also advised and encouraged to do it. I'm thirty-seven in a couple of weeks, yet I have already seen a lot of my friends and colleagues and myself hit by medical issues. It is a very fickle business when it comes to medicals. Having another string to you bow ... not necessarily a university education ... a lot of the guys I worked with in Aberdeen had different businesses, they were interested in computers ... it is definitely worth having a back-up plan. Sadly, however well you plan, it can just take one episode or medical, and your flying career can stop. I would definitely recommend – even if it is aviation-based – that people have another string to their bow" (Helicopter Captain, business charter).

"It still beats working in an office. I might have stayed in the RAF a bit longer. But the air force can get very serious. It is still a good job. It is still fairly well paid. It could be the best job in the world. With a little bit of thought. The only good thing about it is the flying. Everything else about it is very poor. The respect given to us by management is very poor indeed" (A319 Captain, low-cost carrier).

7 Review

Is there anything else you would like to talk about?

"All our customers want is the cheapest possible deal. They don't really understand that it could directly affect safety. Flying is now so cheap it has cheapened the industry." Do you think this is the time to re-regulate the industry. Should we set a minimum seat price with some of the money going towards training, say? "That would be very difficult. We should have more surveys of what pilots think about their airlines. One question could be: 'Does your airline have a just culture?' That might drive some airline managers to try to improve their game. Re-regulation? How do you regulate respect?" (A319 Captain, low-cost carrier).

Conclusion

Despite the element of self-selection bias, both the questionnaire responses and interviews generated a detailed commentary on the aviation industry as it was in 2010–2011. The accounts should be used as a springboard for further sociological investigation. If pilots perceived fatigue to be a problem under CAP371, what will happen under the new FTL scheme introduced by EASA? Some claim the new scheme will see pilots worked harder.[18]

18   On 9 October 2013 the EU Parliament voted to accept EASA's proposed new Europe-wide FTL scheme.

The Lived Reality of Commercial Flying

> [T]he greatest prize of the researcher is to find out the common measure
> or the underlying pattern ...
>
> — ZWEIG, 1961: xi

Introduction

In any capitalistic endeavour, be it oil production, car manufacture, coal-mining or commercial aviation, a balance must be struck between profit and safety.[1] Striking the right balance is never easy – as evidenced, for example, by the driver and passenger deaths attributed to the U.S. automotive industry's eschewing of safety-science in the 1950s and 1960s (Nader, 1965), the 1988 Piper Alpha oil production platform explosion that killed 167 workers (Cullen, 1990) and the 2005 explosion at BP's Texas City oil refinery that killed fifteen (Baker *et al.*, 2007).

Striking the right balance is especially difficult in aviation, one of the world's most competitive and cost-sensitive industries.[2] Aviation's back-story is the need to bear down on costs (Lawton, 2002; Massachusetts Institute of Technology, 2011; Franke and John, 2011). That is the context

---

1   In the United Kingdom this equation finds expression in the Health and Safety Executive's dictum that safety precautions must be 'reasonably practicable'. That is, safety precautions must not be so costly that they threaten the viability of the business.

2   Cost-saving measures are sometimes hotly contested. American Airlines's 2010 scheme to reduce the amount of reserve fuel carried on board its aircraft met with fierce resistance from pilots (Hilkevitch and Johnsson, 2010).

to diarists', respondents' and interviewees' comments, and to the trends identified in this study. Even though diarists, respondents and interviewees said they understood the competitive nature of the business,[3] many queried whether airline managers were striking the right balance between economic efficiency and safety.[4] This concern is echoed by trade unions like BALPA and pressure groups like the European Cockpit Association.

Sleep Debt

The survey results show that pilots accumulate sleep debt.[5] Because sleep debt affects performance it poses a risk to flight safety. One low-cost pilot flew an approach into a U.K. airport with a sleep debt of 16 hours (see case study C4). Over 86% of those who completed the on-line questionnaire ('respondents') said they had flown a sector when knowingly fatigued (Chapter 4, Question 15). Sleep debt is difficult to eliminate. Neither HOTAC nor the home environment are conducive to eliminating sleep debt (because of circadian disruption, extraneous noise, poor environmental conditions, interruptions, the demands of family life, post-flight stress reactions, anticipatory stress, etc.).

---

3   As one Senior First Officer at a full-service airline put it: "I'm a realist. I understand that things are going to get cut. We'll have less time away. Less allowances. It's big business at the end of the day".

4   Workers in other industries express similar concerns.

5   In their survey of fatigue levels amongst night-freight pilots, Gander, Connell and Miller (1998: B32) found that: "During daytime layovers, individual sleep episodes were about three hours shorter than when crewmembers were able to sleep at night ... Crewmembers were three times more likely to report multiple sleep episodes (including naps) on duty days than on non-duty days ... Nevertheless, these additional sleep episodes were insufficient to prevent most crewmembers accumulating sleep debt across trip days".

Sleep debt creates a road safety risk for pilots who elect to drive home. Over 92% of respondents said they had driven home in a state of fatigue (Question 25.a). Nearly 8% of respondents had been involved in an accident while driving home in a state of fatigue (Question 25.d.i). Of these, over 96% believed that fatigue had played a part in the accident (Question 25.d.ii).

Of those who said they had driven home in a fatigued state, over 78% claimed they had reservations about driving home in this condition (Question 25.b). Nearly 68% said they regretted what they had done on arrival (Question 25.c).

Extended Periods of Wakefulness on a Duty Day

Over 86% of respondents said they had experienced a period of continuous wakefulness exceeding 18 hours on a duty day (Question 16). Over 20% said they had experienced a period of continuous wakefulness equal to or exceeding 28 hours. Hersman (2009: 39) explains: "The NTSB's 1994 study of flight crew-related major aviation accidents found that captains who had been awake for more than about 12 hours made significantly more errors than those who had been awake fewer than 12 hours". Caruso and Hitchcock (2010: 193) note: "Fatigue-related impairments can lead to reduced performance on the job ... [T]he odds for a nurse making an error at work increased by three times when work shifts lasted 12.5 hours or longer, compared with 8.5-hour shifts". Rhodes and Gil (2002: 15) note: "By the 18th hour [of wakefulness] the pilot will have great difficulty remembering things he has done or said a few moments ago (short-term memory) and his reaction time will have almost doubled in duration. By the 24th hour his ability to think creatively and make decisions will be dangerously low". The Civil Aviation Authority (2007: 16) explains: "A blood alcohol concentration (BAC) level of 0.085% ... is just over the permitted level for drivers of road vehicles in the UK. This is approximately the level reached ... after 24 hours of continuous wakefulness".

It is not unknown for pilots to unintentionally fall asleep while operating. One pilot wrote: "The company [a low-cost carrier] became more ambitious with their rostering. Due to FTL alleviation on early duties, on returning to LGW I would basically be asleep or nodding off between the Isle of Wight and 1,000ft on approach. After two days 'off' (read sleeping and ironing) I would do 5 days on, each of approximately 12 duty hours. With my drive to work, and a 30 minute bus drive to and from the car park to the crew centre, I would be out of my house for at least 15 hours a day (nine hours for dinner, breakfast and sleep)". Werfelman (2009: 23) notes: "[A] survey by the U.S. National Aeronautics and Space Administration [found that] 80 percent of 1,424 flight crewmembers from regional airlines said they had 'nodded off' during a flight. A survey of 1,488 corporate/executive flight crewmembers found that 71 percent had fallen asleep during flight".

Many of those surveyed experienced long periods of wakefulness on duty days.[6] Pilots' inability to get 'top-up' sleep before reporting for duty contributed to this problem. Pilots who are not tired find it difficult to sleep-to-order. Further, efforts to get pre-report sleep can be frustrated by noise and interruption, both at home and in HOTAC. Over 74% of pilots said they had commenced a duty knowing they were fatigued (Question 14). Although over 77% of respondents described their down-route accommodation as either 'good' or 'excellent' (Question 28.c), only 36.2% said they *could* get all the sleep they needed in their down-route accommodation. For those who said they could not get all the sleep they needed, the most common problems were interruptions from hotel staff (cited by 35%), minimum rest (37%), inability to regulate the room temperature (46%) and noise disturbance (65%) (Question 28.d.ii). Although 76% of respondents said that their airline understood the rest and recreational needs of

---

6   One interviewee, who flew for a low-cost carrier, said: "The five early starts really kill you. Last week I did not get a minute of sleep for my first early. It wasn't massively early. It was a 06:00 report. Maybe I was anxious about work. Maybe it was fear of missing the alarm. They run everything so close all the time, there are rarely any spare crew. So if you are late you get an arse-kicking. The following night, when I was absolutely exhausted, I managed just four hours sleep".

down-route pilots, less than 30% said that hotel staff (clerks, cleaners, etc.) understood the needs of down-route pilots. 86% had asked to be moved to another hotel room, and over 11% to another hotel.[7] The most common problem in each case was noise.

It is the author's experience that Rostering and Crewing Officers proceed on the basis that pilots have the facility to sleep-to-order.[8] Rostering and Crewing Officers' mental model of pilot behaviour is out of step with reality.[9] Further, it appears that CAP371 (and other FTLs) are based on the assumption that pilots can get adequate rest and sleep between duties. The data presented here suggests that the current model of pilots' capacities is inaccurate. Basing a flight-time limitation on an inaccurate model of the pilot lifestyle creates a latent error (see Reason (1990, 2013) for an explanation of latent errors/resident pathogens). An unpropitious intersection of adverse physiological/psychological states (fatigue and stress, for example) and events (attempting to land at an unfamiliar airport in a tropical storm with a novice First Officer who lacks confidence and a passenger who requires medical attention, for example) may activate the FTL latent error, creating accident risk.

A July 2001 survey conducted by Public Opinion Strategies revealed pilot fatigue to be the number one concern for the American travelling public: "Americans overwhelmingly chose adequate rest for pilots as the most important air travel issue. Compared to a list of other issues, including courteous service, adequate cabin and seat room, on-time departures and ticket prices, 82% of survey respondents ranked a pilot that is rested enough to fly as the most important concern for them when flying" (*PR Newswire*, 2001). The Chairman of the California Academy for Physician Assistants (CAPA) commented: "From the recent media coverage of flight delays, airline ticket pricing and a Passenger Bill of Rights it seemed as though passengers were only concerned with getting to their destination

---

7   In some locales there might not be a choice of hotel.
8   The author has spent many hundreds of hours on the flight-deck and is familiar with life down-route.
9   Rostering Departments might wish to distribute this book to their staff.

cheaply and on time. This shows us that when it comes right down to it, Americans want the FAA to spend time making safety a top priority, and that it regulates the flying environment so pilots can do their job safely and effectively" (Miller cited in *PR Newswire*, 2001). There is no reason to believe that the European public's priorities differ from those of the American public.

Roster Instability

While most pilots understand that rosters may be changed at short notice to meet operational demands (a shortage of crews due to illness, for example), roster volatility creates latent risk. As mentioned above, few pilots can sleep-to-order. Nevertheless, most try to do the right thing. A pilot rostered for a night duty will retire in the late afternoon to sleep. The data suggests that few get the sleep they desire. This means that pilots can go for long periods without sleep (see Question 16, above). Extending the duty (a not infrequent occurrence amongst night-freight pilots, for example) augments fatigue risk. Annoyed, pilots sometimes vent their frustrations on Crewing and Rostering Officers. This creates bad feeling and undermines team spirit (a precondition for safe operation). Some pilots vent their frustration by moving to another airline. Turnover erases organisational memory, reducing safety margins.

In their book *The Myth of Work-Life Balance*, Gambles, Lewis and Rapoport (2006: 4) claim that "paid work has become increasingly demanding and invasive in people's lives". To the extent that roster changes thwart pilots' plans for rest and recreation, they may be considered antithetical to a healthy work-life balance. To illustrate the nature of the problem, a night-freight Captain's roster is reproduced below. His roster went through three iterations (5 August, 16 August, 27 September). His experience is typical of the industry.

Night-Freight Roster

The first two rosters (5 August and 16 August) were withdrawn. The last roster was worked (the achieved roster). Pilots comment that roster volatility makes it difficult to organise a successful home and social life (Bennett, 2003, 2006, 2010a). Rest and relaxation help pilots (indeed, all workers) maintain morale, good health and relationships with partners, offspring, relatives and friends:

> A happy social and domestic life is an important foundation for health and well-being. The amount and quality of time spent with family and friends can, however, be affected by unusual patterns of work. A worker who experiences a disrupted social or domestic life may feel isolated, moody or depressed, which can affect their health and performance at work (Health and Safety Executive, 2006: 12).

The hidden costs of roster volatility include negativity, feelings of resentment, poor industrial relations, domestic strain and alienation (Bennett, 2010a). Reviewing the cabin crew lifestyle (which resembles the pilot lifestyle) Partridge and Goodman (2007: 7) comment: "Realities such as a lack of control of lifestyle, being away from family and friends and the difficulties in planning ahead, could begin to deflate the glamour 'bubble'. The physical implications of the job, such as compounded sleep deprivation, jetlag and dehydration can also take their toll".

Rosters

1	2	3	4	5	6	7	8	9	10	11	12	13	14	15	16	17	18	19	20	21
SBY	SBY	21:45	01:40	01:15	03:05	00:30	OFF	OFF	OFF	SBY	REST	00:25	LEJ	19:15	20:35	EMA	OFF	OFF	ROFF	ROFF
12:00	20:00	EMA*	LEJ	LEJ	LEJ	LEJ*				12:00		EMA		LEJ	STR	01:15				
20:00	06:00	LEJ	MRS	CDG	WAW	EMA				20:00		LEJ		STR	LEJ	03:40				
		23:35	03:35	02:55	04:30	02:20						02:10		20:20	21:45	EMA				
			04:20	21:45	19:50							03:10			23:25	EDI				
			MRS	CDG	WAW							LEJ			LEJ	04:40				
			VLC	LEJ	LEJ							STR				19:40				
			05:45	23:20	21:20							04:05				EDI				
			18:40									20:35				EMA				
			VLC									STR				20:45				
			MRS									LEJ								
			19:55									21:45								
			20:40																	
			MRS																	
			LEJ																	
PUBLISHED 5 AUG		22:35																		

1	2	3	4	5	6	7	8	9	10	11	12	13	14	15	16	17	18	19	20	21
08:00	00:10	LEJ	01:40	01:15	03:05	00:30	OFF	OFF	OFF	SBY	REST	00:25	LEJ	19:15	20:35	EMA	OFF			
EMA*	LEJ		LEJ	LEJ	LEJ	LEJ*				12:00		EMA		LEJ	STR	01:15				
LTN	BTS		MRS	CDG	WAW	EMA				20:00		LEJ		STR	LEJ	03:40				
09:35	01:25		03:35	02:55	04:30	02:20						02:10		20:20	21:45	EMA				
10:35	03:30		04:20	21:45	19:50							03:10			23:25	EDI				
LTN*	BTS		MRS	CDG	WAW							LEJ			LEJ	04:40				
LEJ	SOF		VLC	LEJ	LEJ							STR				19:40				
12:15	04:55		05:45	23:20	21:20							04:05				EDI				
	19:05		18:40									20:35				EMA				
	SOF		VLC									STR				20:45				
	BTS		MRS									LEJ								
	20:35		19:55									21:45								
	21:25		20:40																	
	BTS		MRS																	
	LEJ		LEJ																	
	22:40		22:35																	

PUBLISHED 16 AUG

1	2	3	4	5	6	7	8	9	10	11	12	13	14	15	16	17	18	19	20	21
08:00	HSBY	LEJ	01:45	01:15	EMA	OFF	OFF	OFF	OFF	22:00	LEJ	00:30	04:00	HSBY	23:25	EMA	OFF	OFF	ROFF	ROFF
EMA* 00:10		01:00	LEJ	LEJ	01:15					EMA*	01:00	01:30		18:00	LEJ	01:15				
LTN 04:00			LYS	CDG						BRU	ASBY	LEJ		22:00		03:40				
09:35 18:00			03:30	02:55						23:10	22:00	MAD				EMA				
10:35 LEJ			04:45	21:15						23:45		04:25				EDI				
LTN* BRU			LYS	CDG						BRU		20:00				04:40				
LEJ 20:30			TLS	LEJ								MAD				19:40				
12:15 23:45			05:50	22:50								LEJ				EDI				
BRU			18:30	23:25								22:55				EMA				
			TLS	LEJ								ASBY				20:45				
			LYS									23:40								
			19:30																	
			20:40																	
			LYS																	
			LEJ																	
			22:20																	

PUBLISHED
27 SEP

Maintaining a healthy work-life balance benefits not only the individual pilot but also her/his airline. The benefits of balancing the demands of work and home include better retention of pilots, improved motivation, increased productivity, a larger number of applicants for jobs, improved corporate reputation and public image, more stable families (thereby reducing the level of family breakdown – a huge and largely hidden cost to society) and more stable relationships (thereby reducing personal angst and resulting psychological dysfunction). Nearly 80% of respondents said they had felt unduly stressed at home (Question 18). Over 73% of respondents said they had felt unduly stressed at work (Question 19).[10] Over 18% of respondents said they would not describe their home as a restful place (Question 33a). Some respondents cited stress as a factor in a relationship problem/separation/divorce (see the testimonies in Chapter 4).

CAP371: Risk-Management Tool or Productivity Target?

Many pilots claimed that their airline saw the CAP371 FTL more as a target than a legal maximum (of 900 flying hours). Typical comments were: "Captain is on leave tomorrow. He has done 893 flying hours (U.K. max legal hours is 900) in the past 365 days. He was utterly knackered and I felt I needed to be above my game to compensate – which is tough when I have been awake since 07:00" (First Officer, low-cost carrier – turbofan (C4)); "900 flying hours per year is a limit, not a target. The law says this. The law is not enforced"; "[My most intensive period of flying was] 2003 to 2006. 750–800 hours per year. LGW. During the whole of this period I was

---

10   Bor, Field and Scragg (2002: 241) write: "[I]t has been observed that pilots generally dislike being interviewed by mental health professionals (Jones *et al.*, 1997). This is because they do not feel in control of the situation, [and] that goes against their nature. They may feel uncomfortable in a context where they are unfamiliar with the rules and fear the implications of the encounter which could, after all, jeopardize their flying career and their livelihood if it leads to their licence being revoked".

chronically fatigued. It is only with hindsight that I realise this ... On one occasion, after 5 days of lates, approximately 60 hours duty, 18 sectors and the last day running into a day off, I spun my car into the central reservation of the M25 at about 80mph. In my fatigued state I was completely unable to assess the risk of driving at this speed on a waterlogged motorway"; "Flight time limitations in their present form were implemented in a different commercial operating environment. Multi-sector shorthaul operations to maximum hours are now the target, and the norm. This is very tiring and fatiguing. It seems that when FTLs were introduced, shorthaul flightcrew would be unlikely to get to 900 hours on a regular basis. Unfortunately, for many pilots this happens year in, year out, leading many to just about operate within safe boundaries".

CAP393 Air Navigation: The Order and the Regulations (2010: Section 1, Part 20, Page 2) states: "A person must not act as a member of the crew of an aircraft to which this article applies if they know, or suspect that they are suffering from, or, having regard to the circumstances of the flight to be undertaken, are likely to suffer from, such fatigue as may endanger the safety of the aircraft or of its occupants". Regarding operators' responsibilities for managing fatigue, *CAP393* (2010: Section 1, Part 20, Page 3) states: "The operator of an EU-OPS aeroplane must not cause or permit that aeroplane to make a commercial air transport flight unless the operator has taken all such steps as are reasonably practicable to ensure that the provisions of the scheme will be complied with in relation to every person flying in that aeroplane as a member of its crew". Over 13% of respondents said they had refused a duty in the past 12 months because of fatigue (Question 13.a). Of these, 96.5% had refused between one and five duties (Question 13.b).[11]

Another theme that emerged was pilots' reluctance to put their own interests before those of their crew. Camaraderie on the flight deck and a sense of obligation discourage pilots from refusing duties. As one respondent put it: "For acute stress/fatigue I would try to tell Crewing I was unfit

---

11   One pilot said: "I would like to have the option to refuse more than two duties a year without getting into trouble over it". Could it be that some airlines use the threat of the Head Office interview to discourage multiple refusals?

to operate – although when away from home the pressure to get home, 'keep the show on the road', not let down fellow crewmembers and passengers is compelling". 'Professionalism' can mean different things at different times. It can mean either refusing a duty, or struggling on for the sake of one's colleagues and passengers. Circumstance influences pilots' understanding of what it means to be professional. The interpretation is *contingent*. Regulations generally do not take account of the *Realpolitik* of pilots' understanding of their role. This is why a deeper sociological understanding of the culture of aviation is needed. Aviation merits an ongoing sociological audit.

Erosion of Terms and Conditions

Escalating training costs and pressure on benefits and compensation (salaries) are impacting the financial position of some pilots. While those who fly for U.K. airlines are probably not as vulnerable as those who fly for U.S. Airlines,[12] the trend is to cut costs: "Constant and ever-improving methods of operational cost reduction are *de rigueur* ... The obvious way to safeguard a company against ... acute market vulnerability is to decrease operational expenses and increase employee and aircraft productivity" (Lawton, 2002: 3). Where possible costs are passed on to trainees/new recruits. Coupled with university tuition fees in the United Kingdom of up to £9,000, this cost-cutting trend is causing significant levels of indebtedness amongst trainees/new recruits. As one pilot remarked: "Total training costs £118,000

---

12 Between 2001 and 2005 America's legacy carriers cut average wage rates by 7% (Massachusetts Institute of Technology, 2011). In 2009 Chesley Sullenberger, the Captain who successfully ditched his Airbus in New York's Hudson River, addressed the House of Representatives: "It is my personal experience that my decision to remain in the profession I love has come at a great financial cost to me and my family. My pay has been cut 40%, my pension, like most airline pensions, has been terminated ..." (Sullenberger, 2009: 2).

(*ab initio* and two conversion courses). One conversion course of £23,000 paid back by airline over 5 years. Current debt left after repaying for just under 10 years = £62,000. Monthly payments to the bank of £1,050. About 5 years to go". The squeeze is also felt by some veterans. One said: "[My situation is] DIRE!!!! 4th airline. Been at it for 30 years now so ... pay freeze, pay cut, increased taxes, costs, etc".

Regarding airlines' expectation that aspiring pilots bear the financial risks of their training and, indeed, of their mentoring by the airline, Learmount (2010) comments: "The result of this situation is that self-sponsored pilots arrive on line with massive debt – about €100,000 – and having taken the entire risk of their investment on themselves. The airlines accept none of the cost and take none of the risk". When it comes to investing in one of its key resources – the pilot – the airline industry is increasingly risk-averse. Airlines' efforts to offload training costs reflect a strong focus on profits and shareholder value: "[Q]uestions of cost efficiency, operating profitability and competitive behaviour have become the dominant issues facing airline management" (Massachusetts Institute of Technology, 2011).

There was a perception amongst some respondents that airline managements saw pilots as a 'necessary evil'. There was also a suspicion amongst some pilots that cabin crew were being indoctrinated with the view that pilots were under-worked and over-paid. Typical remarks were: "Whereas in my previous job I was proud to serve my country and was well supported, I feel that this job is based on a requirement to buy a resource as cheaply as possible. That does not imply poor management, we have one or two excellent Flight Ops managers, but the reality of commercialism means they will always try to get more from us, for less. This 'race to the bottom' will eventually devalue this profession and all who work within it. My hopes for learning so much from working for a successful company have yet to be realised; it seems that some, but certainly not all, of our manager-colleagues are rewarded for trying to destroy the profession they are supposed to represent"; "Cabin crew are clearly now being trained to believe that pilots are overpaid and under-utilised, and that their chain of command is there to be challenged and questioned. This comes from the staff who train them, who often have a serious axe to grind with pilots, possibly formed on past experiences".

Two findings suggest that pilot morale is not as high as it could be. First, nearly 35% of respondents said that the profession had not met their expectations (of course, it is possible that this group's initial expectations were too high). Secondly, just over 19% of respondents said they would recommend a career in commercial aviation to their offspring (Question 46). 42.7% said they would *not* recommend a career in aviation to their offspring (Question 46).[13]

A Pilot Diaspora

Aviation is a volatile industry. Airlines merge or cease operating. Bases are closed or moved in reorganisations. Pilots may be made redundant when economies slump (Gowrisankaran, 2002; Massachusetts Institute of Technology, 2011). Obliged to 'follow the work' some pilots find themselves commuting long distances to their base. Over 30% of respondents took between 60 and 120 minutes to commute to base (Question 24.a). While 51% of respondents lived 50 miles or less from base, nearly 23% lived between 51–100 miles from base (meaning a car journey of at least one hour). 6.7% of respondents lived between 101–150 miles from base. 14.7% of respondents lived between 151–700 miles from base, and 4.6% lived more than 701 miles from base (Question 21). One correspondent remarked: "I am convinced that my chosen crazy lifestyle is not wholly responsible or healthy. I have been a commercial pilot for over 20 years, and am still a Senior First Officer with [a U.K.-registered full-service carrier] based in London but living in Tokyo".

Because commuting can add several hours to a pilot's working day, some use temporary accommodation close to base. 29.6% of respondents

---

13   A survey published in the 2006 book *A Sociology of Commercial Flight Crew* revealed that thirty-five percent of pilot-respondents would encourage their offspring to become a commercial pilot, while sixty-five percent said they would not.

said they used temporary accommodation (Question 23.a). One pilot commented "[I use temporary accommodation] because I can't commute 2,000 km on a daily basis". One solution to the increasing spatial dislocation of flight crew would be for airlines to provide accommodation, either on-site or off-site. Over 81% of respondents confirmed that their airline did not provide accommodation at or near their designated base (Question 26.a). Over 83% of respondents confirmed that their airline would not subsidise HOTAC for fatigued crew returning to base (Question 27). The lack of provision evidences the trend to offload costs onto employees.

Living away from home may stress the commuter and her/his family. In their book *Geographical Mobility: Family Impacts* Green and Canny (2003: 37) described the potential negative impacts on families of weekly commuting (where a family member rents a room or flat or shares a house close to their place of work):

> [W]hen children were involved in such arrangements, the pressures on families were acknowledged more readily. In such circumstances the employee has two lives – a 'work life' and a 'home life' – with the former often being fulfilled at the expense of the latter ... A male employee with experience of long-distance commuting for over a year ... admitted that it was 'more difficult to live away from the family than I thought'. In this instance the commuting arrangement was not conducive to integration in the destination area and was also unsatisfactory from the employee's perspective for family life.

An employee who lives away from home is more likely to feel isolated. Relationships may come under pressure.[14] There may be an unpicking of the social fabric (Third Sector Foresight, 2010). The social costs of working away from home (broken relationships or marriages, psychological dysfunction and/or delinquency amongst offspring, the undermining of community spirit, the physical and psychological strain on the commuter,

14   Bennett's (2003: 226) investigation into the habits of pilots who worked for a UK-registered low-cost carrier encompassed the itinerant lifestyle: "A number of interviewees lived in temporary accommodation when flying. Some of these pilots commented on the unsatisfactory nature of the arrangement. Isolation and loneliness would seem to be features of this type of existence".

etc.) should be included in any calculation of the aviation industry's net worth. These costs are presently hidden.

Work-Life Balance

Gambles, Lewis and Rapoport (2006: 4) make the following case for balancing the demands of work and home: "[T]ime and energy to connect with others and give and receive care – as parents, children, lovers or friends, or even time to care for ourselves – are crucial for individual and societal well-being". Unfortunately, ever-more aggressive competition and exhortations to achieve, to consume and to 'get behind one's company, industry or country' undermine efforts to balance the demands of work and home (Gambles, Lewis and Rapoport, 2006).

The survey produced evidence that workplace demands intrude into pilots' home lives. As discussed, some pilots use temporary accommodation to mitigate fatigue and stress. This means they can spend a significant amount of time away from home. Pilots who fly long-haul passenger or freight services, or short-haul night-freight services, spend time in HOTAC. Over 95% of respondents said they spent time in HOTAC (Question 28.a). 43% of respondents said they had felt lonely or isolated when staying in down-route HOTAC (Question 28.g). A common coping mechanism was to keep in touch with partners/family members via the telephone or Internet. As one respondent explained: "A lot of time is spent at work … If I can talk to the family I feel I can stay involved in the situation and communications keep me calm". Some pilots said they felt guilty about leaving their family. "I know the guilt I feel leaving my son (and to a lesser extent my husband) is irrational, but it's still sometimes hard to deal with … I always feel slightly guilty being away, but as I am the main earner in our house I have no option to go part time" said one.

One interviewee described how he never seemed to fully recover from work: "The big issue for me at the moment is finishing on a late duty, and starting on an early. It is very difficult in a family home to get appropriate rest prior to earlies ... because the rest of the house is up until 23:00, or 24:00. And so am I, if I'm honest, because I have things to do. Then the alarm goes off at 04:30, and away you go. If you do that four times in the week, you are shattered by the end of the week. You never actually fully recover". Never fully recovering induces chronic fatigue. Caldwell *et al.* (2009: 30) discuss the problem of insufficient recovery time between duties:

> Short-haul (domestic) pilots most frequently blame their fatigue on sleep depriva-
> tion and high workload. Both long- and short-haul pilots commonly associate their
> fatigue with night flights, jet lag, early wakeups, time pressure, multiple flight legs
> and consecutive duty periods without sufficient recovery breaks. Corporate/execu-
> tive pilots experience fatigue-related problems similar to those reported by their
> commercial counterparts.

When at home, peripatetic pilots felt obliged to 'catch up' on chores. As one put it: "The airline does not understand life away from home. You have to cram your life into your one or two days off at home". The SLOGs showed how it could take several days for off-duty pilots to eliminate the sleep debt they had accumulated when operating. They also showed how it could take several days for off-duty pilots to settle back into a normal sleep pattern, whereupon they could look forward to getting the required seven to eight hours sleep per night.

It would seem that neither the hotel nor home environment could guarantee a pilot adequate rest before Report. Over 84% of respondents said they had failed to get adequate rest at home before Report (Question 34.a). Major irritants were telephone calls (cited by 23% of those respond-ents who said they had failed to get adequate rest), extraneous noise (23%), household noise (24%), work-related stress (27%), household duties (43%) and family-related stress (53%) (Question 34.b). One respondent gave the following reasons for his home not being a restful place: "Pressures of family life. Heavy concentration of home-related duties into available time at home, including marital attention, parenthood, finances, home maintenance, social engagements. My marriage is challenging at times – in no small part due to my being away 65% of the time". Another respondent wrote: "Children – a lot to do, and with my partner working in a 'more important' (in his opinion) job than mine, complicated arrangements to keep the show on the road".

There are costs – both to the individual and society – of failing to achieve a reasonable balance between one's working and home life. These costs include guilt; stress; depression; relationship/marital breakdown; alienation from offspring; misbehaviour of offspring; alienation from relatives; alienation from friends; loss of interest in community affairs (civic society); and a less than optimal performance at work.[15] Over 40% of respondents said that relationships with partners/offspring had affected their working life (Question 38). Nearly 20% of respondents said they had sought advice/help for a domestic relationship issue (Question 39.a). Of those who sought advice, very few looked to airline managers for advice/help. Most talked to either a trusted colleague, non-work friend or the family G.P. (Question 39.b).[16] In their survey of fatigue and well being amongst BALPA members working for one airline, Steptoe and Bostock (2011: 3) found that "Levels of self-reported fatigue, sleep problems and symptoms of anxiety and depression were higher than would be expected in a general population".

Industrial Relations and Trust

The data suggests a deterioration in industrial relations, both between pilots and management and, at British Airways in particular, between pilots and cabin crew. Several pilots talked about a 'bonus culture' amongst managers. Typical comments were: "It is in a gradual state of decline and managed by short-term bonus-grabbing people"; "There is a downward trend in terms and conditions. Who is going to borrow £120,000 to become a pilot when they can only expect £15,000 per year on a temporary contract?

---

15   Gambles, Lewis and Rapoport (2006: 64) document feelings of "loneliness and disconnection" amongst workers: "We hear much concern ... about not having invested sufficiently in friendships and other forms of connectedness".

16   When asked whether they had used BALPA's confidential peer-support system, only 2.1% (9/433) of respondents said they had.

Directors are bonus-driven, and don't care if the airline exists in five years
time. The contempt shown to the profession by managers says it all". There
was a feeling that pilots' status was being undermined and that they were
seen by some managers (and cabin crew) more as units of production than
skilled professionals.

A test of pilots' confidence in management is their willingness to seek
managers' advice and help with work problems. Just over 13% of respondents
said they had sought advice/help for a relationship issue with a work colleague
(Question 40.a). Relatively few had consulted a manager (Question 40.b):

Who did you consult (Question 40.b)?[17]

Family G.P.:	0
Authorised Medical Examiner:	0
Partner:	17
Offspring:	0
Trusted (non-work) friend:	15
Trusted colleague:	42
Chief Executive Officer:	0
Personnel Director:	0
Operations Director:	0
Chief Pilot:	5
Fleet Manager:	12
Rostering Manager:	0
Crewing Officer:	0
Other (please specify):	6

Despite some pilots' apparent lack of faith in management and concerns
about the industry in general, there is strong evidence of pilots' enthusi-
asm for flying. Those who talked about the art of flying did so with pride
and fondness. As one interviewee put it: "The flying bug bit me when I
was doing my PPL. It's always different. I like the fact that I get to see the
sun. Even though I'm at work at three in the morning, I like the fact that
my days off are predominantly in the week ... I fly little aeroplanes outside
of work, gliders. I have a love of flying". It is reasonable to conclude that

17   Respondents could select more than one category.

flying is much more a vocation than a job. As indicated above, there is a perception that some airline managements deal with pilots as they would any other worker. This perception raises fears of de-professionalisation.

Just Culture?

A just culture is one of the building blocks of a safe airline. If pilots are certain they will not be victimised for admitting to slips and errors, they are more likely to report them. Only if slips and errors are reported can the airline learn from experience (referred to as organisational learning). If pilots fear they might be victimised (scapegoated) they are less likely to report slips and errors. The under-reporting of slips and errors inhibits organisational learning (Reason, 1990, 1997, 1998, 2013) and makes incidents and accidents more likely. Under-reporting creates an *affordance* for incidents and accidents.

Some statements suggested that the need for a just culture is not universally understood.[18] One diarist remarked: "There is little or no protection for us. There is a culture of 'bullying' by the management ('How dare you be tired') and no protection afforded by the Civil Aviation Authority (who are in bed with the company – the Flight Operations Inspector 'cherry-picks' a bullet Orlando trip once a month to stay current)". One interviewee remarked: "They [managers] went out of their way a couple of years ago when pilots were saying they were fatigued to say: 'You pilots are not fatigued. If you were fatigued it would be a medical issue. You would be off long-term sick. You are just tired. It's up to you to manage your rest. We give you ample time off'. They also made it very clear that if we did not like it, we could leave. That's what the Chief Pilot said. That has continued for the past two years. Why should they pay high-ranking Captains when they can promote from within?" Another interviewee said: "I have reported fairly innocent mistakes

---

18 Even if an airline has a just culture, if pilots *perceive* the culture to be unjust there
    will be under-reporting of slips and errors. Perception is reality.

and it has been blown out of all proportion. That has led me to feel that the airline is not a just airline, and on many occasions I have not reported errors or problems for fear that it may be blown out of proportion. I know many of my colleagues feel the same. There have been occasions when pilots have reported things and it really has not helped them. If they had kept quiet they would not have got into trouble". A third interviewee said: "They like to push this just culture. The 'just culture' is about accountability. They are trying to find someone to pin it on. That is not right at all. You should have a culture where people are willing to put their hand up and say 'I'm sorry, I fucked up. I made this mistake. I'll take any re-training required'. But the culture involves finding a person who is accountable and then disciplining them, or sacking them. I don't think that is safety-minded at all".

FRMS – How Resilient?

One of the criticisms levelled at baseline FTLs like CAP371 is that in catering for every type of operation (from multi-sector short-haul to ultra long-haul to night freight to helicopter operations), they fail to accommodate the nuances of each. One of the benefits of a fatigue risk management system (FRMS) is that each type of operation – indeed, each operator – can develop an FTL that balances the rest and recreation (R&R) needs of flight crew with the operator's business model and operational requirements, such that an adequate margin of safety is maintained while ensuring commercial viability. Jones (2009: 18) puts it this way:

> The [FRMS] philosophy recognises that different influences [work-rate or circadian disruption, for example] will affect levels of fatigue ... and that a 'one size fits all' prescriptive hours limitation scheme cannot effectively regulate for this. In a FRMS every duty will have its own bespoke hours limitations formulated through a process of multi-faceted monitoring and reporting, evaluation, timely modification of limits and procedures, and [an] integral, systematic feedback loop for continuous fatigue risk assessment for that particular operation. It is a performance outcome-driven system relying on a 'just' culture ... intended to be as much proactive as it is reactive.

Operators use qualitative data (pilots' fatigue reports, for example) and quantitative data (Actiwatch read-outs and flight-data trend analysis, for example) to develop and refine their FRMS.[19] Data is the lifeblood of a FRMS. Without data rosters cannot be validated. Because it may augment pilot fatigue, a non-validated roster creates a latent error or resident pathogen. Embedded deep within the airline's operation, pathogenic rosters are difficult to spot. Pilots won't file fatigue reports if they believe those reports will be ignored. Pilots won't file them if they fear they might be victimised. (Pilots who fear victimisation may file sickness reports *in lieu* of fatigue reports. This masks fatigue risk exposure).

To function as intended a FRMS requires committed managers who understand the requirements, a just culture, pilot buy-in and a healthy reporting culture where *not* reporting fatigue is considered deviant. The timely reporting of fatigue can help create a high-reliability operation. Hopkins (2002: 9) says: "[High-reliability organisations (HROs)] have well-developed systems for reporting near misses, process upsets and small and localised failures of all sorts. In short ... they have well-developed reporting cultures". Woods *et al.* (2010: 77) explain: "[HRO] researchers found that through leadership safety objectives, the maintenance of relatively closed systems, functional decentralisation, the creation of a safety culture, redundancy of equipment and personnel and systematic learning, organisations could achieve the consistency and stability required to effect failure-free operations". In a HRO, employee behaviour is characterised by a 'preoccupation with failure' (attentiveness to deviation, error and malfunction) (LaPorte and Consolini, 1991; Hopkins, 2002; Antonsen, 2009).

19 Writing in 2011, Steptoe and Bostock (2011: 4) noted that airline-specific FTL variations necessitated validation by a fatigue risk management system: "CAP371 allows airlines flexibility to implement their own approved Flight Time Limitation schemes in order to balance commercial requirements with aircrews' needs for rest and recovery. Partial or total alleviations from the FTL schema outlined in CAP371 can be granted to airlines which employ a Fatigue Risk Management System (FRMS). A FRMS is a 'scientifically based, data-driven flexible alternative to prescriptive flight and duty time limitations' requiring a continuous process of monitoring and managing fatigue risk (International Civil Aviation Organisation)".

There is some evidence of masking amongst flight crew. For example, one diarist wrote: "My fatigue report has been rejected. The only way to do it is to go sick. It saves a call from the management". There is a perception that some airlines do not operate a just culture. One interviewee, when asked if he had, on any occasion, not reported sick or fatigued for fear of being victimised, replied: "Yes, pretty frequently. On these runs of five earlies, particularly on days four and five you are absolutely buggered. But because it happens all the time you get used to the fact that that is how you feel. So you turn up anyway. If you don't you get snotty e-mails. You get pulled into the office. People get disciplined for being off sick. They have even started saying that people use 'fatigue' far too often. So one of the few things we can say without being questioned is now being questioned, because they think we say it too often. In the last three or four years I have only been off for two days". (Also, see pilots' comments in Chapters 3 and 4).

The problem seems universal: there is a reluctance amongst some U.S. pilots to report fatigue: "Some of the air carrier pilots reported using [fatigue risk management programmes] successfully, whereas other pilots reported that they hesitated to use such programmes because of fear of retribution ... In addition, other pilots reported that they attempted to call in as fatigued but encountered company resistance" (National Transportation Safety Board, 2008: 35–36). Non-reporting and masking undermine fatigue risk management systems. *In extremis* they render fatigue risk management systems unsafe.

Multiple Lines of Responsibility and Control

There is an 'inconsistency of control' at the heart of commercial aviation: while flight crew are responsible in law for the safety of their passengers, aircraft and crew, they often have no control over their rosters (which, as evidenced by the data contained in this report, can influence a flight crew's ability to fly their aircraft safely and efficiently). Even though rosters impact a Captain's ability to discharge her/his legal duty, crew rosters are designed by back-office staff (Crewing Officers, etc.). Consequently, although pilots are able to directly manage many operational risks (like ensuring sufficient fuel is carried to deal with worst-case routing), they are unable to manage the risks associated with rosters. They have a personal responsibility to manage fatigue risk but are unable to directly influence one of the potential sources of that risk – the duty roster. Put another way, pilots' ability to manage fatigue risk is circumscribed by their inability to influence rostering.

Preferential rostering provides one solution to the problem of managing rostering risks. It has long been recognised that some workers are 'day people' while others are 'night people'.[20] The former are at their best during the day, the latter during the night. Preferential rostering does two things. First, it empowers flight crew to manage the fatigue risk associated with rosters. Secondly, it recognises and accommodates the physiological limitations of individual pilots:

> [Preferential rostering] enables crew members to match their schedules with their circadian rhythms, helping to preclude fatigue. Thus a person whose peak performance usually is reached late in the day can shape the schedule to eliminate or minimise early duties while accepting more late duties, a schedule that a 'morning' person would find fatiguing and undesirable (Chittick, 1998: 17).

One pilot remarked: "I have had three weekends off this year (not including leave) ... Eight years of working every weekend, and having very little choice in rostering is not an acceptable way to live".

Pilots and Businesspeople?

Airline managers have suggested to the author that many pilots have second jobs. It has been intimated that pilots' second jobs contribute to acute and chronic fatigue. Just over 3% of respondents said they ran a business from home. (Just over 7% confirmed that another household member ran a

---

20   Caldwell and Caldwell (2003: 93) write: "[V]ariations in their physiological and psychological make-ups will likely make [pilots] differentially responsive to their jobs". Put another way, some pilots are better able to cope with stress and fatigue than others. This is why tailored rosters can help reduce operational risk. Tailored rosters address the issue of variations in physiological and psychological capacity.

business from home). Of those pilots who ran a business from home, 71.5% devoted no more than 10 hours to it in a typical non-flying week. It seems that second jobs are not a safety issue, and that airline managers are wrong to claim they are. The roots of the fatigue problem must lie elsewhere.

Flight Preparation as a Stressor?

Over 28% of respondents felt they did not have enough time and resources to adequately prepare for their duty (Question 51). Problems encountered included lack of time and inadequate information technology. Comments included: "We always need to come in early to cope with the deficiencies in I.T."; "A 45-minute report before pushback is not enough, especially for four sectors, as there is too much paperwork to wade through. I have frequently missed important NOTAM information. A 25-minute turna-round with refuelling supervisor duties is not achievable safely, as it leads to rushed briefing and rushed pre-flight and rushed checklists". From a flight-safety perspective it is best to reduce the level of stress experienced by flight (and cabin) crew prior to operating.

Security Checks as a Stressor?

Over 95% of respondents said that current security measures were 'exces-sive'. No-one said they were too lax. Over three quarters of respondents were of the opinion that passing through security had compromised flight safety. Security checks that were perceived to be excessive acted to stress flight crew. Typical comments were: "Being patronised and humiliated doesn't set you up in the right frame of mind for the day! Being deliber-ately pissed-off 10 minutes before you arrive at the aircraft is not the way to treat people you expect to look after the reputation of the airline. Note, it's especially farcical and idiotic at home base – LHR"; "Body scanners!!! Please do something about this. I am not happy with BALPA's response that they are not a health risk, because in many countries, other unions and medical professionals say they are … or could be. I do not want to die of cancer, or just get cancer because of some useless scanner. Why do we do security clearances if they still insist on treating us like criminals?" From a flight-safety perspective it is best to reduce the level of stress experienced by flight (and cabin) crew prior to operating.

Stress and Fatigue – Advice, Catharsis and Closure

Having identified a problem like fatigue or stress the responsible thing to do is to seek help. Most respondents said they would consult their partner. The following table ranks sources of advice and help in terms of their popularity amongst pilots (from the most popular at the top, to the least popular at the bottom):

Partner
Trusted colleague
Trusted non-work friend
Family G.P.
Fleet Manager
Aviation Medical Examiner
Other (for example, a psychotherapist)
Chief Pilot
Crewing Officer
Offspring
Rostering Manager
Operations Director
Personnel Director
Chief Executive Officer

Typical comments from respondents were: "I could not possibly contemplate talking to anyone in authority within my employer: I have utterly no confidence that the matter would be dealt with properly. My poor wife bears the brunt of things. Her support is sometimes all that keeps me going"; "I feel that most people either don't understand or don't want to sympathise, so I don't raise it with anyone".

There seemed to be a reluctance to broach the subjects of stress and fatigue with the AME, probably because the AME can exert significant leverage over a pilot's career. Interviewees' comments included: "I'd be a little wary [of talking to my AME] because he has the capacity to take my flying licence away. So when I reported sick for stress I actually went to my G.P."; "My present [AME], I guess so. I'm a little scarred by the aviation medical side at the moment. Because our livelihood depends so much on our medical, you are very loathe to bring anything up that isn't really necessary. If I were to have a minor health issue I was unsure about, I would much rather go and confide in my G.P. first, to see what happens, then take it to my AME, rather than the other way around ... because the AME has a duty of care to do things immediately, if they hear something"; "Yes, I could confide in my old [AME]. I could probably confide in my new AME. However, if something in my life was affecting my work I would probably look elsewhere. I'd be worried that he might write something down that might leak to the CAA. If, say, I had a marital problem I would probably chat to my close friends. If things escalated I would probably talk to someone for cash, someone like a psychologist".

Pilots' reluctance to talk to managers could indicate one of two things. Either pilots feel that managers do not have the requisite skills (unlike, say, a psychologist) or they believe they might receive an unsympathetic response. If the reason for pilots' reluctance to confide in managers is fear of having their opinions challenged or dismissed, this says much about the culture of today's airline industry. Self-censorship is not conducive to safe operation. Suppressed (masked) human factors problems generate latent errors/resident pathogens within the socio-technical system of commercial aviation. High-reliability is grounded in self-examination, openness, honesty and a general will to get things right (LaPorte and Consolini, 1991;

Hopkins, 2002; Antonsen, 2009; Woods *et al.*, 2010). A just culture is a prerequisite for safe operation.

Conclusion

Regardless of the possibility of bias in the results of this survey (see comments in Chapter 3) it is clear that from a safety perspective all is not well. Many of the pilots who participated in the 2010–2011 research were worried about the industry's trajectory. Intense competition requires that airlines (and air traffic service providers, maintainers, airports, regulators, manufacturers and so on) do more with less. The recession that began in 2008 has squeezed all the slack out of the system. Locked in a battle for survival the airlines have no choice but to work physical and human capital as hard as possible (Lawton, 2002; Franke and John, 2011; European Cockpit Association, 2012).[21] The challenge for the industry is to ensure that capital is not worked so hard that it breaks. As shown by the aviation industry's steadily improving safety record, so far pilots' physical and psychological reserves have been sufficient to meet whatever new challenges have been thrown at them. However, medical science suggests that pilots' capacities are finite. As Tom Wolfe (1991) explains, even those with the Right Stuff have natural limits.

---

21 The European Cockpit Association (2012: 1) says the airlines have dealt with competition and recession by: "Consolidating (mergers and acquisitions); Reducing costs and capacity; Reducing labour costs and increasing productivity of employees; Opening or acquiring low cost subsidiaries and transferring production there".

CHAPTER SIX

What Have We Learned?

Introduction

The aviation industry is a force for good. It creates opportunity and wealth and, by providing businesspeople and leisure travellers with relatively cheap long-distance transport, brings nations closer together. It accelerates the globalisation of opportunity. And that is a good thing. The direct and indirect employment created by the industry puts money in peoples' pockets and channels tax income to government coffers. The industry is resilient, surviving downturn and crisis:

> [T]he commercial aircraft segment is expected to reach record levels of revenues in 2013, just coming off its best year ever for production in 2012 ... Growth in commercial aircraft manufacturer's revenues is expected to reach record levels in 2013, based on increased production rates and the introduction of the next generation aircraft. It is likely that 2013 may continue the new trend of global production levels above 1,000 aircraft per year for the third year in a row ... Backlogs are expected to continue growing, with airlines continuing to update their fleets with new fuel-efficient aircraft in order to stay competitive (Deloitte, 2013: 3–4).

And yet, as we have seen, there is a dark side to the industry. The search for economy is relentless. Where possible costs are passed on to passengers and employees. Low-cost carriers are especially good at stripping out costs. Passengers are obliged to book on line and pay for even the most basic items (like tea and coffee). Pilots are obliged to pay for training and uniforms and are increasingly employed on zero-hours contracts. Low-cost carriers like Ryanair have taken up vogue employment practices with gusto. Regarding flight operations, the trend is to see flight-time limitations not as maxima but as rostering targets. To date pilots have been able to absorb the additional physiological and psychological pressures that result from being worked as hard as the rules allow. However, the time may come when less restrictive FTLs exhaust pilots' physiological and psychological reserves. Medical science predicts that exhaustion induces error. Most errors are inconsequential (they are trapped by liveware, procedures, hardware or software). Some are not.

Commercial aviation is a complex socio-technical activity that incorporates scientific, technological, social, economic and political elements. Safety performance is an emergent property of the interactions between these elements. Safety performance cannot be divorced from context. It is influenced by social, economic and political factors. For example, the employment of pilots on zero-hours contracts may encourage pilots to report for work when sick. Yes, a pilot who is unwell is obliged by regulation to report sick. However, if a pilot is only paid when s/he reports, the temptation is to report. To characterise this behaviour as 'unprofessional' is to ignore the economic realities of everyday life. Pilots are no more immune from these than anyone else. For young pilots such realities include paying off university and training fees that may exceed £120,000. It is unprofessional of those who regulate and run the industry to ignore employees' necessary economic calculations. It is unprofessional to expect pilots to reason in a vacuum.

Safety as Product

[D]ecision making in aviation operations is considered to be 100 per cent safety-oriented ... this is hardly realistic. Human decision making in operational contexts is a compromise between production and safety goals ... (International Civil Aviation Organisation, 2002: 1.1–1.2).

It is unwise to consider safety in isolation from economics: political economy impinges upon safety. A pilot's performance is an emergent property of multiple interconnected factors. These include a pilot's innate ability, the quality and relevance of their initial and recurrent training, the quality of the hardware and software (standard operating procedures, etc.) at their disposal, the quality of teamwork *and their compensation (salary) and conditions of work.*

Behavioural Impacts of Context – Example

The author consulted to a night-freight airline where management withdrew the down-route meals allowance. Withdrawing the allowance affected pilots' behaviour. Because withdrawal meant that flight crew were left with only one free meal – the hotel breakfast – pilots would make a point of breakfasting. Depending on the time they checked-in, pilots would either go to bed for a couple of hours, get up to eat breakfast, then return to bed (on a full stomach) or take breakfast when they arrived, then go to bed (on a full stomach). It was noted that low-paid First Officers (some of whom kept accommodation in both the U.K. and Germany (the location of the airline's hub) and had loans to pay off) were the most likely to either interrupt or delay their sleep to take breakfast. Acute sleep loss degrades performance. Cumulative sleep loss (sleep debt) degrades performance. Retiring on a full stomach may reduce sleep quality and cause short and long-term health problems (Rhodes and Gil, 2002; Virgin Blue, 2005; Eurocontrol, 2005; Caruso and Hitchcock, 2010).

While safety-assurance methodologies like SHEL make reference to "economic pressures ... compromising the efficacy of the crew's decision-making" (Harle, 1997: 136), they fail to acknowledge the potential impact of a pilot's personal circumstances on her/his flight-deck performance. For safety's sake it is time the nexus between income/lifestyle and performance was explicitly recognised (by regulators, air accident investigators, airline managers, politicians and other parties).

As university and training fees rise the economic pressures on junior flight crew increase (consider the data on indebtedness reproduced in this book). The squeeze on salaries compounds the problem. Pilot impoverishment may affect operational safety. The industry says it wants to achieve a step-change in safety performance. Taking a more holistic view of flight-deck performance – one that references context – will help the aviation industry achieve its objective.

Aviation's most significant achievement – the provision of safe mass transportation – is problematic because it creates the impression that transporting people by air is no more difficult than transporting them by automobile, train or bus. Those who work at the coal-face (pilots, controllers, engineers, dispatchers, etc.) know this to be a falsehood. Back-office staff may prefer to accept the falsehood because it allows them to shunt operational safety into a siding so they can concentrate on maximising shareholder value. Many pilots expressed the view that back-office staff showed little interest in pilots' work and home lives. Many said they felt undervalued. Many suspected that managers saw them more as units of production than skilled professionals. Depersonalisation is one of the characteristics of the capitalist mode of production.

Commercial aviation is not just another means of transportation. By nature the activity creates significant latent risk. Flying passengers at close to the speed of sound miles above the earth in intense cold in a volatile physical environment in a complex machine creates latent risk. Landing an aircraft in a tropical storm at an unfamiliar airport with a fatigued and inexperienced crew creates latent risk. Airline managements need to be reminded of this fact. The industry is laden with risk.

Why Take an Interest in Pilots' Lives When Most Employers Eschew Enlightened Employment Practices?

It is important to take an interest in pilots' lives because what happens outside the airport perimeter influences the quality of flight-deck labour, and because accidents are low-probability but high-consequence. A major accident could consign the airline concerned to the dustbin. Accident costs include the loss of life, hardware and reputation, legal fees, payouts to relatives and elevated insurance premiums. No airline is so big that it cannot be felled by a major accident. Flight-time and company rules that do not reference industry dynamics and the pilot lifestyle may increase the probability of incident and accident. For example, base closures or relocations leave pilots commuting long distances. Unable to relocate (perhaps because of a depressed property market or family circumstance) but determined to work, pilots may commute every day or take unsatisfactory temporary accommodation (as in the risk-laden U.S. practice of 'hot-bunking'). The net result can be a pilot who suffers chronic fatigue. A fatigued pilot is more likely to make mistakes. Preferential rostering demonstrates that the industry *is* capable of attending to difference (albeit in the case of preferential rostering, differences in physiology rather than circumstance). If the industry can make safety-enhancing concessions to pilots on rostering it can make safety-enhancing concessions in other areas, too – like subsidising emergency HOTAC for pilots running late between duties so their time for sleep is not lost to commuting.

It is important to take an interest in pilots' lives because aviation is a noteworthy human achievement that does not deserve short-term, myopic, get-rich-quick management and profit-seeking regulation. One survey respondent put it succinctly: "Fundamentally, aviation is a dangerous business that is only made safe by the professionalism of those who really care. Whereas a control of costs is necessary for success, the pendulum has swung way too far in favour of reducing costs and away from maintaining safety. Huge debts for training, and increasing duty hours, are just two examples of the damage of excessive cost-cutting".

Is aviation a special case? Yes, it is. As a *transformative* endeavour, commercial aviation should be nurtured. Judging aviation against a crude profit-loss benchmark, then regulating and managing it accordingly insults those committed to the industry and the significance of powered flight:

> As a piece of applied science the aeroplane has a place alongside the wheel, gunpowder, the printing press and the steam engine as one of the great levers of change in world history. The effect of aircraft on the way we live has been profound: they have shrunk the world, mingling previously isolated cultures ... [and] created new economic zones (Rendall, 1988: 7).

Because of its impact and potential, the aviation industry deserves more respect than it is presently accorded. Likewise the workforce.

Bibliography

Air Line Pilots Association International (2013). *Looking for a career where the sky is the limit?* Herndon, VA: Air Line Pilots Association International.

Ames, B. C. and Hlavacek, J. D. (1990). 'Vital truths about managing your costs', *Harvard Business Review*, January–February, 140–147.

Anonymous (2013). *The Truth About The Profession*. <http://thetruthabouttheprofession. weebly.com> accessed 13 September 2013.

Ashcroft, M. (2004). 'The Ryan King', *British Industry*, September.

Baker, J. A., Erwin, G., Priest, S., Tebo, P. V., Rosenthal, I., Bowman, F. L., Hendershot, D., Leveson, N., Wilson, D., Gorton, S., Wiegmann, D. A. (2007). *The Report of the B.P. U.S. Refineries Independent Safety Review Panel*. <http://www.csb. gov> accessed 25 November 2008.

Battelle Memorial Institute (1998). *An Overview of the Scientific Literature Concerning Fatigue, Sleep and the Circadian Cycle*. Seattle: Battelle Memorial Institute.

Beaty, D. (1969). *The Human Factor in Aircraft Accidents*. London: Secker and Warburg.

Bellamy, W. (2013). 'IATA Downgrades 2013 Airline Profit Forecast by $1 Billion', *Aviation Today*, 23 September, <http://www.aviationtoday.com/> accessed 24 September 2013.

Bennett, S. A. (1998). 'Challenger – Learning the Lessons', *Risk Management Bulletin*, September, 13–17.

Bennett, S. A. (2003). 'Flight crew stress and fatigue in low-cost commercial air operations – an appraisal', *International Journal of Risk Assessment and Management*, 4 (2), 207–231.

Bennett, S. A. (2006). 'A longitudinal ethnographic study of aircrews' lived experience of flying operations at a low-cost airline', *Risk Management: An International Journal*, 8 (2), 92–117.

Bennett, S. A. (2009). *Londonland: an Ethnography of Labour in a World City*. London: Middlesex University Press.

Bennett, S. A. (2010a). 'A longitudinal ethnographic study of night freight pilots', *Journal of Risk Research*, 13 (6), 701–730.

Bennett, S. A. (2010b). *Contemporary issues: Fatigue impacts of employee commutes*. London: Parliamentary Advisory Council for Transport Safety.

Bennett, S. A. (2010c). 'Human Factors for Maintenance Engineers and Others – A Prerequisite for Success'. In R. Blockley and W. Shyy (eds.), *Encyclopedia of Aerospace Engineering*, pp. 4703–4710. Chichester: Wiley.

Bennett, S. A. (2011). *The Pilot Lifestyle: a sociological study of the commercial pilot's work and home life*. Leicester: Vaughan College, University of Leicester.

Bennett, S. A. (2012a). 'Aviation and corporate social responsibility'. In S. A. Bennett (ed.), *Innovative Thinking in Risk, Crisis and Disaster Management*, pp. 139–171. Farnham: Gower.

Bennett, S. A. (2012b). 'The Air France 447 Accident. Organisationally and Socially Produced?' *The Aerospace Professional*, October, 20–21.

Bennett, S. A. (2013a). 'Pilot Debt: A Safety Issue?' *Air International*, May, 74–77.

Bennett, S. A. (2013b). 'Treat with care', University of Leicester Exchanges, <leicesterexchanges.com/2013/08/07/treat-with-care> accessed 8 September 2013.

Bennett, S. A. and Shaw, A. P. (2003). 'Incidents and accidents on the ramp: does "risk communication" provide a solution?' *Human Factors and Aerospace Safety*, 3 (4), 333–352.

Beynon, H. (1973). *Working for Ford*. London: Penguin.

Binns, D. (2013). 'Buy-buy to reality', *Metro*, 21 October.

Bittner, E. (1967). 'The Police on Skid-Row: A Study of Peace Keeping', *American Sociological Review*, 32 (5), 699–715.

Bjiker, W. (1994). *Of Bicycles, Bakelites, and Bulbs. Toward a Theory of Sociotechnical Change*. Cambridge MA: Massachusetts Institute of Technology Press.

Bor, R., Field, G. and Scragg, P. (2002). 'The mental health of pilots: an overview', *Counselling Psychology Quarterly*, 15 (3), 239–256.

Bor, R. and Hubbard, T. (2006). *Aviation Mental Health: Psychological Implications for Air Transportation*. Aldershot: Ashgate.

Braverman, H. (1974). *Labour and Monopoly Capital*. New York: Monthly Review Press.

British Airline Pilots Association Medical Study Group (1988). *Fit to Fly: A Medical Handbook for Pilots*. Oxford: BSP Professional Books.

British Airline Pilots Association (2013). 'Half of pilots have fallen asleep while flying', <http://www.balpa.org/News-and-campaigns/News/HALF-OF-PILOTS-HAVE-FALLEN-ASLEEP-WHILE-FLYING.aspx> accessed 23 October 2013.

British Broadcasting Corporation (2013). 'Pilot hours regulation plan rejected by MEPs', *BBC News*, 30 September, <http://www.bbc.co.uk> accessed 1 October 2013.

Broadbent, M. (2013). 'Resurgence of low-cost, long-haul', *Air International*, October, 106–109.

Brookes, A. (2002). *Destination Disaster. Aviation Accidents in the Modern Age*. Hersham: Ian Allan.

Burns, R. B. (2000). *Introduction to Research Methods*. Thousand Oaks, CA: Sage.

Cable, V. (2009). *The Storm: The World Economic Crisis and What it Means*. London: Atlantic Books.

Caldwell, J. A. and Caldwell, J. L. (2003). *Fatigue in Aviation. A Guide to Staying Awake at the Stick*. Aldershot: Ashgate.

Campbell, R. D. and Bagshaw, M. (1999). *Human Performance and Limitations in Aviation*. Oxford: Blackwell Science.

Canby, V. (1988). 'Movie Review: Dear America: Letters Home from Vietnam (1987)', *The New York Times*, 16 September.

Carthey, J. and Clarke, J. (2010). *Implementing Human Factors in Healthcare*. London: Patient Safety First.

Caruso, C. C. and Hitchcock, E. M. (2010). 'Strategies for Nurses to Prevent Sleep-Related Injuries and Errors', *Rehabilitation Nursing*, 35 (5), 192–197.

Centerprise Trust (1977). *A People's Autobiography of Hackney*. London: Centerprise Trust.

Cerny, P. G. (2010). 'Globalisation and Statehood'. In M. Beeson and N. Bisley (eds.), *Issues in 21st Century World Politics*, pp. 17–32. Basingstoke: Palgrave Macmillan.

Channel 4 Dispatches (2013). 'Ryanair: Secrets from the Cockpit', broadcast 12 August 2013, over the Channel 4 network.

Chartered Institute of Personnel and Development (2013a). *Employee Outlook: Winter 2012–2013*. London: Chartered Institute of Personnel and Development.

Chartered Institute of Personnel and Development (2013b). *Press Release: Zero hours contracts more widespread than thought – but only minority of zero hours workers want to work more hours*, <www.cipd.co.uk/pressoffice/> accessed 6 September 2013.

Chittick, J. (1998). 'Preferential scheduling for aircrew can help address problem of short-term accumulated fatigue', *ICAO Journal*, 53 (3), 16–17.

Civil Aviation Authority (2003). *CAA PAPER 2003/8 A Review of In-flight Napping Strategies – Updated 2003*. London: Civil Aviation Authority.

Civil Aviation Authority (2004). *CAP371. The Avoidance of Fatigue In Aircrews*. London: Civil Aviation Authority Safety Regulation Group.

Civil Aviation Authority (2007). *Aircrew Fatigue: A Review of Research Undertaken on Behalf of the UK Civil Aviation Authority: Issue 2*. London: Civil Aviation Authority.

Civil Aviation Authority (2012). *CAP393. Air Navigation: The Order and the Regulations*. London: Civil Aviation Authority.

Civil Aviation Safety Authority (2012). *Fatigue Management for the Australian Aviation Industry. Fatigue Management Strategies for Aviation Workers: A Training and Development Workbook*. Canberra: Civil Aviation Safety Authority.

Comisión de Investigación de Accidentes e Incidentes de Aviación Civil (2013). *Report IN-010/2010*. Madrid: Comisión de Investigación de Accidentes e Incidentes de Aviación Civil.

Control of Major Accident Hazards Competent Authority (2011). *Buncefield: Why did it happen?* Berkshire: HSE Books.

Cook, T. D. and Campbell, D. T. (1979). *Quasi-experimentation: design and analysis issues for field settings*. Skokie, Ill: Rand McNally.

Cooper, C. L., Dewe, P. J. and O'Driscoll, M. P. (2001). *Organisational Stress: A Review and Critique of Theory, Research and Applications*. Thousand Oaks: Sage.

Couturié, B. and Dewhurst, R. (1987). 'Dear America: Letters Home from Vietnam', HBO/Taurus Films, broadcast 3 April 1988, over the HBO network.

Crandall, R. L. (2008). *Remarks of Robert L. Crandall, The Wings Club, Tuesday, June 10, 2008*, <http://www.wingsclub.org/eventspeeches_2008-06.html> accessed 5 October 2013.

Cullen, W. D. (1990). *The public inquiry into the Piper Alpha Disaster. Department of Energy*. London: HMSO.

Cullen, W. D. (2001). *The Ladbroke Grove rail inquiry Part 2: Report*. London: HMSO.

Cusick, J. (2013). 'Fall in wages puts Britain in Europe's bottom four', *The Independent*, 11 August, <http://www.independent.co.uk/> accessed 5 September 2013.

Daily Mail (2010). 'Why a happy marriage can ease the pain of arthritis', *Daily Mail*, 17 November.

Dekker, S. W. A. (2005). *Ten Questions about Human Error*. New Jersey: Lawrence Erlbaum.

Dekker, S. W. A. (2008). *Just culture: balancing safety and accountability*. Aldershot: Ashgate Publishing Co.

Dekker, S. W. A. (2008). 'Just culture: who gets to draw the line?' *Cognition, Technology and Work*, 11 (3), 177–185.

Dekker, S. W. A. (2012). *Just Culture: Balancing Safety and Accountability* (Second Ed.). Farnham: Ashgate.

Dekker, S. W. A. (2013). 'Production and safety are not opposites', *Hindsight*, Summer, 8–9.

Deloitte (2013). *2013 Global aerospace and defence industry outlook. Expect defence to shrink while commercial aerospace sets new records*. New York: Deloitte.

Denison (2009). *Corporate culture in global business*. <http://corporateculture.wordpress.com/2009/05/15/what-is-organizational-culture-i%E2%80%99ll-know-it-when-i-see-it/> accessed 8 September 2013.

Dorrian, J., Baulk, S. D. and Dawson D. (2011). 'Work hours, workload, sleep and fatigue in Australian Rail Industry employees', *Applied Ergonomics*, 42 (2), 202–209.

Duke, N. and Lanchbery, E. (eds.) (1964). *The Crowded Sky*. London: Corgi Books.

Durkheim, E. (1950/1895). *The rules of the sociological method*. New York: Free Press.

Edmonds, L. (2013). 'Pilot admits that he and his co-pilot were both asleep just minutes before they were due to land their freight flight', <http://www.dailymail.co.uk/news/article-2436633/Pilot-admits-pilot-asleep-just-minutes-land-freight-flight.html#ixzz2ja76R5ri > accessed 3 November 2013.

Eurocontrol (2005). *Fatigue and Sleep Management*. Brussels: Eurocontrol.

European Aviation Safety Agency/Moebus Aviation (2008). *Scientific and Medical Evaluation of Flight Time Limitations*. Zurich: Moebus Aviation.

European Aviation Safety Agency (2013). 'EASA welcomes new flight time limitations rules', <https://easa.europa.eu/communications/press-releases/EASA-press-release.php?id=124> accessed 14 November 2013.

European Cockpit Association (2012). *Reflection paper to the global dialogue forum on the effects of the global economic crisis on the civil aviation industry*. Brussels: European Cockpit Association.

European Cockpit Association (2013a). *Pilots' Position*. <https:// www.eurocockpit.be/pages/pilots-position> accessed 14 October 2013.

European Cockpit Association (2013b). *Press Release: Better protection for safety reporting in EU aviation*. Brussels: European Cockpit Association.

European Regions Airline Association (2013a). *Press Release: European aviation safety is not at risk*, 21 January <www.eraa.org> accessed 25 January 2013.

European Regions Airline Association (2013b). *Press Release: ERA applauds MEPs' endorsement of FTL proposal*, 9 October <www.eraa.org> accessed 14 November 2013.

European Transport Safety Council (2013). *ETSC Position on Flight Time Limitations*. Brussels: European Transport Safety Council.

Federal Aviation Administration (2009). 'Medical Facts for Pilots', *Aeronautical Information Manual*. Washington, D.C.: Federal Aviation Administration.

Federal Aviation Administration (2010). *Federal Register. Part II Department of Transportation. 14 CFR Parts 117 and 121 Flightcrew Member Duty and Rest Requirements; Proposed Rule*. Washington, D.C.: Federal Aviation Administration.

Fennell, D. (1988). *Investigation into king's cross underground fire. Department of transport*. London: HMSO.

Franke, M. and John, F. (2011). 'What comes next after recession? – Airline industry scenarios and potential end games', *Journal of Air Transport Management*, 17 (1), 19–26.

Freeman, S. (2009). 'A Crowded Hub Away From Home', *The Washington Post*, 4 August.

Fulcher, J. (2004). *Capitalism*. Oxford: Oxford University Press.

Gander, P. H., Gregory, K. B., Connell, L. J., Graeber, R. C., Miller, D. L. and Rose-kind, M. R. (1998). 'Flight crew fatigue IV: Overnight cargo operations', *Aviation, Space and Environmental Medicine*, 69 (suppl. 9), 26–36.

Gilbert, N. (2001). *Researching Social Life*. London: Sage.

Ginnett, R. C. (1990). 'Airline cockpit crew'. In J. R. Hackman (ed.) *Groups that work (and those that don't): Creating conditions for effective teamwork*, pp. 427–448. San Francisco: Jossey-Bass.

Glendon, I. A., Clarke, S. G. and McKenna, E. F. (2006). *Human Safety and Risk Management*. London: Taylor and Francis.

Global Aviation Information Network (2004). *Roadmap to a just culture: Enhancing the safety environment. Global Aviation Information Network. Group E: Flight Ops/ATC Ops Safety Information Sharing Working Group*. Alexandria, VA: Flight Safety Foundation.

Goode, J. H. (2003). 'Are pilots at risk of accidents due to fatigue?' *Journal of Safety Research*, 34, 309–313.

Gowrisankaran, G. (2002). *Competition and Regulation in the Airline Industry*. San Francisco: Federal Reserve Bank of San Francisco.

Greater Manchester Low Pay Unit (1995). *Workers' Voices: Accounts of Working Life in Britain in the Nineties*. Manchester: Greater Manchester Low Pay Unit.

Green, A. E. and Canny, A. (2003). *Geographical Mobility: Family Impacts*. Bristol: The Policy Press.

Guerra, T. (2013). 'What Is the Average Yearly Salary of an Airline Baggage Handler?' *Chron*, <http://work.chron.com/average-yearly-salary-airline-baggage-handler-9525.html> accessed 19 October 2013.

Gunn, R. W. and Gullickson, B. R. (2004). 'The Normalisation of Deviance', *Strategic Finance*, March, <http://www.paci.com.au/downloads_public/risk/11_NormalisationOfDeviance.pdf> accessed 25 September 2013.

Hackman, J. R. (1998). 'Why teams don't work'. In R. S. Tindale and L. Heath (eds.) *Theory and research on small groups*, pp. 245–267. New York: Plenum.

Haertner, A. (2011). *Frauen im Cockpit: Eine ethnographische Studie über weibliche Berufsbilder und Berufspraxis (Female Pilots: An ethnographic study of female professional praxis in a male domain)*. Leicester: Vaughan College, University of Leicester.

Hall, S. (1989). 'The Meaning of New Times'. In S. Hall and M. Jacques (eds.), *New Times: The changing face of politics in the 1990s*, pp. 116–134. London: Lawrence and Wishart.

Harris, D. (2005). 'Drinking and flying: causes, effects and the development of effective countermeasures'. In D. Harris and H. Muir (eds.), *Contemporary Issues in Human Factors and Aviation Safety*, pp. 297–317. Aldershot: Ashgate.

Hayes, P. (2013). '2012: the safest year ever for air travel again', *Hindsight*, Summer, pp. 42–43.

Health and Safety Executive (2002). *Safety Culture: A review of the literature*. Sheffield: Health and Safety Laboratory.

Health and Safety Executive (2006). *Managing shift work. Health and Safety Guidance*. Sudbury: HSE Books.

Helm, T. (2013). 'Two-tier job market leaves "millions stuck on low pay"', *The Observer*, 1 September, 1.

Hersman, D. A. P. (2009). 'Fighting Fatigue: A Team Effort', *Aerosafety World*, June.

Hilkevitch, J. and Johnsson, J. (2010). 'Cost-cutting measure fuels debate at American Airlines. Company directive to fly with less fuel angers pilots, worries safety experts', *The Chicago Tribune*, 27 June.

Hollnagel, E. (2004). *Barriers and Accident Prevention*. Aldershot: Ashgate.

Hopkins, A. (2002). *Safety Culture, Mindfulness and Safe Behaviour: Converging Ideas?* Canberra: Australian National University.

International Airport Review (2013). 'MEPs must support FTL proposal, says ERA', *International Airport Review*, 27 September, <http://www.internationalairportreview.com> accessed 2 October 2013.

International Civil Aviation Organisation (2002). *Line Operations Safety Audit (LOSA)*. Montreal: International Civil Aviation Organisation.

Jeffrey, K. (2013). 'Review: Lord Cullen – what have we learned from Piper Alpha?' *Finding Petroleum*, 16 September, <http://www.findingpetroleum.com> accessed 2 October 2013.

Johnson, R. (2004). 'Cover story: Lord of the wings', *Times Online*, 1 August, <http://www.timesonline.co.uk> accessed October 20 2004.

Johnson, S. (2013). 'The Average Salary of a Regional Airline Pilot', *Chron*, <http://work.chron.com/average-salary-regional-airline-pilot-5985.html> accessed October 19 2013.

Johnston, K. (2013). 'Airlines on a new course', *Boston Globe*, 2 April, <http://www.boston.com/business/news> accessed 12 August 2013.

Jones, R. (2009). *Fatigue Risk Management System: Introduction into a Long-haul Airline*, unpublished MSc dissertation, City University, London.

Joseph Rowntree Foundation (2003). *The effects on families of job relocations*. York: Joseph Rowntree Foundation.

Katholieke Radio Omroep (KRO) Brandpunt Reporter (2012). 'Mayday, Mayday'. Broadcast 28 December 2012.

Keohane, R. O. and Nye, J. S. (1977). *Power and Interdependence: World Politics in Transition*. Boston: Little, Brown and Company.

King, C. (2011). 'Under Pressure', *The Log*, February/March.

Koehler, M., Esquivias, P. and Varadarajan, R. (2009). 'Cutting to fit', *Airline Business*, November.

Koivu, H. (2013). 'Safety versus cost. The rush-hour years of aviation', *Hindsight*, Summer, 60–64.

Krause, S. S. (1996). *Aircraft Safety: Accident Investigations, Analyses and Applications*. New York: McGraw-Hill.

Labour Research Department (2013). *Zero hours contracts increase across all sectors*. <http://www.lrdpublications.org.uk> accessed 27 August 2013.

Latour, B. (1991). 'Technology is Society Made Durable'. In J. Law (ed.) *A Sociology of Monsters. Essays on Power, Technology and Domination*, Sociological Review Monograph 38, pp. 103–131.

Lavrakas, P. J. (ed.) (2008). *Encyclopedia of Survey Research Methods*. Thousand Oaks, CA: Sage.

Lawton, T. C. (2002). *Cleared for Take-Off. Structure and strategy in the low-fare airline business*. Aldershot: Ashgate.

Leadbeater, C. (1989). 'Thatcherism and Progress'. In S. Hall and M. Jacques (eds.) *New Times: The changing face of politics in the 1990s*, pp. 395–411. London: Lawrence and Wishart.

Learmount, D. (2010). 'Training: jobs for tomorrow', *Flight International*, 31 March.

Levin, A. (2009). 'Alcohol tests catch 11 pilots a year', *USA Today*, 11 December.

MacKenzie, D and Wajcman, J. (eds.) (1985) *The Social Shaping of Technology*. Milton Keynes: Open University Press.

Massachusetts Institute of Technology (2011). *Airline Industry Overview*. <http://mit.edu/airlines/> accessed 6 March 2011.

Mathieu, J. E., Heffner, T. S., Goodwin, G. F., Salas, E. and Cannon-Bowers, J. A. (2000). 'The influence of shared mental models on team process and performance', *Journal of Applied Psychology*, 85, 284–93.

Marx, K. (1992). *Capital: A critique of political economy, Volume 3*. London: Penguin.

Marx, D. (2001). *Patient safety and the 'just culture': a primer for health care executives*. New York: Columbia University.

Mason, R. (2013). 'Zero-hours pay rates "40% below average", claims Chuka Umunna', *The Guardian*, 20 August, <http://www.theguardian.com/> accessed 6 September 2013.

Mason, R. O. (2004). 'Can a culture be lethal?' *Organisational Dynamics*, 33 (2), 128–142.

Mass Observation Archive (2001). *A brief history of Mass-Observation*. <http://www.massobs.org.uk/history.html/> accessed 29 October 2013.

Mass Observation (2009). *War Factory (originally published 1943)*. London: Faber and Faber.

Massey, R. (2012). 'Ryanair is "courting disaster" by flying planes with near-empty fuel tanks to cut costs', *Mail Online*, 19 September, <www.dailymail.co.uk/news/article-2205314/> accessed 1 September 2013.

Miller, J. C. (2005). *Operational Risk Management of Fatigue Effects. AFRL Report 20050073*. Brooks City-Base, TX: United States Air Force Research Laboratory.

Millward, D. (2010). What's wrong with getting on your bike? *Daily Telegraph*, 28 June.

Morrison, S. A. and Winston, C. (1995). *The Evolution of the Airline Industry*. Washington: The Brookings Institution.

Morrison, S. A. and Winston, C. (2005). *What's Wrong with the Airline Industry? Diagnosis and Possible Cures. Hearing before the Subcommittee on Aviation, Committee on Transportation and Infrastructure, United States House of Representatives, September 28, 2005*. Boston: Northeastern University.

Mostrous, A. (2013). 'Crisis is over and we're ready for the "new normal", say British workers', *The Times*, 28 October, 3.

MSP Solutions (2007). *Aircraft Maintenance, Repair and Overhaul Market Study*. Reigate: MSP Solutions.

Murray, R. (1989). 'Fordism and Post-Fordism'. In S. Hall and M. Jacques (eds.) *New Times: The changing face of politics in the 1990s*, pp. 38–53. London: Lawrence and Wishart.

Nader, R. (1965). *Unsafe at Any Speed: The designed-in dangers of the American automobile*. New York: Grossman Publishers.

National Careers Service (2013). *Airline Pilot*. <https://nationalcareersservice.direct.gov.uk/advice/planning/jobprofiles/Pages/airlinepilot.aspx> accessed 23 October 2013.

National Transportation Safety Board (2008). *Runway Overrun During Landing, Shuttle America Inc., Doing Business as Delta Connection Flight 6448, Embraer ERJ-170, N862RW, Cleveland, Ohio, February 18, 2007*. Washington, D.C.: National Transportation Safety Board.

National Transportation Safety Board (2010). *Loss of Control on Approach, Colgan Air, Inc. Operating as Continental Connection Flight 3407, Bombardier DHC-8-400, N200WQ Clarence Centre, New York February 12, 2009*. Washington, D.C.: National Transportation Safety Board.

Oborne, P. (2010). 'The coalition speaks with many voices', *The Week*, 2 October.

Oliver, M. (2002). 'Selby crash motorist receives five year sentence', *The Guardian*, 11 January.

Olsen, R. (2008). 'Self-selection bias'. In P. J. Lavrakas (ed.), *Encyclopedia of Survey Research Methods*, pp. 809–811. Thousand Oaks, CA: Sage.

O'Brien, D. (2013). 'Ryanair. To: All Pilots. Re: Capt John Goss', <http://ryanair-dontcarecrew.blogspot.co.uk/2013/08/ryanair-memo-profit-priority-capt-john.html> accessed 1 September 2013.

Partridge, C. and Goodman, T. (2007). 'Psychological aspects of the role of cabin crew', *Counselling at Work*, Spring, 6–11.

Perrow, C. (1984). *Normal Accidents*. New York: Basic Books.

Perrow, C. (1999). *Normal Accidents: Living with high-risk technologies*. Princeton, N.J.: Princeton University Press.

Petzinger, T. (1995). *Hard Landing. How the Epic Contest for Power and Profits Plunged the Airlines into Chaos*. London: Aurum.

Pinch, T. (1996). The social construction of technology: A review. In R. Fox (ed.), *Technological change: Methods and themes in the history of technology*, pp. 17–35. Amsterdam: Harwood Academic Publishers.

PR Newswire (2001). 'Pilots Group Urges FAA to Heed Public Opinion by Updating Current Flight and Duty Time Regulations', *PR Newswire*, 24 July.

Pyper, D. and McGuinness, F. (2013). *Zero-hours contracts*. London: House of Commons Library.

Rash, C. E. and Manning, S. D. (2009). 'Stressed Out', *AeroSafety World*, August, 38–42.

Rasmussen, J. (1997). 'Risk management in a dynamic society: a modelling problem', *Safety Science*, 27, 183–213.

Rasmussen, J. (1999). 'The concept of human error: is it useful for the design of safe systems?' *Safety Science Monitor*, 3.

Ray, L. (2010). 'Losing its Luster', *ATW Online*, 1 May, <http://atwonline.com> accessed 27 May 2010.

Reason, J. (1990). *Human Error*. Cambridge: Cambridge University Press.

Reason, J. (1997). *Managing the risks of organisational accidents*. Aldershot: Ashgate.

Reason, J. (1998). 'Achieving a safe culture: Theory and practice', *Work and Stress*, 12 (3), 293–306.

Reason, J. (2013). *A Life in Error. From little slips to big disasters*. Farnham: Ashgate.

Rendall, I. (1988). *Reaching for the Skies*. London: BBC Books.

Rhodes, W. and Gil, V. (2002). *Fatigue Management Guide for Canadian Marine Pilots: A Trainer's Handbook*. York, Ontario: Rhodes and Associates.

Rickard, J. W. (2010). *Air Safety Group: A brief history*. London: Air Safety Group.

Rosekind, M. and Gregory, K. (2009). *The Moebus Aviation Report on 'Scientific and Medical Evaluation of Flight Time Limitations': Invalid, Insufficient and Risky*. <www.ryanair.com/doc/news/2009/mar090607.pdf> accessed 23 October 2013.

Rosness, R. (2009). 'Derailed Decisions: The Evolution of Vulnerability on a Norwegian Railway Line'. In C. Owen, P. Béguin and G. Wackers (eds.), *Risky Work*

Environments. Reappraising Human Work Within Fallible Systems, pp. 53–80. Aldershot: Ashgate.

Rossow, M. (2012). *Engineering Ethics Case Study: The Challenger Disaster.* <http://www.cedengineering.com/upload/Ethics%20Challenger%20Disaster.pdf> accessed 25 September 2013.

Ruitenberg, B. (2002). 'Court case against Dutch controllers', *The Controller*, 41, 22–5.

Ryanair Holdings plc. (2013). *Annual Report 2013.* <http://www.ryanair.com/doc/investor/2013/final_annual_report_2013_130731.pdf> accessed 1 September 2013.

Sampson, A. (1984). *Empires of the Sky. The Politics, Contests and Cartels of World Airlines.* London: Hodder and Stoughton.

Sarker, M. A. R., Chowdhury, G. H. and Zaman, L. (2012). 'Sustainability and Growth of Low Cost Airlines: An Industry Analysis in Global Perspective', *American Journal of Business and Management*, 1, 162–171.

Scott, M. (2004). 'From airline pilot to airline machine-minder', *The Log*, October.

Sharkey, J. (2011). 'Since Sept. 11, Years of Change for Airlines', *The New York Times*, 5 September, <www.nytimes.com> accessed 14 September 2013.

Snook, S. (2000). *Friendly Fire: The Accidental Shootdown of U.S. Black Hawks over Northern Iraq.* Princeton, New Jersey: Princeton University Press.

Steptoe, A. and Bostock, S. (2011). *A survey of fatigue and well-being among commercial airline pilots. Final report 7th February 2011. Survey commissioned by BALPA.* London: University College London Psychobiology Group.

Strauss, S. (2010). 'Pilot Fatigue – fatigue and flight operations', *Focus on Commercial Aviation Safety*, Winter.

Sullenberger, C. B. (2009). *Statement of Captain Chesley B. Sullenberger III, Captain, US Airways Flight 1549, before the Subcommittee on Aviation, Committee on Transportation and Infrastructure, United States House of Representatives, February 24, 2009.* Washington, D.C.: United States House of Representatives.

Swan, J. (1995). *Human Performance for Pilots Simplified.* Thatcham: Swan Aviation Publishers.

The Canadian Nuclear Safety Commission (2013). *Human Performance: Managing Worker Fatigue and Hours of Work. Regulatory Document REGDOC-2.2.1.* Ottawa: The Canadian Nuclear Safety Commission.

The Economist (1998). 'Behind Branson', *The Economist*, 19 February, <www.economist.com/> accessed 14 September 2013.

The Guardian (2013). 'Ryanair pilots call for inquiry into reporting of safety concerns', *The Guardian*, 12 August, <http://www.theguardian.com/business/> accessed 20 August 2013.

The Independent (2001). 'Hart guilty of Selby train crash deaths', *The Independent*, 13 December.

The Institute of Medicine of the National Academies (2009). *Resident Duty Hours: Enhancing sleep, supervision and safety*. Washington D.C.: The National Academies Press.

The Sydney Morning Herald (2012). 'Low-fuel emergency landings "perfectly safe", says Ryanair boss', 24 August, *The Sydney Morning Herald*, <http://www.smh.com.au/travel/travel-incidents/> accessed 1 September 2013.

Theobald, R. (1994). *Understanding Industrial Society. A Sociological Guide*. London: Macmillan.

Third Sector Foresight (2010). *Personal Mobility*, <http://www.3s4.org.uk> accessed 2 December 2010.

Trades Union Congress (2010). *Home working helps to drive commute times down to 10 year low*. London: Trades Union Congress.

Transport Canada (2007). *Developing and Implementing a Fatigue Risk management System*. Montreal: Transport Canada.

Transport Canada (2008). *Fatigue Risk Management System for the Canadian Aviation Industry. Trainer's Handbook. TP 14578E*. Ottawa: Transport Canada.

Transport Canada (2008). *Fatigue Risk Management System for the Canadian Aviation Industry. Fatigue Management Strategies for Employees*. Ottawa: Transport Canada.

Tuckman, B. (1965). 'Developmental sequence in small groups', *Psychological Bulletin*, 63, 384–99.

Turner, B. A. (1976). 'The organisational and interorganisational development of disasters', *Administrative Science Quarterly*, 21, 378–397.

Turner, B. A. (1978). *Man Made Disasters*. London: Wykeham.

United Kingdom National Work Stress Network (2013). *Work Stress*. <www.workstress.net> accessed 25 October 2013.

United States Bureau of Labour Statistics (2013). *Occupational Employment Statistics: Occupational Employment and Wages, May 2012*. <http://www.bls.gov/oes/current> accessed 14 August 2013.

Uttal, B. (1983). 'The corporate culture vultures', *Fortune Magazine*, 17 October.

Vaughan, D. (1997). *The Challenger Launch Decision. Risky Technology, Culture and Deviance at NASA*. Chicago: University of Chicago Press.

Virgin Blue (2005). *Fit for Duty*. Brisbane: Virgin Blue.

Waters, M. (1995). *Globalisation*. London: Routledge.

Watson, T. J. (2003). *Sociology, Work and Industry: Fourth Edition*. London: Routledge.

Weir, D. T. H. (1996). 'Risk and disaster: the role of communications breakdown in plane crashes and business failure'. In C. Hood and D. K. C. Jones (eds.), *Debates in Risk Management*, pp. 114–126. London: UCL Press.

Werfelman, L. (2009). 'Easing Fatigue', *AeroSafety World*, March, pp. 22–27.

Wiener, E. L., Kanki, B. G. and Helmreich, R. L. (eds.) (1993). *Cockpit Resource Management*. San Diego: Academic Press.

Wolfe, T. (1991). *The Right Stuff*. London: Picador.

Woods, D. D., Dekker, S., Cook, R., Johannesen, L. and Sarter, N. (2010). *Behind Human Error: Second Edition*. Farnham: Ashgate.

Wright, O. (2013). 'You thought Ryanair's attendants had it bad? Wait 'til you hear about their pilots. Staff memo warns that signing letter airing safety fears would be "gross misconduct"', *The Independent*, 17 May, <http://www.independent.co.uk/news/> accessed 5 August 2013.

Zellner, W. and Rothman, A. (1992). 'The Airline Mess', *Businessweek*, 5 July, <http://www.businessweek.com/stories/1992-07-05/the-airline-mess> accessed 20 September 2013.

Zweig, F. (1948). *Men in the Pits*. London: Victor Gollancz.

Zweig, F. (1952). *Women's Life and Labour*. London: Victor Gollancz.

Zweig, F. (1961). *The worker in an affluent society: family life and industry*. London: Heinemann.